Taste *of* Home
comfort food classics

TASTE OF HOME BOOKS • RDA ENTHUSIAST BRANDS, LLC • MILWAUKEE, WI

Visit us at **tasteofhome.com** for other
Taste of Home books and products.

International Standard Book Number:
979-8-88977-097-8

Chief Content Officer: Jason Buhrmester
Content Director: Mark Hagen
Creative Director: Raeann Thompson
Associate Creative Director: Jami Geittmann
Senior Editor: Christine Rukavena
Editor: Hazel Wheaton
Senior Art Director: Courtney Lovetere
Art Director: Jennifer Ruetz
Manager, Production Design:
Satyandra Raghav
Senior Print Publication Designers:
Jogesh Antony, Bipin Balakrishnan
Production Artist: Nithya Venkatakrishnan
Deputy Editor, Copy Desk: Ann M. Walter
Senior Copy Editor: Elizabeth Pollock Bruch
Contributing Copy Editors: Nancy J. Stohs,
Pam Grandy

Cover Photography:
Photographer: Dan Roberts
Set Stylist: Stephanie Marchese
Food Stylist: Josh Rink

Pictured on front cover:
Fried Chicken & Waffles, p. 139

Pictured on back cover:
Apple Pie, p. 23; The Ultimate Chicken
Noodle Soup, p. 28; Cinnamon Swirl
Bread, p. 74

Printed in China
1 3 5 7 9 10 8 6 4 2

Mile-High Chicken
Potpie, Page 21

Contents

Classic Pizza, Page 17

Bacon Cheeseburgers, Page 20

Strawberry Pretzel Dessert, Page 207

Creamy Macaroni & Cheese, Page 24

Overnight Cinnamon Rolls, Page 16

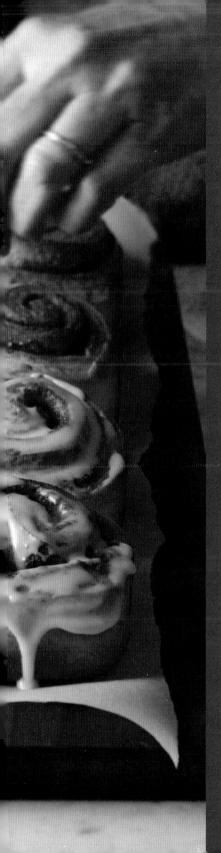

The All-Time Top 25

25 The Best Beef Stew

Our best beef stew recipe has tons of flavor. The blend of herbs and the addition of red wine and balsamic vinegar takes a comforting classic to the next level.

—James Schend, Pleasant Prairie, WI

Prep: 30 min. • **Cook:** 2 hours
Makes: 6 servings (2¼ qt.)

- 1½ lbs. beef stew meat, cut into 1-in. cubes
- ½ tsp. salt, divided
- 6 Tbsp. all-purpose flour, divided
- ½ tsp. smoked paprika
- 1 Tbsp. canola oil
- 3 Tbsp. tomato paste
- 2 tsp. herbes de Provence
- 2 garlic cloves, minced
- 2 cups dry red wine
- 2 cups beef broth
- 1½ tsp. minced fresh rosemary, divided
- 2 bay leaves
- 3 cups cubed peeled potatoes
- 3 cups coarsely chopped onions (about 2 large)
- 2 cups sliced carrots
- 2 Tbsp. cold water
- 2 Tbsp. balsamic or red wine vinegar
- 1 cup fresh or frozen peas
  Additional fresh rosemary, optional

1. In a small bowl, toss beef and ¼ tsp. salt. In a large bowl, combine 4 Tbsp. flour and paprika. Add beef, a few pieces at a time; toss to coat.
2. In a Dutch oven, brown the beef in oil over medium heat. Stir in tomato paste, herbes de Provence and garlic; cook until fragrant and color starts to darken slightly. Add wine; cook until mixture just comes to a boil. Simmer until reduced by half, about 5 minutes. Stir in broth, 1 tsp. rosemary and bay leaves.

Bring to a boil. Reduce heat; cover and simmer until meat is almost tender, about 1½ hours.
3. Add potatoes, onions and carrots. Cover; simmer until meat and vegetables are tender, about 30 minutes longer.
4. Discard bay leaves. In a small bowl, combine the remaining ½ tsp. rosemary, remaining ¼ tsp. salt and remaining 2 Tbsp. flour.

Add cold water and vinegar; stir until smooth. Stir into stew. Bring to a boil; add peas. Cook, stirring, until thickened, about 2 minutes. If desired, top with additional fresh rosemary.
1½ cups 366 cal., 11g fat (3g sat. fat), 71mg chol., 605mg sod., 40g carb. (9g sugars, 6g fiber), 28g pro.
Diabetic exchanges 3 lean meat, 2½ starch, ½ fat.

24. Chicken-Fried Steak & Gravy

As a child, I learned from my grandmother how to make chicken-fried steak. I taught my daughters, and when my granddaughters are older, I'll show them, too.
—Donna Cater, Fort Ann, NY

Takes: 30 min. • **Makes:** 4 servings

- 1¼ cups all-purpose flour, divided
- 2 large eggs
- 1½ cups 2% milk, divided
- 4 beef cubed steaks (6 oz. each)
- 1¼ tsp. salt, divided
- 1 tsp. pepper, divided
  Oil for frying
- 1 cup water

1. Place 1 cup flour in a shallow bowl. In a separate shallow bowl, whisk eggs and ½ cup milk until blended. Sprinkle steaks with ¾ tsp. each salt and pepper. Dip in flour to coat both sides; shake off excess. Dip in egg mixture, then again in flour.

2. In a large cast-iron or other heavy skillet, heat ¼ in. oil over medium heat. Add the steaks; cook until golden brown and a thermometer reads 160°, 4-6 minutes on each side. Remove from pan; drain on paper towels. Keep warm.

3. Remove all but 2 Tbsp. oil from pan. Stir in the remaining ¼ cup flour, ½ tsp. salt and ¼ tsp. pepper until smooth; cook and stir over medium heat until golden brown, 3-4 minutes. Gradually whisk in water and the remaining 1 cup milk.

Bring to a boil, stirring constantly; cook and stir until thickened, 1-2 minutes. Serve with steaks.

1 steak with ⅓ cup gravy 563 cal., 28g fat (5g sat. fat), 148mg chol., 839mg sod., 29g carb. (4g sugars, 1g fiber), 46g pro.

Which Cut is Best?

Tough, cheap cuts of steak like cubed or round steak work best here. Cubed steaks are from the round, and they've already tenderized by the butcher. You can tenderize your own round steaks at home by buying thin steaks and pounding them with a mallet to roughly a ¼-in. thickness.

23 Cheesy Broccoli Soup

Basic ingredients have never tasted or looked so good. The green broccoli florets and the brilliant orange carrots make my rich soup a colorful addition to any table.
—Evelyn Massner, Oakville, IA

Prep: 5 min. • **Cook:** 30 min.
Makes: 8 servings (2 qt.)

- 2 cups sliced fresh carrots
- 2 cups broccoli florets
- 1 cup sliced celery
- 1½ cups chopped onion
- ½ cup butter
- ¾ cup all-purpose flour
- 1 can (10½ oz.) condensed chicken broth, undiluted
- 4 cups whole milk
- ½ lb. Velveeta, cubed

1. In a large saucepan, bring 2 qt. water to a boil. Add carrots, broccoli and celery; cover and boil for 5 minutes. Drain, remove the vegetables and set aside.
2. In the same saucepan, saute onion in butter. Add flour and stir to make smooth paste. Gradually add chicken broth and milk. Cook until mixture thickens, 8-10 minutes. Add vegetables; heat until tender. Add cheese; heat until cheese is melted.
1 cup 472 cal., 31g fat (19g sat. fat), 88mg chol., 1033mg sod., 32g carb. (17g sugars, 3g fiber), 18g pro.

22 Buffalo Chicken Wings

Hot wings got their start in Buffalo, New York, in the kitchen of a bar. Although there was no game on at the time, today spicy wings and cool sauces are traditional game-day fare. Cayenne, red sauce and spices keep these tangy Buffalo chicken wings good and hot, just like the originals.
—Nancy Chapman, Center Harbor, NH

Prep: 10 min. • **Cook:** 10 min./batch
Makes: about 4 dozen

- 5 lbs. chicken wings
   Oil for frying
- 1 cup butter, cubed
- ¼ cup Louisiana-style hot sauce
- ¾ tsp. cayenne pepper
- ¾ tsp. celery salt
- ½ tsp. onion powder
- ½ tsp. garlic powder
   Optional: Celery ribs and ranch or blue cheese salad dressing

1. Cut chicken wings into 3 sections; discard wing tip sections. In an electric skillet, heat 1 in. oil to 375°. Fry wings in oil, a few at a time, for 3-4 minutes on each side or until chicken juices run clear. Drain on paper towels.
2. Meanwhile, in a small saucepan, melt butter. Stir in the hot sauce and spices. Place chicken in a large bowl; add sauce and toss to coat. Remove to a serving plate with a slotted spoon. Serve with celery and ranch or blue cheese dressing if desired.
Note Uncooked chicken wing sections (wingettes) may be substituted for whole chicken wings.
1 piece 126 cal., 12g fat (4g sat. fat), 25mg chol., 105mg sod., 0 carb. (0 sugars, 0 fiber), 5g pro.

1. Sprinkle roast with salt and pepper. In a Dutch oven, brown roast in oil on all sides. Transfer to a 6-qt. slow cooker. Add the mushrooms, onions, broth, wine, tomato sauce, parsnips, celery, carrots, garlic, bay leaves, thyme and chili powder. Cover and cook on low for 6-8 hours or until the meat is tender.

2. Remove meat and vegetables to a serving platter; keep warm. Discard bay leaves. Skim fat from cooking juices; transfer juices to a small saucepan. Bring liquid to a boil. Combine cornstarch and water until smooth; gradually stir into the pan. Bring to a boil; cook and stir for 2 minutes or until thickened. Serve with mashed potatoes, meat and vegetables.

4 oz. cooked beef with ⅔ cup vegetables and ½ cup gravy 310 cal., 14g fat (5g sat. fat), 89mg chol., 363mg sod., 14g carb. (4g sugars, 3g fiber), 30g pro. **Diabetic exchanges** 4 lean meat, 2 vegetable, 1½ fat.

"This is a wonderful recipe, rich and delicious. The combo of red wine, tomato sauce and beef broth makes the gravy so flavorful. I didn't include parsnips, but added large chunks of potato towards the end of the cooking process. I added a splash of Worcestershire, too. I was short on time, so I simmered this on the stove instead of in a slow-cooker. It was ready to eat in 2½ hours. Really delicious. I'll make it again...soon!"

—Theresa419, tasteofhome.com

21 Contest-Winning Pot Roast

Packed with wholesome veggies and tender beef, this is one company-special entree all ages will like. Serve mashed potatoes alongside to soak up every last drop of the beefy gravy.
—Angie Stewart, Topeka, KS

Prep: 25 min. • **Cook:** 6 hours
Makes: 10 servings

- 1   boneless beef chuck roast (3 to 4 lbs.)
- ½   tsp. salt
- ¼   tsp. pepper
- 1   Tbsp. canola oil
- 1½   lbs. sliced fresh shiitake mushrooms
- 2½   cups thinly sliced onions
- 1½   cups reduced-sodium beef broth
- 1½   cups dry red wine or additional reduced-sodium beef broth
- 1   can (8 oz.) tomato sauce
- ¾   cup chopped peeled parsnips
- ¾   cup chopped celery
- ¾   cup chopped carrots
- 8   garlic cloves, minced
- 2   bay leaves
- 1½   tsp. dried thyme
- 1   tsp. chili powder
- ¼   cup cornstarch
- ¼   cup water
     Mashed potatoes

20 Queso Baked Nachos

I modified a nachos recipe I found, and my family loved it! It is now a regular at all our parties or any time we're craving nachos.
—Denise Wheeler, Newaygo, MI

Prep: 25 min. • **Bake:** 10 min.
Makes: 12 servings

- 1 lb. ground beef
- 1 envelope taco seasoning
- ¾ cup water
- 1 pkg. (13 oz.) tortilla chips
- 1 cup refried beans
- 1 jar (15½ oz.) salsa con queso dip
- 2 plum tomatoes, chopped
- ¼ cup minced fresh chives, optional
- ½ cup sour cream

1. Preheat oven to 350°. In a large skillet, cook and crumble beef over medium heat until no longer pink, 5-7 minutes; drain. Stir in taco seasoning and water; bring to a boil. Reduce heat; simmer, uncovered, until thickened, about 5 minutes, stirring occasionally.
2. In an ungreased 13x9-in. baking pan, layer a third each of the chips, beans, beef mixture and queso dip. Repeat layers twice.
3. Bake, uncovered, until heated through, 10-15 minutes. Top with tomatoes and, if desired, chives; serve immediately with sour cream on the side.
1 serving 313 cal., 16g fat (5g sat. fat), 29mg chol., 786mg sod., 32g carb. (2g sugars, 2g fiber), 11g pro.

"So tasty and easy! I used regular salsa queso dip on one end of the pan and white cheese dip on the other—my husband and I loved it both ways."
—Grammy Debbie, tasteofhome.com

19 Picnic Fried Chicken

For our family, it's not a picnic unless there's fried chicken! This is a Golden Oldie recipe for me—I've used it many times through the years.
—Edna Hoffman, Hebron, IN

Prep: 30 min. + marinating
Cook: 40 min. • **Makes:** 6 servings

- 1 broiler/fryer chicken (3 lbs.), cut up
- ¾ to 1 cup buttermilk

Coating
- 1½ to 2 cups all-purpose flour
- 1½ tsp. salt
- ½ tsp. pepper
- ½ tsp. garlic powder
- ½ tsp. onion powder
- 1 Tbsp. paprika
- ¼ tsp. ground sage
- ¼ tsp. ground thyme
- ⅛ tsp. baking powder
  Oil for frying

1. Pat chicken pieces dry with paper towels; place in a large flat dish. Pour buttermilk over chicken; cover and refrigerate at least 1 hour or overnight.
2. Combine the dry ingredients in a shallow dish. Add chicken pieces, 1 at a time, and turn to coat. Lay coated pieces on waxed paper for 15 minutes to allow coating to dry (this will help coating cling during frying).
3. In a Dutch oven or deep skillet, heat ½ in. oil over medium heat to 350°. Fry chicken in batches, uncovered, turning occasionally, until the coating is dark golden brown and the meat is no longer pink, 7-8 minutes per side. Drain on paper towels.
5 oz. cooked chicken 623 cal., 40g fat (7g sat. fat), 106mg chol., 748mg sod., 26g carb. (2g sugars, 1g fiber), 38g pro.

18 Mom's Meat Loaf

Mom made the best meat loaf, and now I do too. When I first met my husband, he wasn't a meat loaf guy, but this recipe won him over.

—Michelle Beran, Claflin, KS

Prep: 15 min.
Bake: 1 hour + standing
Makes: 6 servings

- 2 large eggs, lightly beaten
- ¾ cup 2% milk
- ⅔ cup finely crushed saltines
- ½ cup chopped onion
- 1 tsp. salt
- ½ tsp. rubbed sage
  Dash pepper
- 1½ lbs. lean ground beef (90% lean)
- 1 cup ketchup
- ½ cup packed brown sugar
- 1 tsp. Worcestershire sauce

1. Preheat oven to 350°. In a large bowl, combine the first 7 ingredients. Add beef; mix lightly but thoroughly. Shape into an 8x4-in. loaf; place in an ungreased 15x10x1-in. baking pan.
2. In a small bowl, combine the remaining ingredients, stirring to dissolve sugar; remove ½ cup for sauce. Spread remaining mixture over meat loaf.
3. Bake 60-65 minutes or until a thermometer inserted in the meat loaf reads 160°. Let stand 10 minutes before slicing. Serve with the reserved sauce.
1 piece 366 cal., 12g fat (5g sat. fat), 135mg chol., 1086mg sod., 38g carb. (31g sugars, 0 fiber), 26g pro.

Meat Loaf Tips

What can I do with leftover meat loaf? Our favorite use for leftover meat loaf is sandwiches. Gently fry thick slices in a skillet to give them a crisp edge, then layer them between slices of bread with your favorite burger toppings. Thin slices make an excellent filling for meat loaf gyros. You can also chop up the meat loaf and make chili, use it as a pizza topping or a taco filling, or use it in pasta dishes such as beef Bolognese.

What makes meat loaf juicy? The combination of crushed saltines, milk and eggs ensure this meat loaf turns out juicy. The saltines absorb moisture, which is released as the loaf cooks, preventing it from drying out. You could substitute broth or use bread crumbs, but the goal is to add dry and wet ingredients to the ground beef. Be sure to let the loaf rest. Slicing it too soon will release the juices from inside instead of allowing them to redistribute within the loaf

17 Homemade Buttermilk Biscuits

The recipe for these four-ingredient biscuits has been handed down for many generations in our family.
—Fran Thompson, Tarboro, NC

Takes: 30 min. • **Makes:** 8 biscuits

- ½ cup cold butter, cubed
- 2 cups self-rising flour
- ¾ cup buttermilk
  Melted butter

1. In a large bowl, cut butter into flour until mixture resembles coarse crumbs. Stir in buttermilk just until moistened.
2. Turn onto a lightly floured surface; knead 3-4 times. Pat or lightly roll to ¾-in. thickness. Cut with a floured 2½-in. biscuit cutter.
3. Place on a greased baking sheet. Bake at 425° until golden brown, 11-13 minutes. Brush tops with butter. Serve warm.
Note As a substitute for each cup of self-rising flour, place 1½ tsp. baking powder and ½ tsp. salt in a measuring cup. Add all-purpose flour to measure 1 cup.
1 biscuit 222 cal., 12g fat (7g sat. fat), 31mg chol., 508mg sod., 24g carb. (1g sugars, 1g fiber), 4g pro.

16 Spicy Touchdown Chili

Football, cool weather and chili just seem to go together. Whether I'm cheering on the local team on a Friday night or enjoying a Saturday afternoon of Oklahoma Sooner football with some friends, I enjoy serving this chili on game day.
—Chris Neal, Quapaw, OK

Prep: 30 min. • **Cook:** 4 hours
Makes: 12 servings (3 qt.)

- 1 lb. ground beef
- 1 lb. bulk pork sausage
- 2 cans (16 oz. each) kidney beans, rinsed and drained
- 2 cans (15 oz. each) pinto beans, rinsed and drained
- 2 cans (14½ oz. each) diced tomatoes with mild green chiles, undrained
- 1 can (14½ oz.) diced tomatoes with onions, undrained
- 1 can (12 oz.) beer
- 6 bacon strips, cooked and crumbled
- 1 small onion, chopped
- ¼ cup chili powder
- ¼ cup chopped pickled jalapeno slices
- 2 tsp. ground cumin
- 2 garlic cloves, minced
- 1 tsp. dried basil
- ¾ tsp. cayenne pepper
  Optional: Shredded cheddar cheese, sour cream and chopped green onions

1. In a large skillet, cook beef over medium heat until no longer pink, 6-8 minutes, crumbling beef; drain. Transfer to a 6-qt. slow cooker. Repeat with sausage.
2. Stir in the next 13 ingredients. Cook, covered, on low until heated through, 4-5 hours.
3. Top individual servings with cheddar cheese, sour cream and green onions as desired.
1 cup 365 cal., 15g fat (5g sat. fat), 48mg chol., 901mg sod., 34g carb. (7g sugars, 9g fiber), 22g pro.

15 Best Spaghetti & Meatballs

This classic recipe makes a big batch and is perfect for family meals and entertaining. One evening we had unexpected company. Since I had some of these meatballs in the freezer, I warmed them up as appetizers. Everyone raved!

—Mary Lou Koskella, Prescott, AZ

Prep: 30 min. • **Cook:** 2 hours
Makes: 16 servings

- 2 Tbsp. olive oil
- 1½ cups chopped onions
- 3 garlic cloves, minced
- 2 cans (12 oz. each) tomato paste
- 3 cups water
- 1 can (29 oz.) tomato sauce
- ⅓ cup minced fresh parsley
- 1 Tbsp. dried basil
- 2 tsp. salt
- ½ tsp. pepper

Meatballs

- 4 large eggs, lightly beaten
- 2 cups soft bread cubes (cut into ¼-in. pieces)
- 1½ cups 2% milk
- 1 cup grated Parmesan cheese
- 3 garlic cloves, minced
- 2 tsp. salt
- ½ tsp. pepper
- 3 lbs. ground beef
- 2 Tbsp. canola oil
- 2 lbs. spaghetti, cooked

1. In a Dutch oven, heat olive oil over medium heat. Add onions; saute until softened. Add garlic; cook 1 minute longer. Stir in tomato paste; cook 3-5 minutes. Add next 6 ingredients. Bring to a boil. Reduce heat; simmer, covered, for 50 minutes.
2. Combine the first 7 meatball ingredients. Add beef; mix lightly but thoroughly. Shape mixture into 1½-in. balls.

3. In a large skillet, heat canola oil over medium heat. Add meatballs; brown in batches until no longer pink. Drain. Add to sauce; bring to a boil. Reduce heat; simmer, covered, until flavors are blended, about 1 hour, stirring occasionally. Serve with hot cooked spaghetti.
½ cup sauce with 4 meatballs and 1¼ cups spaghetti 519 cal., 18g fat (6g sat. fat), 106mg chol., 1043mg sod., 59g carb. (8g sugars, 4g fiber), 30g pro.

Oven Option

Instead of frying, you can bake the meatballs at 400° on a rack over a rimmed baking sheet until golden brown, about 20 minutes.

14 Overnight Cinnamon Rolls

Each of these soft rolls is packed with cinnamon flavor. I like to try different fun fillings, too. They are definitely worth the overnight wait—perfect for special mornings, or any morning at all!

—Chris O'Connell, San Antonio, TX

Prep: 35 min. + chilling
Bake: 20 min. • **Makes:** 2 dozen

- 2 pkg. (¼ oz. each) active dry yeast
- 1½ cups warm water (110° to 115°)
- 2 large eggs, room temperature
- ½ cup butter, softened
- ½ cup sugar
- 2 tsp. salt
- 5¾ to 6¼ cups all-purpose flour

Cinnamon Filling
- 1 cup packed brown sugar
- 4 tsp. ground cinnamon
- ½ cup softened butter

Glaze
- 2 cups confectioners' sugar
- ¼ cup half-and-half cream
- 2 tsp. vanilla extract

1. In a small bowl, dissolve yeast in warm water. In a large bowl, combine eggs, butter, sugar, salt, yeast mixture and 3 cups flour; beat on medium speed until smooth. Stir in enough remaining flour to form a very soft dough (dough will be sticky). Do not knead. Cover; refrigerate overnight.

2. In a small bowl, mix brown sugar and cinnamon. Turn out dough onto a floured surface; divide in half. Roll 1 portion into an 18x12-in. rectangle. Spread with ¼ cup butter to within ½ in. of edges; sprinkle evenly with half of the brown sugar mixture.

3. Roll up jelly-roll style, starting with a long side; pinch seam to seal. Cut into 12 slices. Place in a greased 13x9-in. baking pan, cut side down. Repeat with the remaining dough and filling.

4. Cover with kitchen towels; let rise in a warm place until doubled, about 1 hour. Preheat oven to 375°.

5. Bake for 20-25 minutes or until lightly browned. In a small bowl, mix confectioners' sugar, cream and vanilla; spread over warm rolls.

1 roll 278 cal., 9g fat (5g sat. fat), 39mg chol., 262mg sod., 47g carb. (23g sugars, 1g fiber), 4g pro.

13 Classic Pizza

This recipe is a hearty, zesty main dish with a crisp, golden crust. Feel free to add your favorite toppings.
—Marianne Edwards, Lake Stevens, WA

Prep: 25 min. + rising
Bake: 25 min.
Makes: 2 pizzas (3 servings each)

- 1 pkg. (¼ oz.) active dry yeast
- 1 tsp. sugar
- 1¼ cups warm water (110° to 115°)
- ¼ cup canola oil
- 1 tsp. salt
- 3½ to 4 cups all-purpose flour
- 1 can (15 oz.) tomato sauce
- 3 tsp. dried oregano
- 1 tsp. dried basil
  Optional: 2 cups toppings of your choice (sliced pepperoni, cooked crumbled sausage, chopped onion, sliced mushrooms, chopped green pepper or sliced olives)
- 2 cups shredded part-skim mozzarella cheese

1. In large bowl, dissolve yeast and sugar in warm water; let stand for 5 minutes. Add oil and salt. Stir in flour, 1 cup at a time, until a soft dough forms.
2. Turn onto a floured surface; knead until smooth and elastic, 2-3 minutes. Place in a greased bowl; turn once to grease the top. Cover and let rise in a warm place until doubled, about 45 minutes.
3. Punch down dough; divide in half. Press each half into a greased 12-in. pizza pan. Combine the tomato sauce, oregano and basil; spread over crusts. If desired, add toppings. Sprinkle with cheese.
4. Bake at 400° for 25-30 minutes or until crust is lightly browned.
1 serving 485 cal., 18g fat (5g sat. fat), 24mg chol., 972mg sod., 63g carb. (3g sugars, 4g fiber), 18g pro.

12 Chicken & Dumplings

This classic, savory casserole is one of my husband's favorites. He loves the fluffy dumplings with plenty of gravy.
—Sue Mackey, Jackson, WI

Prep: 30 min. • **Bake:** 40 min.
Makes: 8 servings

- ½ cup chopped onion
- ½ cup chopped celery
- ¼ cup butter, cubed
- 2 garlic cloves, minced
- ½ cup all-purpose flour
- 2 tsp. sugar
- 1 tsp. salt
- 1 tsp. dried basil
- ½ tsp. pepper
- 4 cups chicken broth
- 1 pkg. (10 oz.) frozen green peas
- 4 cups cubed cooked chicken

Dumplings
- 2 cups biscuit/baking mix
- 2 tsp. dried basil
- ⅔ cup 2% milk

1. Preheat oven to 350°. In a large saucepan, saute onion and celery in butter until tender. Add garlic; cook 1 minute longer. Stir in flour, sugar, salt, basil and pepper until blended. Gradually add broth; bring to a boil. Cook and stir 1 minute or until thickened; reduce heat. Add peas and cook 5 minutes, stirring constantly. Stir in the chicken. Pour into a greased 13x9-in. baking dish.
2. For dumplings, in a small bowl, combine baking mix and basil. Stir in milk with a fork until moistened. Drop by tablespoonfuls into mounds over chicken mixture.
3. Bake, uncovered, 30 minutes. Cover and bake 10 minutes longer or until a toothpick inserted in a dumpling comes out clean.
1 serving 393 cal., 17g fat (7g sat. fat), 80mg chol., 1313mg sod., 33g carb. (6g sugars, 3g fiber), 27g pro.

11 🕐 The Best Ever Grilled Cheese Sandwich

Spreading a mixture of mayo and butter on the bread creates a delightfully crispy crust with the well-loved, wonderful flavor of butter one expects on a classic grilled cheese sandwich.
—Josh Rink, Milwaukee, WI

Takes: 25 min. • **Makes:** 4 servings

- 6 Tbsp. butter, softened, divided
- 8 slices sourdough bread
- 3 Tbsp. mayonnaise
- 3 Tbsp. finely shredded Manchego or Parmesan cheese
- ⅛ tsp. onion powder
- ½ cup shredded sharp white cheddar cheese
- ½ cup shredded Monterey Jack cheese
- ½ cup shredded Gruyere cheese
- 4 oz. Brie cheese, rind removed and sliced

1. Spread 3 Tbsp. butter on 1 side of the bread slices. Toast the bread, butter side down, in a large skillet or electric griddle over medium-low heat until golden brown, 2-3 minutes, remove. In a small bowl, mix together the mayonnaise, Manchego cheese, onion powder and the remaining 3 Tbsp. butter. In a second bowl, combine the cheddar, Monterey Jack and Gruyere cheeses.
2. To assemble sandwiches, top toasted side of 4 bread slices with sliced Brie. Sprinkle the cheddar cheese mixture evenly over Brie. Top with the remaining bread slices, toasted side facing inward. Spread the mayonnaise mixture on the outsides of each sandwich. Place in same skillet, and cook until the bread is golden brown and the cheese is melted, 5-6 minutes on each side. Serve immediately.
1 sandwich 659 cal., 49g fat (27g sat. fat), 122mg chol., 1017mg sod., 30g carb. (3g sugars, 1g fiber), 24g pro.

10 Bacon Cheeseburgers

I usually serve these juicy burgers when we have company. Guests rave about the flavorful cheesy topping.
—Wendy Sommers, West Chicago, IL

Takes: 30 min. • **Makes:** 6 servings

- 1½ lbs. ground beef
- 3 Tbsp. finely chopped onion
- ½ tsp. garlic salt
- ½ tsp. pepper
- 1 cup shredded cheddar cheese
- ⅓ cup canned sliced mushrooms
- 6 bacon strips, cooked and crumbled
- ¼ cup mayonnaise
- 6 hamburger buns, split
  Optional: Lettuce leaves and tomato slices

1. Combine beef, onion, garlic salt and pepper. Shape into 6 patties, ¾ in. thick. In a small bowl, combine the cheese, mushrooms, bacon and mayonnaise; chill.

2. Grill burgers, covered, over medium heat until a thermometer reads 160°, 5-7 minutes on each side. During the last 3 minutes, spoon ¼ cup of the cheese mixture onto each burger. Serve on buns, with lettuce and tomato if desired.

1 burger 480 cal., 29g fat (12g sat. fat), 86mg chol., 778mg sod., 23g carb. (4g sugars, 2g fiber), 30g pro.

9 Chocolate Cake

Years ago, I drove four hours to a cake contest, holding my entry on my lap the whole way. But it paid off! One bite and you'll see why this velvety beauty was named the best chocolate cake recipe and won first prize.
—Sandy Johnson, Tioga, PA

Prep: 30 min.
Bake: 30 min. + cooling
Makes: 16 servings

- 1 cup butter, softened
- 3 cups packed brown sugar
- 4 large eggs, room temperature
- 2 tsp. vanilla extract
- 2⅔ cups all-purpose flour
- ¾ cup baking cocoa
- 3 tsp. baking soda
- ½ tsp. salt
- 1⅓ cups sour cream
- 1⅓ cups boiling water

Frosting
- ½ cup butter, cubed
- 3 oz. unsweetened chocolate, chopped
- 3 oz. semisweet chocolate, chopped
- 5 cups confectioners' sugar
- 1 cup sour cream
- 2 tsp. vanilla extract

1. Preheat oven to 350°. Grease and flour three 9-in. round baking pans.

2. In a large bowl, cream butter and brown sugar until light and fluffy, 5-7 minutes. Add eggs, 1 at a time, beating well after each addition. Beat in vanilla. In another bowl, whisk flour, cocoa, baking soda and salt; add to the creamed mixture alternately with sour cream, beating well after each addition. Stir in water until blended.

3. Transfer batter to prepared pans. Bake until a toothpick comes out clean, 30-35 minutes. Cool in pans 10 minutes; remove to wire racks to cool completely.

4. For frosting, in a metal bowl over simmering water, melt butter and chocolates; stir until smooth. Cool slightly.

5. In a large bowl, combine the confectioners' sugar, sour cream and vanilla. Add the chocolate mixture; beat until smooth. Spread frosting between layers and over top and side of cake. Refrigerate any leftovers.

1 piece 685 cal., 29g fat (18g sat. fat), 115mg chol., 505mg sod., 102g carb. (81g sugars, 3g fiber), 7g pro.

8 Mile-High Chicken Potpie

Classic chicken potpie gets extra homey when it's loaded with a creamy filling and baked tall in a springform pan. This deep-dish marvel is perfect for Sunday dinners.
—Shannon Norris, Cudahy, WI

Prep: 40 min. + chilling
Bake: 50 min. + cooling
Makes: 6 servings

- 1 large egg, separated
- 4 to 6 Tbsp. cold water, divided
- 2 cups all-purpose flour
- ¼ tsp. salt
- ⅔ cup cold butter, cubed

Filling
- 3 Tbsp. butter
- 2 medium potatoes, peeled and cut into ½-in. cubes
- 4 medium carrots, thinly sliced
- 2 celery ribs, finely chopped
- ¼ cup finely chopped onion
- 3 Tbsp. all-purpose flour
- 2 Tbsp. chicken bouillon granules
- 1½ tsp. dried tarragon
- ½ tsp. coarsely ground pepper
- 1½ cups half-and-half cream
- 2½ cups cubed cooked chicken
- 1½ cups fresh peas or frozen peas
- ½ to 1 tsp. celery seed

1. In a small bowl, beat egg yolk with 2 Tbsp. water. In a large bowl, combine flour and salt; cut in butter until crumbly. Gradually add the yolk mixture, tossing with a fork; add additional water 1 Tbsp. at a time, as needed, until dough forms a ball. Divide dough into 2 portions, 1 with three-quarters of the dough and 1 with the remainder. Shape each portion into a disk; cover and refrigerate 1 hour or overnight.

2. For filling, in a Dutch oven, melt butter. Saute potatoes, carrots, celery and onion until crisp-tender, 5-7 minutes. Stir in flour, bouillon, tarragon and pepper. Gradually stir in cream. Bring to a boil; cook and stir until thickened, about 2 minutes. Stir in chicken and peas; set aside to cool completely.

3. On a lightly floured surface, roll out larger portion of dough to fit the bottom and up the side of an 8-in. springform pan. Place dough in pan; add cooled filling. Roll the remaining dough to fit over the top. Place over filling. Trim, seal and flute edge. Cut slits in top. Chill for at least 1 hour.

4. Lightly beat egg white with 1 tsp. water. Brush over the top crust; sprinkle with celery seed. Place pie on a rimmed baking tray.

5. Bake at 400° until crust is golden brown and filling is bubbly, 50-55 minutes. Cool on a wire rack for at least 30 minutes before serving.

1 piece 700 cal., 38g fat (22g sat. fat), 183mg chol., 1282mg sod., 58g carb. (8g sugars, 6g fiber), 29g pro.

7 Apple Pie

I remember coming home sullen one day because we'd lost a softball game. Grandma, in her wisdom, suggested that maybe a slice of hot apple pie would make me feel better. She was right.
—Maggie Greene, Granite Falls, WA

Prep: 20 min. + chilling
Bake: 1 hour + cooling
Makes: 8 servings

    Dough for double-crust pie
⅓ cup sugar
⅓ cup packed brown sugar
¼ cup all-purpose flour
1 tsp. ground cinnamon
¼ tsp. ground ginger
¼ tsp. ground nutmeg
6 to 7 cups thinly sliced peeled tart apples
1 Tbsp. lemon juice
1 Tbsp. butter
1 large egg white
    Optional: Turbinado or coarse sugar, ground cinnamon, vanilla bean ice cream and caramel sauce

1. Preheat oven to 375°. On a lightly floured surface, roll half the dough to a ⅛-in.-thick circle; transfer to a 9-in. pie plate. Chill while preparing filling. In a small bowl, combine sugars, flour and spices. In a large bowl, toss apples with lemon juice. Add the sugar mixture; toss to coat. Add filling to crust; dot with butter.
2. Roll the remaining dough to a ⅛-in.-thick circle; cut into 1-in.-wide strips. Arrange over filling in a lattice pattern. Trim and seal strips to edge of bottom crust; flute edge. Beat egg white until foamy; brush over crust. If desired, sprinkle with turbinado sugar and ground cinnamon.

3. Bake on the lowest rack until crust is golden brown and filling is bubbly, 60-70 minutes; cover with foil halfway if crust begins to get too dark. Cool on a wire rack. If desired, serve with ice cream and caramel sauce.

Dough for double-crust pie
Combine 2½ cups all-purpose flour and ½ tsp. salt; cut in 1 cup cold butter until crumbly. Gradually add ⅓ to ⅔ cup ice water, tossing with a fork until dough holds together when pressed. Divide dough in half. Shape each into a disk; wrap and refrigerate 1 hour.
1 piece 467 cal., 25g fat (15g sat. fat), 64mg chol., 331mg sod., 58g carb. (26g sugars, 2g fiber), 5g pro.

Apple Pie Tips

What are the best apples to use in pies? In the Test Kitchen, we prefer Granny Smith apples for pies because of their tart flavor and ability to hold their shape. If you like more sweetness, we recommend Braeburn, Golden Delicious or Jonagold.

How many apples are in 6 cups? Typically, 1 medium apple yields 1⅓ cups sliced. For 6 cups of sliced apples, you will need about 5 medium-sized peeled apples.

How can I keep the bottom of my apple pie from getting soggy? Allow the bottom crust to heat more rapidly than the rest of the pie. Place a baking sheet in the oven while it preheats, then bake your pie on the sheet.

5 Basic Homemade Bread

If you'd like to learn how to make bread, here's a wonderful place to start. This easy bread recipe bakes up deliciously golden brown. There's nothing like the homemade aroma wafting through my kitchen as it bakes.
—Sandra Anderson, New York, NY

Prep: 20 min. + rising
Bake: 30 min.
Makes: 2 loaves (16 pieces each)

    1   pkg. (¼ oz.) active dry yeast
    3   Tbsp. plus ½ tsp. sugar
    2¼ cups warm water (110° to 115°)
    1   Tbsp. salt
    6¼ to 6¾ cups bread flour
    2   Tbsp. canola oil

1. Dissolve yeast and ½ tsp. sugar in warm water; let stand until bubbles form on surface. Whisk together the remaining 3 Tbsp. sugar, salt and 3 cups flour. Stir oil into yeast mixture; pour into flour mixture and beat until smooth. Stir in enough remaining flour, ½ cup at a time, to form a soft dough.
2. Turn dough onto a floured surface; knead until smooth and elastic, 8-10 minutes. Place in a greased bowl; turn once to grease the top. Cover and let rise in a warm place until doubled, 1½ to 2 hours.
3. Punch dough down. Turn onto a lightly floured surface; divide dough in half. Shape each into a loaf. Place in 2 greased 9x5-in. loaf pans. Cover and let rise until doubled, 1 to 1½ hours.
4. Bake at 375° until loaf is golden brown and sounds hollow when tapped or has reached an internal temperature of 200°, 30-35 minutes. Remove from pans to wire racks to cool.
1 piece 102 cal., 1g fat (0 sat. fat), 0 chol., 222mg sod., 20g carb. (1g sugars, 1g fiber), 3g pro.

6 Creamy Macaroni & Cheese

This is the ultimate mac and cheese. It's saucy, thick and rich, with wonderful cheddar flavor. Once you taste it, you'll be hooked.
—Cindy Hartley, Chesapeake, VA

Prep: 20 min. • **Bake:** 35 min.
Makes: 6 servings

    2   cups uncooked elbow
        macaroni
    ½   cup butter, cubed
    ½   cup all-purpose flour
    1½ to 2 cups 2% milk
    1   cup sour cream
    8   oz. cubed Velveeta
    ¼   cup grated Parmesan cheese
    ½   tsp. salt
    ½   tsp. ground mustard
    ½   tsp. pepper
    2   cups shredded cheddar cheese

1. Cook macaroni according to the package directions.
2. Meanwhile, preheat oven to 350°. In a large saucepan, melt butter. Stir in flour until smooth. Gradually add 1½ cups milk. Bring to a boil; cook and stir 2 minutes or until thickened. Reduce heat; stir in sour cream, Velveeta, Parmesan cheese, salt, mustard and pepper until smooth and cheese is melted. Add more milk as needed to reach desired consistency.
3. Drain macaroni; toss with cheddar cheese. Transfer to a greased 3-qt. baking dish. Stir in cream sauce.
4. Bake, uncovered, 35-40 minutes or until golden brown and bubbly.
1 cup 653 cal., 46g fat (30g sat. fat), 143mg chol., 1141mg sod., 35g carb. (8g sugars, 1g fiber), 25g pro.

4 Best Lasagna

Want to know how to make lasagna for a casual holiday meal? You can't go wrong with this deliciously rich and meaty lasagna. My grown sons and daughter-in-law request it for their birthdays, too.

—Pam Thompson, Girard, IL

Prep: 1 hour
Bake: 50 min. + standing
Makes: 12 servings

- 9   lasagna noodles
- 1¼ lbs. bulk Italian sausage
- ¾   lb. ground beef
- 1   medium onion, diced
- 3   garlic cloves, minced
- 2   cans (one 28 oz., one 15 oz.) crushed tomatoes
- 2   cans (6 oz. each) tomato paste
- ⅔   cup water
- 2   to 3 Tbsp. sugar
- 3   Tbsp. plus ¼ cup minced fresh parsley, divided
- 2   tsp. dried basil
- ¾   tsp. fennel seed
- ¾   tsp. salt, divided
- ¼   tsp. coarsely ground pepper
- 1   large egg, lightly beaten
- 1   carton (15 oz.) ricotta cheese
- 4   cups shredded part-skim mozzarella cheese
- ¾   cup grated Parmesan cheese

1. Cook noodles according to package directions; drain. Meanwhile, in a Dutch oven, cook sausage, beef and onion over medium heat 8-10 minutes or until meat is no longer pink, breaking up meat into crumbles. Add garlic; cook 1 minute. Drain.
2. Stir in tomatoes, tomato paste, water, sugar, 3 Tbsp. parsley, basil, fennel, ½ tsp. salt and pepper; bring to a boil. Reduce heat; simmer, uncovered, 30 minutes, stirring occasionally.
3. In a small bowl, mix egg, ricotta cheese and the remaining ¼ cup parsley and ¼ tsp. salt.

4. Preheat oven to 375°. Spread 2 cups of the meat sauce into an ungreased 13x9-in. baking dish. Layer with 3 noodles and a third of the ricotta mixture. Sprinkle with 1 cup mozzarella cheese and 2 Tbsp. Parmesan cheese. Repeat layers twice. Top with the remaining meat sauce and cheeses (dish will be full).
5. Bake, covered, 25 minutes. Bake, uncovered, 25 minutes longer or until bubbly. Let stand 15 minutes before serving. If desired, top with additional parsley and Parmesan cheese.

1 piece 519 cal., 27g fat (13g sat. fat), 109mg chol., 1013mg sod., 35g carb. (10g sugars, 4g fiber), 35g pro.

"The only lasagna recipe I'll make! 2 Tbsp. sugar takes it to the sweeter side so I don't add as much. I make the meat sauce for stuffed shells too. So good!"

—**Christina968, tasteofhome.com**

3 Sunday Dinner Mashed Potatoes

Sour cream and cream cheese give these potatoes their delicious flavor. The dish can be prepped in advance and is special enough to serve guests.

—Melody Mellinger, Myerstown, PA

Prep: 35 min. • **Bake:** 20 min.
Makes: 8 servings

- 5 lbs. potatoes, peeled and cubed
- 1 cup sour cream
- 1 pkg. (8 oz.) cream cheese, softened
- 3 Tbsp. butter, divided
- 1 tsp. salt
- 1 tsp. onion salt
- ¼ tsp. pepper

1. Place potatoes in a Dutch oven; cover with water. Cover and bring to a boil. Cook until very tender, 20-25 minutes; drain well.
2. In a large bowl, mash potatoes. Add the sour cream, cream cheese, 2 Tbsp. butter, salt, onion salt and pepper; beat until fluffy.
3. Transfer to a greased 2-qt. baking dish. Dot with remaining 1 Tb. butter. Bake, uncovered, at 350° until heated through, 20-25 minutes.
¾ cup 300 cal., 13g fat (9g sat. fat), 43mg chol., 617mg sod., 40g carb. (4g sugars, 3g fiber), 5g pro.

2 Big & Buttery Chocolate Chip Cookies

Our version of the classic cookie is based on a recipe from a California bakery called Hungry Bear. The cookie is big, thick and chewy—perfect for dunking.

—Irene Yeh, Mequon, WI

Prep: 35 min. + chilling
Bake: 10 min./batch
Makes: about 2 dozen

- 1 cup butter, softened
- 1 cup packed brown sugar
- ¾ cup sugar
- 2 large eggs, room temperature
- 1½ tsp. vanilla extract
- 2⅔ cups all-purpose flour
- 1¼ tsp. baking soda
- 1 tsp. salt
- 1 pkg. (12 oz.) semisweet chocolate chips
- 2 cups coarsely chopped walnuts, toasted

1. In a large bowl, beat butter and sugars until blended. Beat in eggs and vanilla. In a small bowl, whisk flour, baking soda and salt; gradually beat into butter mixture. Stir in chocolate chips and walnuts.
2. Shape ¼ cupfuls of dough into balls. Flatten each ball to ¾-in. thickness (2½-in. diameter), smoothing edges as necessary. Place in an airtight container, separating layers with waxed paper or parchment; refrigerate, covered, overnight.
3. To bake, place dough portions 2 in. apart on parchment-lined baking sheets; let stand at room temperature 30 minutes before baking. Preheat oven to 400°.
4. Bake until edges are golden brown (centers will be light), 10-12 minutes. Cool on pans 2 minutes. Remove to wire racks to cool.
1 cookie 311 cal., 19g fat (8g sat. fat), 38mg chol., 229mg sod., 35g carb. (23g sugars, 2g fiber), 4g pro.

1 The Ultimate Chicken Noodle Soup

My first Wisconsin winter was so cold, all I wanted to eat was soup. This recipe is in heavy rotation at our house from November to April.
—Gina Nistico, Denver, CO

Prep: 15 min.
Cook: 45 min. + standing
Makes: 10 servings (about 3½ qt.)

- 2½ lbs. bone-in chicken thighs
- ½ tsp. salt
- ½ tsp. pepper
- 1 Tbsp. canola oil
- 1 large onion, chopped
- 1 garlic clove, minced
- 10 cups chicken broth
- 4 celery ribs, chopped
- 4 medium carrots, chopped
- 2 bay leaves
- 1 tsp. minced fresh thyme or ¼ tsp. dried thyme
- 3 cups uncooked kluski or other egg noodles (about 8 oz.)
- 1 Tbsp. chopped fresh parsley
- 1 Tbsp. lemon juice
  Optional: Additional salt and pepper

1. Pat chicken dry with paper towels; sprinkle with salt and pepper. In a 6-qt. stockpot, heat oil over medium-high heat. Add chicken in batches, cook until dark golden brown, 3-4 minutes. Remove chicken from pan; discard all but 2 Tbsp. drippings.

2. Add onion to drippings; cook and stir over medium-high heat until tender, 4-5 minutes. Add garlic; cook 1 minute longer. Add broth, stirring to loosen browned bits from pan. Bring to a boil. Return chicken to pan. Add celery, carrots, bay leaves and thyme. Reduce heat; simmer, covered, until chicken is tender, 25-30 minutes.

3. Transfer chicken to a plate. Remove soup from heat. Add noodles; let stand, covered, until noodles are tender, 20-22 minutes.

4. Meanwhile, when chicken is cool enough to handle, remove meat from bones; discard bones. Shred meat into bite-sized pieces. Return meat to stockpot. Stir in parsley and lemon juice. If desired, adjust seasoning with additional salt and pepper. Discard bay leaves.

1⅓ cups 239 cal., 12g fat (3g sat. fat), 68mg chol., 1176mg sod., 14g carb. (3g sugars, 2g fiber), 18g pro.

Chicken Noodle Soup Tips

What can I add for even more flavor? Cooking chicken in broth already gives it great flavor. But to kick it up a notch, stir in 1 Tbsp. of chicken bouillon granules.

Can I use chicken breasts? Yes! If you prefer, replace the thighs with bone-in chicken breasts. Once they reach an internal temperature of 165°, set the chicken on a plate, let it cool and then shred.

Is chicken noodle soup really good for you? Not only is this a feel-good dish, it's good for you, too! It's loaded with protein and vegetables and will keep you hydrated when you're feeling sick.

Touchdown Brat
Sliders, Page 56

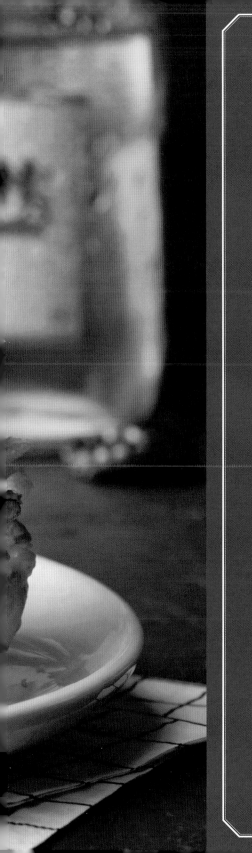

Pub Grub & Party Bites

Antipasto Platter

We entertain often, and antipasto is one of our favorite crowd-pleasers. Guests love having their choice of so many delicious nibbles, including pepperoni and cubes of provolone.
—Teri Lindquist, Gurnee, IL

Prep: 10 min. + chilling
Makes: 16 servings (3 qt.)

- 1 jar (24 oz.) pepperoncini, drained
- 1 can (15 oz.) garbanzo beans or chickpeas, rinsed and drained
- 2 cups halved fresh mushrooms
- 2 cups halved cherry tomatoes
- ½ lb. provolone cheese, cubed
- 1 can (6 oz.) pitted ripe olives, drained
- 1 pkg. (3½ oz.) sliced pepperoni
- 1 bottle (8 oz.) Italian vinaigrette dressing
     Lettuce leaves

1. In a large bowl, combine the pepperoncini, beans, mushrooms, tomatoes, provolone cheese, olives and pepperoni. Pour vinaigrette over mixture; toss to coat.
2. Refrigerate at least 30 minutes or overnight. Arrange on a lettuce-lined platter. Serve with toothpicks.
1 cup 178 cal., 13g fat (4g sat. fat), 15mg chol., 852mg sod., 8g carb. (2g sugars, 2g fiber), 6g pro.

"This is a keeper. Is wonderful as the recipe is written and easy to throw together. Took this to a friend's house and everyone loved it. It could easily be varied if you don't have or can't find certain ingredients."
—Elise21, tasteofhome.com

Bacon Cheddar Potato Skins

Both crisp and hearty, this restaurant-quality snack is one that my family requests often.
—Trish Perrin, Keizer, OR

Takes: 30 min. • **Makes:** 8 servings

- 4   large baking potatoes, baked
- 3   Tbsp. canola oil
- 1   Tbsp. grated Parmesan cheese
- ½   tsp. salt
- ¼   tsp. garlic powder
- ¼   tsp. paprika
- ⅛   tsp. pepper
- 8   bacon strips, cooked and crumbled
- 1½ cups shredded cheddar cheese
- ½   cup sour cream
- 4   green onions, sliced

1. Preheat oven to 475°. Cut potatoes in half lengthwise; scoop out pulp, leaving a ¼-in. shell (save pulp for another use). Place potato skins on a greased baking sheet.
2. Combine oil with cheese, salt, garlic powder, paprika and pepper; brush over both sides of the potato skins.
3. Bake until crisp, about 7 minutes on each side. Sprinkle bacon and cheddar cheese inside the skins. Bake until cheese is melted, about 2 minutes longer. Top with sour cream and onions. Serve immediately.
1 potato skin 350 cal., 19g fat (7g sat. fat), 33mg chol., 460mg sod., 34g carb. (2g sugars, 4g fiber), 12g pro.

Shrimp Cocktail

During the '60s, shrimp cocktail was one of the most popular party foods around. And it's still a crowd favorite. It's the one appetizer that I serve for every special occasion as well as for munchie meals.

—Peggy Allen, Pasadena, CA

Prep: 30 min. + chilling
Makes: about 6 dozen
(1¼ cups sauce)

- 3 qt. water
- 1 small onion, sliced
- ½ medium lemon, sliced
- 2 sprigs fresh parsley
- 1 Tbsp. salt
- 5 whole peppercorns
- 1 bay leaf
- ¼ tsp. dried thyme
- 3 lbs. uncooked shrimp (26-30 per lb.), peeled and deveined (tails on)

Sauce
- 1 cup chili sauce
- 2 Tbsp. lemon juice
- 2 Tbsp. prepared horseradish
- 4 tsp. Worcestershire sauce
- ½ tsp. salt
   Dash cayenne pepper
   Lemon wedges, optional

1. In a Dutch oven, combine the first 8 ingredients; bring to a boil. Add shrimp. Reduce heat; simmer, uncovered, until shrimp turn pink, 4-5 minutes.
2. Drain shrimp and immediately rinse in cold water. Refrigerate until cold, 2-3 hours. For sauce, in a small bowl, combine the next 6 ingredients. Refrigerate until serving.
3. Arrange shrimp on a serving platter; serve with sauce and, if desired, lemon wedges.
1 oz. cooked shrimp with about 2 tsp. sauce 59 cal., 1g fat (0 sat. fat), 66mg chol., 555mg sod., 4g carb. (2g sugars, 0 fiber), 9g pro.

Easy Buffalo Chicken Dip

Everyone will simply devour this savory and delicious dip with shredded chicken throughout. The spicy kick makes it perfect football-watching food, and the recipe always brings raves.

—Janice Foltz, Hershey, PA

Takes: 30 min. • **Makes:** 4 cups

- 1 pkg. (8 oz.) reduced-fat cream cheese
- 1 cup reduced-fat sour cream
- ½ cup Louisiana-style hot sauce
- 3 cups shredded cooked chicken breast
   Assorted crackers

1. Preheat oven to 350°. In a large bowl, beat cream cheese, sour cream and hot sauce until smooth; stir in chicken.
2. Transfer to an 8-in. square baking dish coated with cooking spray. Cover and bake until heated through, 18-22 minutes. Serve warm, with crackers.
3 Tbsp. 77 cal., 4g fat (2g sat. fat), 28mg chol., 71mg sod., 1g carb. (1g sugars, 0 fiber), 8g pro.

Walking Tacos

These walking tacos are perfect for an on-the-go dinner, a campfire meal or an easy game-night supper. The ingredients go right into the chip bags!

Beverly Matthews, Richland, WA

Prep: 10 min. • **Cook:** 30 min.
Makes: 5 servings

- 1 lb. ground beef
- 1 envelope reduced-sodium chili seasoning mix
- ¼ tsp. pepper
- 1 can (10 oz.) diced tomatoes and green chiles
- 1 can (15 oz.) Ranch Style beans (pinto beans in seasoned tomato sauce)
- 5 pkg. (1 oz. each) corn chips
  Toppings: Shredded cheddar cheese, sour cream and sliced green onions

1. In a large skillet, cook beef over medium heat until no longer pink, breaking into crumbles, 6-8 minutes; drain. Stir in chili seasoning mix, pepper, tomatoes and beans; bring to a boil. Reduce heat; simmer, uncovered, until thickened, 20-25 minutes, stirring occasionally.

2. Just before serving, cut open corn chip bags. Add beef mixture and toppings.

1 serving 530 cal., 28g fat (6g sat. fat), 56mg chol., 1017mg sod., 44g carb. (5g sugars, 6g fiber), 24g pro.

"If you cut the bag along the long edge, they are easier to fill and eat."

—JulieGr, tasteofhome.com

Sweet Tea Boysenberry Shandy

I love an ice-cold beer on a hot summer day. I also love sweet tea, so one day I got the great idea to mix the two. Wow! It was absolutely delish. I experimented with different flavorings, and this combination was my favorite.
—Kelly Williams, Forked River, NJ

Prep: 10 min.
Cook: 5 min. + chilling
Makes: 12 servings (2¼ qt.)

- 1½ cups water
- 4 tea bags
- ¾ cup sugar
- ¾ cup boysenberry syrup
- 4 cups cold water
- 3 bottles (12 oz. each) beer or white ale, chilled
- 1 medium orange, sliced, optional

1. In a large saucepan, bring water to a boil; remove from heat. Add tea bags; steep, covered, 3-5 minutes, according to taste. Discard tea bags. Stir in sugar and syrup until dissolved. Stir in cold water. Transfer to a 3-qt. pitcher; refrigerate until cold.
2. Stir beer into tea mixture; serve immediately. If desired, top with orange slices.
¾ cup 137 cal., 0 fat (0 sat. fat), 0 chol., 5mg sod., 29g carb. (26g sugars, 0 fiber), 0 pro.

Air-Fryer Potato Chips

For Christmas last year, I received an air fryer. Potato chips are simple to make in it and are an essential, crispy side for lunch.

Melissa Obernesser, Oriskany, NY

Prep: 20 min. + soaking
Cook: 15 min./batch
Makes: 6 servings

> 2   large potatoes
>   Olive oil-flavored cooking spray
> ½   tsp. sea salt
>   Minced fresh parsley, optional

1. Preheat air fryer to 360°. Using a mandoline or vegetable peeler, cut potatoes into very thin slices. Transfer to a large bowl; add enough ice water to cover. Soak for 15 minutes; drain. Add more ice water and soak another 15 minutes.
2. Drain potatoes; place on towels and pat dry. Spritz potatoes with cooking spray; sprinkle with salt. In batches, place potato slices in a single layer on greased tray in air-fryer basket. Cook until crisp and golden brown, 15-17 minutes, stirring and turning every 5-7 minutes. If desired, sprinkle with parsley.
1 cup 148 cal., 1g fat (0 sat. fat), 0 chol., 252mg sod., 32g carb. (2g sugars, 4g fiber), 4g pro. **Diabetic exchanges** 2 starch.

Air-Frying Benefits

Air-fried food isn't necessarily healthy, but the method does cut down on the calories from fat that would otherwise be used to deep-fry foods.

Herb & Cheese-Stuffed Burgers

Tired of the same old ground beef burgers? This quick-fix alternative, with its creamy cheese filling, will wake up your taste buds.
—Sherri Cox, Lucasville, OH

Takes: 30 min. • **Makes:** 4 servings

> ¼   cup shredded cheddar cheese
> 2   Tbsp. cream cheese, softened
> 2   Tbsp. minced fresh parsley
> 3   tsp. Dijon mustard, divided
> 2   green onions, thinly sliced
> 3   Tbsp. dry bread crumbs
> 2   Tbsp. ketchup
> ½   tsp. salt
> ½   tsp. dried rosemary, crushed
> ¼   tsp. dried sage leaves
> 1   lb. lean ground beef (90% lean)
> 4   hamburger buns, split
>   Optional toppings: Lettuce leaves and tomato slices

1. In a small bowl, mix cheddar cheese, cream cheese, parsley and 1 tsp. mustard. In another bowl, mix green onions, bread crumbs, ketchup, seasonings and remaining mustard. Add beef; mix lightly but thoroughly.
2. Shape mixture into 8 thin patties. Spoon cheese mixture onto the center of 4 patties; top with remaining patties, pressing edges firmly to seal.
3. Grill burgers, covered, over medium heat or broil 4 in. from heat until a thermometer reads 160°, 4-5 minutes on each side. Serve on buns with toppings as desired.
1 burger 383 cal., 16g fat (7g sat. fat), 86mg chol., 861mg sod., 29g carb. (5g sugars, 1g fiber), 29g pro.

Amazing Mac & Cheese Pizza

I love pizza, and I love macaroni and cheese. After lots of experimenting, I figured out a wonderful way to combine the two. The pizza is a big hit among my colleagues, friends and family!

—Martha Muellenberg, Vermillion, SD

Prep: 20 min. • **Bake:** 35 min.
Makes: 8 servings

- 1   cup uncooked elbow macaroni
- 1   loaf (1 lb.) frozen pizza dough, thawed
- 2   tsp. olive oil
- ½   tsp. dried rosemary, crushed
- 8   slices American cheese
- 1   pkg. (8 oz.) shredded Velveeta cheese
- 2   cups shredded part-skim mozzarella cheese
- ¾   cup shredded cheddar cheese
- 8   bacon strips, cooked and crumbled
- ¼   tsp. dried oregano

1. Preheat oven to 400°. Cook macaroni according to package directions; drain.
2. Press dough into a greased 14-in. pizza pan. Brush with oil; sprinkle with rosemary. Top with American cheese.
3. Toss together shredded cheeses; sprinkle half of the mixture over pizza. Toss remaining cheese mixture with bacon, oregano and macaroni; distribute over top. Bake until crust is golden brown and cheese is melted, 35-40 minutes.
1 piece 514 cal., 27g fat (14g sat. fat), 80mg chol., 1127mg sod., 38g carb. (4g sugars, 1g fiber), 27g pro.

Sweet & Spicy Jalapeno Poppers

There's no faster way to get a party started than with bacon-wrapped hot poppers. Prep them ahead and bake them just before serving. Even your hot-pepper-intolerant guests will love these.

—Dawn Onuffer, Crestview, FL

Takes: 30 min. • **Makes:** 1 dozen

- 6   jalapeno peppers
- 4   oz. cream cheese, softened
- 2   Tbsp. shredded cheddar cheese
- 6   bacon strips, halved widthwise
- ¼   cup packed brown sugar
- 1   Tbsp. chili seasoning mix

1. Cut jalapenos in half lengthwise and remove seeds; set aside. In a small bowl, beat cheeses until blended. Spoon into pepper halves. Wrap a half-strip of bacon around each pepper half.
2. Combine brown sugar and chili seasoning; coat peppers with sugar mixture. Place in a greased 15x10x1-in. baking pan.
3. Bake at 350° until bacon is firm, 18-20 minutes.
Note Wear disposable gloves when cutting hot peppers; the oils can burn skin. Avoid touching your face.
1 stuffed pepper half 66 cal., 5g fat (3g sat. fat), 15mg chol., 115mg sod., 3g carb. (3g sugars, 0 fiber), 2g pro.

Mini Corn Dogs

Bring a county fair favorite into your home with these bite-sized corn dogs! I make my own by wrapping cornmeal dough around mini hot dogs. Kids and the young at heart love them.

—Geralyn Harrington, Floral Park, NY

Takes: 30 min. • **Makes:** 2 dozen

1⅔ cups all-purpose flour
⅓ cup cornmeal
3 tsp. baking powder
1 tsp. salt
3 Tbsp. cold butter
1 Tbsp. shortening
1 large egg, room temperature
¾ cup 2% milk
24 miniature hot dogs

Honey Mustard Sauce
⅓ cup honey
⅓ cup prepared mustard
1 Tbsp. molasses

1. In a large bowl, combine the first 4 ingredients. Cut in butter and shortening until mixture resembles coarse crumbs. Beat egg and milk. Stir into dry ingredients until a soft dough forms; dough will be sticky.

2. Turn onto a generously floured surface; knead 6-8 times or until smooth, adding additional flour as needed. Roll out to ¼-in. thickness. Cut with a 2¼-in. biscuit cutter. Fold each dough circle over a hot dog and press edge to seal. Place on greased baking sheets.

3. Bake at 450° until golden brown, 10-12 minutes. In a small bowl, combine the sauce ingredients. Serve with corn dogs.

1 corn dog 109 cal., 5g fat (2g sat. fat), 18mg chol., 306mg sod., 14g carb. (5g sugars, 0 fiber), 3g pro.

Cuban Sliders

Bake till these wonderful little rolls are lightly toasted and the cheese melts. The leftovers keep really well in the fridge, and they make a lovely cold snack. Followers of my blog go nuts for these!

—Serene Herrera, Dallas, TX

Takes: 30 min. • **Makes:** 2 dozen

- 2 pkg. (12 oz. each) Hawaiian sweet rolls
- 1¼ lbs. thinly sliced deli ham
- 9 slices Swiss cheese (about 6 oz.)
- 24 dill pickle slices

Topping
- ½ cup butter, cubed
- 2 Tbsp. finely chopped onion
- 2 Tbsp. Dijon mustard

1. Preheat oven to 350°. Without separating rolls, cut each package of rolls in half horizontally; arrange bottom halves in a greased 13x9-in. baking pan. Layer with ham, cheese and pickles; replace the top halves of the rolls.

2. In a microwave, melt butter; stir in onion and mustard. Drizzle over rolls. Bake, covered, 10 minutes. Uncover; bake until golden brown and heated through, 5-10 minutes longer.

1 slider 191 cal., 10g fat (5g sat. fat), 42mg chol., 532mg sod., 17g carb. (6g sugars, 1g fiber), 10g pro.

How To Melt Butter, Mess-Free

To melt butter without spattering all over the microwave, repurpose that butter wrapper you'd have otherwise tossed out. Cover the cup or bowl with the wrapper before melting a stick of butter.

Buffalo Chicken Meatballs

I like to make these game-day appetizer meatballs with blue cheese or ranch salad dressing for dipping. If I make them for a meal, I often skip the dressing and instead serve the meatballs with blue cheese polenta on the side. Yum!

—Amber Massey, Argyle, TX

Prep: 15 min. • **Bake:** 20 min.
Makes: 2 dozen

- ¾ cup panko bread crumbs
- ⅓ cup plus ½ cup Louisiana-style hot sauce, divided
- ¼ cup chopped celery
- 1 large egg white
- 1 lb. lean ground chicken
  Optional: Ranch or blue cheese salad dressing and chopped celery leaves

1. Preheat oven to 400°. In a large bowl, combine bread crumbs, ⅓ cup hot sauce, celery and egg white. Add chicken; mix lightly but thoroughly.
2. Shape into twenty-four 1-in. balls. Place on a greased rack in a shallow baking pan. Bake 20-25 minutes or until cooked through.
3. Toss meatballs with remaining hot sauce. If desired, drizzle with salad dressing and sprinkle with celery leaves.

1 meatball 33 cal., 1g fat (0 sat. fat), 14mg chol., 338mg sod., 1g carb. (0 sugars, 0 fiber), 4g pro.

Add Some Healthy Crunch

To add variety and color, serve celery and carrot sticks alongside these meatballs.

Fresh Shrimp & Avocado Nachos

I'm a fan of shrimp, and my family loves nachos. When I combined these favorites and added fresh avocado, the result was a cool and satisfying snack.

—Teri Schloessmann, Tulsa, OK

Prep: 30 min. + chilling
Makes: 10 servings

- 4 plum tomatoes, chopped
- 3 tomatillos, husked and chopped
- 4 jalapeno peppers, seeded and finely chopped
- 1 small onion, chopped
- ¼ cup minced fresh cilantro
- 3 Tbsp. olive oil
- 3 Tbsp. lime juice, divided
- 2 Tbsp. seasoned rice vinegar
- 2 garlic cloves, minced
- 1½ tsp. sea salt
- ½ tsp. dried oregano
- 1 lb. peeled and deveined cooked shrimp (31-40 per lb.), coarsely chopped
- 2 medium ripe avocados, peeled and pitted, divided
- ½ cup sour cream
- 8 cups tortilla chips
- 1 cup shredded lettuce

1. In a large bowl, combine tomatoes, tomatillos, peppers, onion, cilantro, oil, 1 Tbsp. lime juice, vinegar, garlic, sea salt and oregano. Cover and refrigerate until chilled, at least 30 minutes. Stir in shrimp.
2. For avocado cream, mash 1 avocado with sour cream and 1 Tbsp. lime juice until smooth. Cube remaining avocado and toss with remaining 1 Tbsp. lime juice.
3. To serve, arrange chips on a large platter. Top with shrimp mixture, cubed avocado, lettuce and avocado cream. Serve immediately.
Note Wear disposable gloves when cutting hot peppers; the oils can burn skin. Avoid touching your face.
1 serving 264 cal., 16g fat (3g sat. fat), 72mg chol., 542mg sod., 20g carb. (3g sugars, 3g fiber), 12g pro.

Spanakopita Pinwheels

I'm enthralled with spanakopita, and this spinach and feta pinwheel recipe was a quick and easy way to enjoy the pie. I have used it for get-togethers and family events with great success.
—Ryan Palmer, Windham, ME

Prep: 30 min. + cooling
Bake: 20 min. • **Makes:** 2 dozen

- 1 medium onion, finely chopped
- 2 Tbsp. olive oil
- 1 tsp. dried oregano
- 1 garlic clove, minced
- 2 pkg. (10 oz. each) frozen chopped spinach, thawed and squeezed dry
- 2 cups crumbled feta cheese
- 2 large eggs, lightly beaten
- 1 pkg. (17.3 oz.) frozen puff pastry, thawed

1. In a small skillet, saute onion in oil until tender. Add oregano and garlic; cook 1 minute longer. Add spinach; cook 3 minutes longer or until liquid is evaporated. Transfer spinach mixture to a large bowl; cool.
2. Add feta cheese and eggs to spinach mixture; mix well. Unfold puff pastry. Spread each sheet with half the spinach mixture to within ½ in. of edges. Roll up jelly-roll style. Cut each into twelve ¾-in. slices. Place cut side down on greased baking sheets.
3. Bake at 400° for 18-22 minutes or until golden brown. Serve warm.
1 pinwheel 197 cal., 13g fat (5g sat. fat), 39mg chol., 392mg sod., 14g carb. (1g sugars, 3g fiber), 7g pro.

"This was a great app that I served to guests. It took minimal time to put together and was fun to eat."
—rwippel, tasteofhome.com

Chunky Chicken Salad with Grapes & Pecans

This chicken salad with grapes is ready in a snap when using rotisserie chicken and a few quick chops of pecans, sweet onion and celery.
—Julie Sterchi, Campbellsville, KY

Takes: 25 min. • **Makes:** 8 servings

- ½ cup mayonnaise
- 2 Tbsp. sour cream
- 1 Tbsp. lemon juice
- ⅛ tsp. salt
- ⅛ tsp. pepper
- 4 cups shredded rotisserie chicken
- 1¼ cups seedless red grapes, halved
- ½ cup chopped pecans
- ½ cup chopped celery
- ¼ cup chopped sweet onion, optional
   Optional: Lettuce leaves or whole wheat bread slices

In a large bowl, combine the first 5 ingredients. Add the chicken, grapes, pecans, celery and, if desired, onion; mix lightly to coat. If desired, serve with lettuce leaves or whole wheat bread.
¾ cup chicken salad 311 cal., 22g fat (4g sat. fat), 70mg chol., 180mg sod., 6g carb. (5g sugars, 1g fiber), 21g pro.

Mini Burgers with the Works

I started preparing these mini burgers several years ago as a creative way to use up bread crusts accumulating in my freezer. Their tiny size makes them simply irresistible.
—Linda Lane, Bennington, VT

Takes: 30 min. • **Makes:** 1 dozen

- ¼ lb. ground beef
- 3 slices American cheese
- 4 slices white bread (heels of loaves recommended)
- 2 Tbsp. prepared Thousand Island salad dressing
- 2 pearl onions, thinly sliced
- 4 baby dill pickles, thinly sliced
- 3 cherry tomatoes, thinly sliced

1. Shape beef into twelve 1-in. patties. Place on a microwave-safe plate lined with paper towels. Cover with another paper towel; microwave on high for 1 minute or until meat is no longer pink. Cut each slice of cheese into fourths; set aside.

2. Using a 1-in. round cookie cutter, cut out 6 circles from each slice of bread. Spread half the bread circles with dressing. Layer with burgers, cheese, onions, pickles and tomatoes. Top with the remaining bread circles; secure with toothpicks.

1 burger 68 cal., 3g fat (1g sat. fat), 11mg chol., 153mg sod., 5g carb. (1g sugars, 0 fiber), 4g pro.

Meatball Pizza

I always keep meatballs and pizza crusts in the freezer to make this specialty on the spur of the moment. Add a tossed salad and you have a delicious dinner.
—Mary Humeniuk-Smith, Perry Hall, MD

Takes: 25 min. • **Makes:** 8 servings

- 1 prebaked 12-in. pizza crust
- 1 can (8 oz.) pizza sauce
- 1 tsp. garlic powder
- 1 tsp. Italian seasoning
- ¼ cup grated Parmesan cheese
- 1 small onion, halved and sliced
- 12 frozen fully cooked Italian meatballs (½ oz. each), thawed and halved
- 1 cup shredded part-skim mozzarella cheese
- 1 cup shredded cheddar cheese

1. Preheat oven to 350°. Place crust on an ungreased 12-in. pizza pan or baking sheet.
2. Spread sauce over crust; sprinkle with garlic powder, Italian seasoning and Parmesan cheese. Top with onion and meatballs; sprinkle with remaining cheeses. Bake 12-17 minutes or until cheese is melted. If desired, top with additional Parmesan cheese.
1 serving 320 cal., 16g fat (8g sat. fat), 35mg chol., 754mg sod., 28g carb. (3g sugars, 2g fiber), 17g pro.

"So good. My only change—I added a few fresh mushrooms. Delicious pizza!"
—K., tasteofhome.com

Soft Beer Pretzel Nuggets

What goes together better than beer and pretzels? Not much that I can think of. That's why I put them together into one recipe. I'm always looking for new ways to combine fun flavors. I love the way this recipe turned out!

—Alyssa Wilhite, Whitehouse, TX

Prep: 1 hour + rising
Bake: 10 min./batch
Makes: 8 dozen

 1   bottle (12 oz.) amber beer or nonalcoholic beer
 1   pkg. (¼ oz.) active dry yeast
 2   Tbsp. unsalted butter, melted
 2   Tbsp. sugar
1½ tsp. salt
 4   to 4½ cups all-purpose flour
10   cups water
 ⅔   cup baking soda

Topping
 1   large egg yolk
 1   Tbsp. water
     Coarse salt, optional

1. In a small saucepan, heat beer to 110°-115°; remove from heat. Stir in yeast until dissolved. In a large bowl, combine butter, sugar, salt, yeast mixture and 3 cups flour; beat on medium speed until smooth. Stir in enough remaining flour to form a soft dough (dough will be sticky).
2. Turn dough onto a floured surface; knead until smooth and elastic, 6-8 minutes. Place in a greased bowl, turning once to grease the top. Cover and let rise in a warm place until doubled, about 1 hour.
3. Preheat oven to 425°. Punch dough down. Turn onto a lightly floured surface; divide and shape into 8 balls. Roll each into a 12-in. rope. Cut each rope into 1-in. pieces.

4. In a Dutch oven, bring 10 cups water and baking soda to a boil. Drop nuggets, 12 at a time, into boiling water. Cook for 30 seconds. Remove with a slotted spoon; drain well on paper towels.
5. Place on greased baking sheets. In a small bowl, whisk egg yolk and 1 Tbsp. water; brush over pretzels. Sprinkle with coarse salt if desired. Bake 10-12 minutes or until golden brown. Remove from pans to a wire rack to cool.

Freeze option Freeze cooled pretzel nuggets in airtight containers. To use, thaw at room temperature or, if desired, microwave on high 20-30 seconds or until heated through.

6 pretzel nuggets 144 cal., 2g fat (1g sat. fat), 8mg chol., 302mg sod., 26g carb. (2g sugars, 1g fiber), 4g pro.
Pretzel Rolls Divide dough into 8 pieces and shape each into a ball; roll each into a 14-in. rope. Starting at 1 end of each rope, loosely wrap dough around itself to form a coil. Boil, top and bake as directed. You can also make traditional pretzels with the same dough.

Sauce 'Em Up

Serve honey mustard, warmed process cheese sauce or even nacho dip alongside these nuggets for tasty dipping.

Air-Fryer Mozzarella Sticks

Deep-fried mozzarella sticks are one of our favorite appetizers. I figured out how to make them at home without having to haul out the deep fryer.
—Mary Merchant, Barre, VT

Prep: 15 min. + freezing
Cook: 10 min. • **Makes:** 1 dozen

- 2 cups dry bread crumbs
- 3 Tbsp. all-purpose flour
- 3 large eggs
- 2 Tbsp. water
- 1 Tbsp. Italian seasoning
- 1 tsp. garlic powder
- ¼ tsp. pepper
- 12 sticks string cheese
- Cooking spray
- 1 cup marinara sauce or meatless pasta sauce, warmed
  Chopped fresh basil, optional

1. In a small skillet, toast bread crumbs until lightly browned, about 1-2 minutes. Cool completely.

2. Place flour in a shallow bowl. In another shallow bowl, beat eggs and water. In a third shallow bowl, combine bread crumbs, Italian seasoning, garlic powder and pepper. Coat cheese sticks with flour, then dip into egg mixture and coat with bread crumb mixture. Repeat egg and bread crumb coatings. Cover and freeze for 8 hours or overnight.

3. Preheat air fryer to 400°. Place cheese in a single layer on a greased tray in air-fryer basket; spritz with cooking spray. Cook until golden brown and heated through, 6-8 minutes, turning halfway through cooking and spritzing with additional cooking spray. Allow to stand 3-5 minutes before serving. Serve with marinara or pasta sauce for dipping. If desired, sprinkle with fresh basil.

Note Cook times vary dramatically among brands of air fryers. Refer to your air-fryer manual for general cook times and adjust if necessary.

1 piece 148 cal., 8g fat (4g sat. fat), 46mg chol., 384mg sod., 10g carb. (2g sugars, 1g fiber), 11g pro.

Prosciutto Pinwheels

These sensational appetizers are a lot easier to make than they look. With just a few ingredients, they're a snap!
—Kaitlyn Benito, Everett, WA

Prep: 20 min. • **Bake:** 15 min.
Makes: 20 appetizers

- 1 sheet frozen puff pastry, thawed
- ¼ cup sweet hot mustard
- ¼ lb. sliced prosciutto or deli ham, chopped
- ½ cup shredded Parmesan cheese

1. Unfold puff pastry. Spread mustard over pastry to within ½ in. of edges. Sprinkle with prosciutto and cheese. Roll up 1 side to the middle of the dough; roll up the other side so the 2 rolls meet in the center. Using a serrated knife, cut into ½-in. slices.
2. Place on greased baking sheets. Bake at 400° until puffed and golden brown, 11-13 minutes. Serve warm.
Freeze option Freeze cooled appetizers in freezer containers, separating layers with waxed paper. To use, reheat appetizers on a greased baking sheet in a 400° oven until crisp and heated through.
1 appetizer 86 cal., 5g fat (1g sat. fat), 6mg chol., 210mg sod., 8g carb. (0 sugars, 1g fiber), 3g pro.

Bloody Mary

Horseradish makes this one of the best Bloody Mary recipes in the world. Without the horseradish, you'll have a more traditional drink, and without the alcohol, you'll have a Virgin Mary. Serve with a stalk of celery, dill pickle spear or olives.
—*Taste of Home* Test Kitchen

Takes: 10 min. • **Makes:** 1 serving

- ¼ tsp. plus ⅛ tsp. celery salt, divided
- 1½ to 2 cups ice cubes, divided
- 2 oz. vodka
- 1 cup tomato juice, chilled
- 1 Tbsp. lemon juice
- 1½ tsp. lime juice
- ¾ tsp. Worcestershire sauce
- ½ tsp. prepared horseradish, optional
- ⅛ tsp. pepper
- ⅛ tsp. hot pepper sauce

Optional Garnishes
   Celery rib, pickle spear, green and ripe olives, cucumber slice and/or cocktail shrimp

1. Using water, moisten rim of a highball glass. Sprinkle ¼ tsp. celery salt on a small plate; dip rim into salt. Discard remaining celery salt from plate. Fill a shaker three-fourths full with ice. Place remaining ice in prepared glass.
2. Add vodka, juices, Worcestershire sauce, horseradish if desired, pepper, remaining celery salt and pepper sauce to shaker; cover and shake until condensation forms on exterior, 10-15 seconds. Strain into prepared glass. Garnish as desired.
1½ cups 180 cal., 1g fat (0 sat. fat), 0 chol., 1110mg sod., 12g carb. (7g sugars, 1g fiber), 2g pro.
Batch of Bloody Marys (4 servings) Place 1 cup ice in a 2-qt. pitcher. Add 1 cup vodka, 4 cups tomato juice, ¼ cup lemon juice, 2 Tbsp. lime juice, 1 Tbsp. Worcestershire sauce, 2 tsp. prepared horseradish if desired, ½ tsp. celery salt, ½ tsp. pepper and ½ tsp. hot pepper sauce; stir to combine. Serve over ice.

Chipotle Turkey Club Sandwich

We're crazy for BLTs. A nearby roadside stand carries gorgeous tomatoes every summer. We load up, then stuff our sandwiches with the usual suspects, plus smoked turkey and cheese.

—Pamela Shank, Parkersburg, WV

Takes: 15 min. • **Makes:** 4 servings

- ¼ cup reduced-fat chipotle mayonnaise
- 8 slices whole wheat bread, toasted
- 8 lettuce leaves
- ½ lb. thinly sliced deli smoked turkey
- 16 cooked center-cut bacon strips
- 4 slices reduced-fat Swiss cheese
- 8 slices tomato

Spread mayonnaise over 4 slices of toast. Layer with lettuce, turkey, bacon, cheese and tomato; top with remaining toast.

1 sandwich 416 cal., 18g fat (5g sat. fat), 70mg chol., 1265mg sod., 30g carb. (5g sugars, 4g fiber), 37g pro.

Make Your Own Chipotle Mayo

It's easy to make your own chipotle mayo. In a food processor, combine 1 cup mayonnaise with ¼ cup Dijon mustard, 1 to 2 seeded chipotle peppers in adobe sauce, 2 Tbsp. white wine vinegar and 1 Tbsp. minced garlic. Cover and process until well blended.

Maryland Corn Pops

Fresh-picked sweet corn is a big thing in Maryland. Here's my homespun version of Mexican street corn that brings in local bay flavors.

—Kristie Schley, Severna Park, MD

Prep: 25 min. • **Grill:** 10 min.
Makes: 2 dozen

- 8 medium ears sweet corn, husked
- 2 Tbsp. canola oil
- 1½ cups mayonnaise
- 1½ tsp. garlic powder
- ¼ tsp. freshly ground pepper
- 24 corncob holders
- 2 cups crumbled feta cheese
- 2 Tbsp. seafood seasoning
- ¼ cup minced fresh cilantro
  Lime wedges, optional

1. Brush all sides of corn with oil. Grill, covered, over medium heat until tender and lightly browned, 10-12 minutes, turning occasionally. Remove from grill; cool slightly.
2. Meanwhile, in a small bowl, mix mayonnaise, garlic powder and pepper. Cut each ear of corn into thirds. Insert 1 corncob holder into each piece. Spread corn with mayonnaise mixture; sprinkle with cheese, seafood seasoning and cilantro. If desired, serve with lime wedges.
1 corn pop 164 cal., 14g fat (3g sat. fat), 10mg chol., 336mg sod., 7g carb. (2g sugars, 1g fiber), 3g pro.

Lobster Tartlets

I love lobster, so I created these gems. They are perfect appetizers for a cocktail party or family dinner. Top with chives or green onions for color.
—Lorraine Caland, Shuniah, ON

Takes: 25 min. • **Makes:** 2½ dozen

- ½ cup shredded white cheddar cheese
- ½ cup shredded provolone cheese
- ½ cup cooked lobster meat or 1 can (6½ oz.) flaked lobster meat, drained
- ⅓ cup finely chopped sweet red pepper
- 2 Tbsp. finely chopped green onion (white portion only)
- 2 Tbsp. mayonnaise
  Dash seafood seasoning
- 2 pkg. (1.9 oz. each) frozen miniature phyllo tart shells
  Paprika, optional

Preheat oven to 350°. In a small bowl, combine the first 7 ingredients. Spoon mixture into tart shells. Place filled shells on an ungreased baking sheet. Bake until shells are lightly browned and filling is heated through, 12-15 minutes. If desired, sprinkle with paprika before serving.
1 tartlet 76 cal., 4g fat (1g sat. fat), 8mg chol., 78mg sod., 6g carb. (0 sugars, 0 fiber), 3g pro.

Taylor's Jalapeno Poppers

If you own a barbecue joint like I do, you pretty much dream about barbecue in your sleep. Jalapeno poppers are one of my favorite appetizers, and this recipe is a unique way to combine two foods I love. These are popular on the menu at my restaurant. Try stuffing the peppers with cooked chicken or beef, too.
—Taylor Hicks, Las Vegas, NV

Prep: 35 min. • **Cook:** 5 min./batch
Makes: 6 servings

- 6 large jalapeno peppers
  Oil for deep-fat frying
- 1 cup refrigerated fully cooked barbecued shredded pork (about 8 oz.)
- 1 cup shredded mild cheddar cheese
- ¼ cup barbecue sauce
- 1 cup all-purpose flour
- 1 cup cornstarch
- 3 tsp. salt
- 3 tsp. paprika
- 12 oz. beer
  White barbecue sauce, optional

1. Cut off stem end of jalapenos. Using the tip of a small knife, remove seeds and membrane. In a large saucepan, bring 8 cups water to a boil. Add jalapenos; cook, uncovered, just until crisp-tender, 2-3 minutes. Remove and immediately drop into ice water. Drain and pat completely dry.
2. In an electric skillet or deep fryer, heat oil to 375°. In a small bowl, mix pork, cheese and barbecue sauce; spoon into jalapenos. In another bowl, whisk flour, cornstarch, salt and paprika; stir in beer just until moistened.
3. Using tongs, dip stuffed jalapenos into batter; fry in batches until golden brown, 3-4 minutes. Drain on paper towels. If desired, serve with white barbecue sauce.
Note Wear disposable gloves when cutting hot peppers; the oils can burn skin. Avoid touching your face.
1 appetizer 209 cal., 8g fat (4g sat. fat), 30mg chol., 870mg sod., 23g carb. (8g sugars, 1g fiber), 10g pro.

Touchdown Brat Sliders

It's game time when these minis make an appearance. Two things my husband loves—beer and brats—get stepped up a notch with crunchy flavored chips.

—Kirsten Shabaz, Lakeville, MN

Prep: 20 min. • **Cook:** 30 min.
Makes: 16 sliders

- 5   thick-sliced bacon strips, chopped
- 1   lb. uncooked bratwurst links, casings removed
- 1   large onion, finely chopped
- 2   garlic cloves, minced
- 1   pkg. (8 oz.) cream cheese, cubed
- 1   cup dark beer or nonalcoholic beer
- 1   Tbsp. Dijon mustard
- ¼   tsp. pepper
- 16 dinner rolls, split and toasted
- 2   cups cheddar and sour cream potato chips, crushed

1. In a large cast-iron or other heavy skillet, cook bacon over medium heat until crisp. Remove to paper towels with a slotted spoon; drain, reserving drippings. Cook bratwurst and onion in drippings over medium heat until meat is no longer pink, breaking into crumbles. Add garlic; cook 1 minute longer. Drain well.

2. Stir in the cream cheese, beer, mustard and pepper. Bring to a boil. Reduce heat; simmer, uncovered, until thickened, 15-20 minutes, stirring occasionally. Stir in bacon. Spoon ¼ cup onto the bottom half of each roll; sprinkle with chips. Replace tops.

1 slider 354 cal., 24g fat (10g sat. fat), 62mg chol., 617mg sod., 23g carb. (2g sugars, 2g fiber), 10g pro.

Seasoned Crab Cakes

These scrumptious crab cakes won first place at the National Hard Crab Derby in Crisfield, Maryland. I entered them on a whim after trying many crab cake recipes for my family.
—Betsy Hedeman, Timonium, MD

Prep: 20 min. + chilling
Cook: 10 min. • **Makes:** 8 crab cakes

- 3 cans (6 oz. each) crabmeat, drained, flaked and cartilage removed
- 1 cup cubed bread
- 2 large eggs
- 3 Tbsp. mayonnaise
- 3 Tbsp. half-and-half cream
- 1 Tbsp. lemon juice
- 1 Tbsp. butter, melted
- 1½ tsp. seafood seasoning
- 1 tsp. Worcestershire sauce
- 1 tsp. salt
- ½ cup dry bread crumbs
- ½ cup canola oil

1. In a large bowl, combine crab and bread cubes. In another bowl, whisk the eggs, mayonnaise, cream, lemon juice, butter, seafood seasoning, Worcestershire sauce and salt. Add to crab mixture and mix gently (mixture will be moist).
2. Place bread crumbs in a shallow dish. Drop the crab mixture by ⅓ cupfuls into crumbs; shape each into a ¾-in.-thick patty. Carefully turn to coat. Cover and refrigerate for at least 2 hours.
3. In a large skillet, cook crab cakes in oil for 4-5 minutes on each side or until golden brown and crispy.
1 crab cake 197 cal., 15g fat (3g sat. fat), 81mg chol., 640mg sod., 8g carb. (1g sugars, 0 fiber), 7g pro.

No-Guilt Beefy Nachos

Nachos you can feel good about! This meaty topping has less fat and sodium than typical nacho beef because you use lean meat and make your own seasoning.
—Carol Betz, Grand Rapids, MI

Prep: 15 min. • **Cook:** 4 hours
Makes: 20 servings (2½ qt.)

- 2 lbs. lean ground beef (90% lean)
- 1 can (15 oz.) Ranch Style beans (pinto beans in seasoned tomato sauce), undrained
- 2 Tbsp. chili powder
- 1 Tbsp. brown sugar
- 2 tsp. ground cumin
- 2 tsp. ground coriander
- 1 tsp. dried oregano
- 1 tsp. cayenne pepper
- 1 Tbsp. cider vinegar
- ¾ tsp. salt
  Baked tortilla chips
  Optional: Shredded cheddar cheese, lettuce, sour cream and guacamole

Combine first 8 ingredients in a 4-qt. slow cooker. Cook, covered, on low until meat is crumbly, 4-6 hours. Stir in vinegar and salt. Serve with tortilla chips and, if desired, toppings.
½ cup 99 cal., 4g fat (2g sat. fat), 28mg chol., 232mg sod., 5g carb. (1g sugars, 1g fiber), 10g pro.

Pepperoni Pan Pizzas

I've spent years trying to come up with the perfect pizza crust and sauce, and they're paired up in this recipe. I fix this crispy pizza for my family often, and it really satisfies my husband and three sons.
—Susan Lindahl, Alford, FL

Prep: 30 min. • **Bake:** 10 min.
Makes: 2 pizzas (9 pieces each)

2¾ to 3 cups all-purpose flour
1   pkg. (¼ oz.) active dry yeast
¼   tsp. salt
1   cup warm water (120° to 130°)
1   Tbsp. canola oil
Sauce
1   can (14½ oz.) diced tomatoes, undrained
1   can (6 oz.) tomato paste
1   Tbsp. canola oil
1   tsp. salt

½   tsp. each dried basil, oregano, marjoram and thyme
¼   tsp. garlic powder
¼   tsp. pepper
Pizzas
1   pkg. (3½ oz.) sliced pepperoni
5   cups shredded part-skim mozzarella cheese
¼   cup grated Parmesan cheese
¼   cup grated Romano cheese

1. In a large bowl, combine 2 cups flour, yeast and salt. Add water and oil; beat until smooth. Add enough remaining flour to form a soft dough.
2. Turn onto a floured surface; knead until smooth and elastic, 5-7 minutes. Cover and let stand for 10 minutes. Meanwhile, in a small bowl, combine tomatoes, tomato paste, oil and seasonings.

3. Divide dough in half; press into two 15x10x1-in. baking pans coated with cooking spray. Prick dough generously with a fork. Bake at 425° until lightly browned, 12-16 minutes.
4. Spread sauce over crusts; top with pepperoni and cheeses. Bake until cheese is melted, 8-10 minutes. Cut into squares.
Freeze option Bake crusts and assemble pizzas as directed. Securely wrap and freeze unbaked pizzas. To use, unwrap pizzas; bake as directed, increasing time as necessary.
2 pieces 460 cal., 23g fat (10g sat. fat), 56mg chol., 1096mg sod., 39g carb. (4g sugars, 3g fiber), 25g pro.

Quick Jalapeno Hush Puppies

The crunchy exterior of these southern-style snacks is a nice contrast to the moist cornbread. Jalapeno peppers and hot sauce add a hint of heat.

—*Taste of Home* Test Kitchen

Prep: 15 min. • **Cook:** 5 min./batch
Makes: 2½ dozen

- 1½ cups yellow cornmeal
- ½ cup all-purpose flour
- 1 tsp. baking powder
- 1 tsp. salt
- 2 large eggs, room temperature, lightly beaten
- ¾ cup 2% milk
- 2 jalapeno peppers, seeded and minced
- ¼ cup finely chopped onion
- 1 tsp. Louisiana-style hot sauce
  Oil for deep-fat frying

1. In a large bowl, combine the cornmeal, flour, baking powder and salt. In another bowl, beat the eggs, milk, jalapenos, onion and hot sauce. Stir into dry ingredients just until combined.

2. In a cast-iron or other heavy skillet, heat oil to 375°. Drop batter by tablespoonfuls, a few at a time, into hot oil. Fry until golden brown on both sides, about 5 minutes. Drain on paper towels. Serve warm.

Note Wear disposable gloves when cutting hot peppers; the oils can burn skin. Avoid touching your face.

1 hush puppy 56 cal., 3g fat (0 sat. fat), 14mg chol., 94mg sod., 7g carb. (0 sugars, 1g fiber), 1g pro.

Honey BBQ Wings

I received the recipe for these yummy wings from a cousin on Vancouver Island during a visit there a few years ago. They're an appealing appetizer, but also a favorite for Sunday lunch with rice and a salad.

—Joan Airey, Rivers, MB

Prep: 15 min. • **Bake:** 50 min.
Makes: about 2 dozen

- 2½ lbs. chicken wings
- ½ cup barbecue sauce
- ½ cup honey
- ½ cup soy sauce

Cut chicken wings into 3 sections; discard wing tip section. Place in a greased 13x9-in. baking dish. Combine barbecue sauce, honey and soy sauce; pour over wings. Bake, uncovered, at 350° for 50-60 minutes or until chicken juices run clear.

Note Uncooked chicken wing sections (wingettes) may be substituted for whole chicken wings.

1 piece 86 cal., 4g fat (1g sat. fat), 15mg chol., 380mg sod., 8g carb. (8g sugars, 0 fiber), 6g pro.

Cranberry Meatballs

Lots of people have asked me for this recipe. But I knew I had a real winner when my grandmother asked me for it!
—Tammy Neubauer, Ida Grove, IA

Prep: 20 min. • **Bake:** 20 min.
Makes: 6 dozen

- 2 large eggs, lightly beaten
- 1 cup cornflake crumbs
- ⅓ cup ketchup
- 2 Tbsp. dried minced onion
- 2 Tbsp. soy sauce
- 1 Tbsp. dried parsley flakes
- ½ tsp. salt
- ¼ tsp. pepper
- 2 lbs. ground pork

Sauce
- 1 can (14 oz.) jellied cranberry sauce
- 1 cup ketchup
- 3 Tbsp. brown sugar
- 1 Tbsp. lemon juice

1. Preheat oven to 350°. Mix the first 8 ingredients. Add pork; mix lightly but thoroughly. Shape into 1-in. meatballs. Place on a greased rack in a 15x10x1-in. pan. Bake until a thermometer reads 160°, 20-25 minutes. Drain meatballs on paper towels.
2. In a large skillet, cook and stir sauce ingredients over medium heat until blended. Stir in meatballs; heat through.
1 meatball 58 cal., 2g fat (1g sat. fat), 16mg chol., 142mg sod., 6g carb. (4g sugars, 0 fiber), 3g pro.

Crispy Beer-Battered Fish

A local restaurant made a similar breading for shrimp po' boys, but we think this version s better. I serve it with a ranch dressing and hot sauce mixture as a dip.
—Jenny Wenzel, Gulfport, MS

Prep: 25 min. • **Cook:** 5 min./batch
Makes: 4 servings

- ½ cup cornstarch
- 1½ tsp. baking powder
- ¾ tsp. salt
- ½ tsp. Creole seasoning
- ¼ tsp. paprika
- ¼ tsp. cayenne pepper
- 1 cup all-purpose flour, divided
- ½ cup 2% milk
- ⅓ cup beer or nonalcoholic beer
- 2 cups crushed unsalted top saltines (about 40)
- 4 cod fillets (6 oz. each)
   Oil for deep-fat frying

1. In a shallow bowl, combine the cornstarch, baking powder, salt, Creole seasoning, paprika, cayenne and ½ cup flour. Stir in milk and beer until smooth. Place crackers and remaining flour in separate shallow bowls. Coat fillets with flour, then dip in batter and coat with crackers.
2. In an electric skillet or deep-fat fryer, heat oil to 375°. Fry fish in batches for 2-3 minutes on each side or until golden brown. Drain on paper towels.
Note If you don't have Creole seasoning, you can make your own using ¼ tsp. each salt, garlic powder and paprika; and a pinch each of dried thyme, ground cumin and cayenne pepper.
1 fillet 513 cal., 27g fat (3g sat. fat), 66mg chol., 775mg sod., 35g carb. (2g sugars, 1g fiber), 30g pro.

Frozen Strawberry Daiquiris

When I was in my early 20s, I went on a Carnival Cruise to the Caribbean. I fell for the frozen strawberry daiquiris on board, so I wanted to come up with my own version when I got home. I think this is pretty darn close!
—James Schend, Pleasant Prairie, WI

Takes: 10 min. • **Makes:** 5 servings

- 1¼ cups rum
- ¾ cup thawed limeade concentrate
- 1 pkg. (15½ oz.) frozen sweetened sliced strawberries
- 2 to 2½ cups ice cubes
  Optional: Fresh strawberries and lime slices

In a blender, combine the rum, limeade concentrate, strawberries and ice. Cover and process until smooth and thickened (use more ice for thicker daiquiris). Pour into 5 cocktail glasses. If desired, garnish with fresh strawberries and lime slices.
1 cup 299 cal., 0 fat (0 sat. fat), 0 chol., 7mg sod., 45g carb. (41g sugars, 2g fiber), 1g pro.

Chili Coney Dogs

From the youngest kids to the oldest adults, everyone in our family loves these hot dogs. They're so easy to throw together in the morning or even the night before.
—Michele Harris, Vicksburg, MI

Prep: 20 min. • **Cook:** 4 hours
Makes: 8 servings

- 1 lb. lean ground beef (90% lean)
- 1 can (15 oz.) tomato sauce
- ½ cup water
- 2 Tbsp. Worcestershire sauce
- 1 Tbsp. dried minced onion
- ½ tsp. garlic powder
- ½ tsp. ground mustard
- ½ tsp. chili powder
- ½ tsp. pepper
  Dash cayenne pepper
- 8 hot dogs
- 8 hot dog buns, split
  Optional: Shredded cheddar cheese, relish and chopped onion

1. In a large skillet, cook beef over medium heat until no longer pink, 6-8 minutes, breaking into crumbles; drain. Stir in tomato sauce, water, Worcestershire sauce, dried minced onion and seasonings.
2. Place hot dogs in a 3-qt. slow cooker; top with beef mixture. Cook, covered, on low 4-5 hours or until heated through. Serve on buns with toppings as desired.
1 chili dog 371 cal., 20g fat (8g sat. fat), 53mg chol., 992mg sod., 26g carb. (5g sugars, 2g fiber), 21g pro.

"This was an easy, tasty recipe. My husband said it was a cross between traditional chili dogs and sloppy joes. What I liked was that the recipe uses pantry staples, no special ingredients, and it comes together fast. This will be a repeat in our house."

—tkuehl, tasteofhome.com

Cinnamon Swirl
Bread, Page 74

Bakery Breads

Traditional Chocolate Chip Muffins

Muffins are one of my favorite things to bake, and these are the best. I always keep some in the freezer for breakfast on the run. I can zap one in the microwave before I head out the door.

—Kelly Kirby, Mill Bay, BC

Prep: 15 min. • **Bake:** 25 min.
Makes: 1 dozen

- ½ cup butter, softened
- 1 cup sugar
- 2 large eggs, room temperature
- 1 cup plain yogurt
- 1 tsp. vanilla extract
- 2 cups all-purpose flour
- 1 tsp. baking soda
- ½ tsp. baking powder
- ½ tsp. salt
- ¾ cup semisweet chocolate chips

Topping
- ¼ cup semisweet chocolate chips
- 2 Tbsp. brown sugar
- 2 Tbsp. chopped walnuts, optional
- 1 tsp. ground cinnamon

1. Preheat oven to 350°. Cream butter and sugar until light and fluffy, 5-7 minutes. Add eggs, 1 at a time, beating well after each addition. Beat in yogurt and vanilla. Combine flour, baking soda, baking powder and salt; add to creamed mixture just until moistened. Fold in chocolate chips. Fill 12 paper-lined muffin cups two-thirds full.
2. Combine the topping ingredients; sprinkle over batter. Bake until a toothpick inserted in the center comes out clean, 25-30 minutes. Cool for 5 minutes before removing from pan to wire rack. Serve warm.
1 serving 308 cal., 13g fat (8g sat. fat), 58mg chol., 319mg sod., 45g carb. (28g sugars, 1g fiber), 5g pro.

Buttery Cornbread

A friend gave me this recipe several years ago, and it's my favorite. I love to serve the melt-in-your-mouth cornbread hot from the oven with butter and syrup. It gets rave reviews on holidays and at potluck dinners.
—Nicole Callen, Auburn, CA

Prep: 15 min. • **Bake:** 25 min.
Makes: 15 servings

- ⅔ cup butter, softened
- 1 cup sugar
- 3 large eggs, room temperature
- 1⅔ cups 2% milk
- 2⅓ cups all-purpose flour
- 1 cup cornmeal
- 4½ tsp. baking powder
- 1 tsp. salt

1. Preheat oven to 400°. In a large bowl, cream butter and sugar until light and fluffy, 5-7 minutes. Combine eggs and milk. Combine flour, cornmeal, baking powder and salt; add to the creamed mixture alternately with the egg mixture.
2. Pour batter into a greased 13x9-in. baking pan. Bake until a toothpick inserted in center comes out clean, 22-27 minutes. Cut into squares; serve warm.
1 piece 262 cal., 10g fat (6g sat. fat), 61mg chol., 395mg sod., 38g carb. (15g sugars, 1g fiber), 5g pro.

Keep it Together
If your cornbread is falling apart, too much flour could be the culprit. An excess of cornmeal can also cause cornbread to be too crumbly, so adjust these ingredients a bit in your go-to recipe if needed.

Date Pecan Tea Bread

Packed with dates and pecans, this already excellent bread is even better with a chunky cream cheese spread.
—Carole Resnick, Cleveland, OH

Prep: 20 min.
Bake: 65 min. + cooling
Makes: 1 loaf (16 pieces) and ½ cup spread

- 2½ cups chopped dates
- 1½ cups boiling water
- 1½ tsp. baking soda
- 1¾ cups all-purpose flour
- ¼ tsp. each ground cloves, cinnamon, ginger and nutmeg
- 2 Tbsp. butter, softened
- 1¼ cups sugar
- 1 large egg, room temperature
- 2 tsp. vanilla extract
- 1½ cups coarsely chopped pecans

Spread
- 3 oz. cream cheese, softened
- 2 Tbsp. chopped dates
- 2 Tbsp. coarsely chopped pecans
- 1 Tbsp. 2% milk

1. Preheat oven to 350°. Place dates in a large bowl. Combine boiling water and baking soda; pour over dates. In a small bowl, combine the flour and spices.

2. In a large bowl, beat butter and sugar until crumbly. Beat in egg and vanilla. Add the flour mixture alternately with the date mixture. Stir in pecans.

3. Pour into a greased and floured 9x5-in. loaf pan. Bake until a toothpick inserted in the center comes out clean, 65-75 minutes. Cool 10 minutes, then remove from pan to wire rack to cool completely.

4. Combine spread ingredients. Refrigerate, covered, for 1 hour. Serve with bread.

1 piece with 1½ tsp. spread
312 cal., 13g fat (3g sat. fat), 23mg chol., 154mg sod., 50g carb. (35g sugars, 4g fiber), 4g pro.

Jelly Doughnuts

No need to run to the bakery for jelly doughnuts! I've been fixing these sweet treats for my family for years.
—Kathy Westendorf, Westgate, IA

Prep: 30 min. + rising
Cook: 10 min.
Makes: 16 doughnuts

- 2 pkg. (¼ oz. each) active dry yeast
- ½ cup warm water (110° to 115°)
- ½ cup warm 2% milk (110° to 115°)
- ⅓ cup butter, softened
- 1⅓ cups sugar, divided
- 3 large egg yolks, room temperature
- 1 tsp. salt
- 3 to 3¾ cups all-purpose flour
- 3 Tbsp. jelly or jam
- 1 large egg white, lightly beaten
  Oil for deep-fat frying

1. In a small bowl, dissolve yeast in warm water. In a large bowl, combine milk, butter, ⅓ cup sugar, egg yolks, salt, yeast mixture and 3 cups flour; beat until smooth. Stir in enough of the remaining flour to form a soft dough (do not knead).
2. Place in a greased bowl, turning once to grease top. Cover and let rise in a warm place until doubled, about 45 minutes.
3. Punch down dough. Turn out onto a lightly floured surface; knead about 10 times. Divide dough in half.
4. Roll out each portion to ¼-in. thickness; cut with a floured 2½-in. round cutter. Place about ½ tsp. jelly in the center of half the circles; brush edges with egg white. Top with remaining circles; press edges to seal tightly. Place on a greased baking sheet. Cover and let rise until doubled, about 45 minutes.
5. In an electric skillet or deep-fat fryer, heat oil to 375°. Fry doughnuts, a few at a time, until golden brown, 1-2 minutes on each side.

Drain on paper towels. Roll warm doughnuts in the remaining 1 cup sugar.
1 doughnut 270 cal., 12g fat (3g sat. fat), 45mg chol., 188mg sod., 38g carb. (19g sugars, 1g fiber), 4g pro.

Bread Machine Naan

Chewy yeast-raised flatbread is a snap to make in a bread machine. Serve with your favorite Indian dishes to soak up the mouthwatering sauces.
—Shannon Ventresca, Middleboro, MA

Prep: 1½ hours.
Cook: 5 min./batch
Makes: 6 servings

- ¾ cup warm 2% milk (70° to 80°)
- ¾ cup plain yogurt
- 1 large egg, room temperature, beaten
- 2 Tbsp. canola oil
- 2 tsp. sugar
- 1 tsp. salt
- 1 tsp. baking powder
- 4 cups bread flour
- 2 tsp. active dry yeast

1. In bread machine pan, place all ingredients in order suggested by manufacturer. Select dough setting (check dough after 5 minutes of mixing; add 1 to 2 Tbsp. of water or flour if needed).
2. When cycle is completed, turn dough onto a lightly floured surface. Divide into 6 portions; shape into balls. Roll each ball into a ¼-in.-thick oval. Let rest for 5 minutes.
3. Brush tops with water. In a greased large skillet over medium-high heat, cover and cook 1 piece of dough, wet side down, for 1 minute. Turn; cover and cook 30 seconds longer or until golden brown. Repeat with the remaining dough.
1 naan 363 cal., 7g fat (2g sat. fat), 42mg chol., 502mg sod., 64g carb. (4g sugars, 2g fiber), 14g pro.

Parmesan-Ranch Pan Rolls

Mom taught me this easy recipe, which is perfect for feeding a crowd. There is never a crumb left over. Mom used her own bread dough, but using frozen dough is my shortcut.
—Trisha Kruse, Eagle, ID

Prep: 30 min. + rising
Bake: 20 min. • **Makes:** 1½ dozen

- 2 loaves (1 lb. each) frozen bread dough, thawed
- 1 cup grated Parmesan cheese
- ½ cup butter, melted
- 1 envelope buttermilk ranch salad dressing mix
- 1 small onion, finely chopped

1. On a lightly floured surface, divide dough into 18 portions; shape each portion into a ball. In a small bowl, combine the cheese, butter and ranch dressing mix.
2. Roll balls in cheese mixture; arrange in 2 greased 9-in. square baking pans. Sprinkle with onion. Cover and let rise in a warm place until doubled, about 45 minutes.
3. Meanwhile, preheat oven to 350°. Bake until golden brown, 20-25 minutes. Remove from pans to wire racks to cool.
1 roll 210 cal., 8g fat (4g sat. fat), 17mg chol., 512mg sod., 26g carb. (2g sugars, 2g fiber), 7g pro.

Pull-Apart Caramel Coffee Cake

The first time I made this delightful breakfast treat for a brunch party, it was a huge hit. Now I get requests every time family or friends do anything around the breakfast hour! I always keep the four simple ingredients on hand.
—Jaime Keeling, Keizer, OR

Prep: 10 min. • **Bake:** 25 min.
Makes: 16 servings

- 2 tubes (12 oz. each) refrigerated buttermilk biscuits
- 1 cup packed brown sugar
- ½ cup heavy whipping cream
- 1 tsp. ground cinnamon

1. Preheat oven to 350°. Cut each biscuit into 4 pieces; arrange evenly in a 10-in. fluted tube pan coated with cooking spray. In a small bowl, mix the remaining ingredients until blended; pour over biscuits.
2. Bake 25-30 minutes or until golden brown. Cool in pan for 5 minutes before inverting onto a serving plate.
5 pieces 204 cal., 8g fat (3g sat. fat), 10mg chol., 457mg sod., 31g carb. (16g sugars, 0 fiber), 3g pro.

"It couldn't get any simpler to whip up this great cake! For the two of us, I cut the recipe in half and baked it in a pie pan."

—Robby1, tasteofhome.com

Morning Crispies

These large cinnamon-sugar pastries make quite an impression. Serve them with brunch or as an afternoon treat.

—Emily Goad, Franklin, IN

Prep: 30 min. + rising
Bake: 15 min. + cooling
Makes: 1½ dozen

- 1 pkg. (¼ oz.) active dry yeast
- ½ cup warm water (110° to 115°)
- 1 cup warm whole milk (110° to 115°)
- 2 cups sugar, divided
- ½ cup canola oil
- 1¼ tsp. salt
- 2 large eggs, room temperature
- 1½ tsp. lemon extract
- 5½ to 6 cups all-purpose flour
- 6 Tbsp. butter, softened, divided
- 1 Tbsp. ground cinnamon

1. In a large bowl, dissolve yeast in water; let stand for 5 minutes. Add milk, ½ cup sugar, oil, salt, eggs, extract and 2 cups flour; beat well. Stir in enough of the remaining flour to make a soft dough.

2. Turn out onto a floured surface; knead until smooth and elastic, 6-8 minutes. Place in a greased bowl, turning once to grease top. Cover and let rise in a warm place until doubled, about 1 hour.

3. Punch down dough. Turn out onto a floured surface and roll out into a ¼-in.-thick rectangle. Spread with 2 Tbsp. butter; sprinkle with ⅓ cup sugar. Fold in half lengthwise; roll out to ¼-in. thickness. Spread with 2 Tbsp. butter and sprinkle with ⅓ cup sugar.

4. Fold in half widthwise; roll out to ¼-in. thickness. Spread with remaining butter and sprinkle with ⅓ cup sugar. Fold in half lengthwise; roll out to an 18x10-in. rectangle.

5. Combine cinnamon and the remaining ½ cup sugar; sprinkle half over the dough to within ¼ in. of all edges. Roll up dough jelly-roll style, starting with a short side; pinch seam to seal.

6. Cut roll into ½-in. slices and place on greased baking sheets (4 to 6 slices per sheet). Cover with waxed paper and flatten with palm of hand. Sprinkle with remaining cinnamon sugar. Let stand for 30 minutes.

7. Preheat oven to 400°. Bake until golden brown, 12-15 minutes. Immediately remove from pans to wire racks to cool completely.

1 pastry 334 cal., 11g fat (3g sat. fat), 32mg chol., 209mg sod., 53g carb. (23g sugars, 1g fiber), 5g pro.

Challah

Eggs lend to the richness of this traditional challah bread recipe. The attractive golden color and delicious flavor make it hard to resist.
—*Taste of Home* Test Kitchen

Prep: 30 min. + rising
Bake: 30 min.
Makes: 2 loaves (16 pieces each)

- 2 pkg. (¼ oz. each) active dry yeast
- 1 cup warm water (110° to 115°)
- ½ cup canola oil
- ⅓ cup sugar
- 1 Tbsp. salt
- 4 large eggs, room temperature
- 6 to 6½ cups all-purpose flour

Topping

- 1 large egg
- 1 tsp. cold water
- 1 Tbsp. sesame or poppy seeds, optional

1. In a large bowl, dissolve yeast in warm water. Add oil, sugar, salt, eggs and 4 cups flour. Beat until smooth. Stir in enough remaining flour to form a firm dough. Turn out onto a floured surface; knead until smooth and elastic, 6-8 minutes. Place in a greased bowl, turning once to grease top. Cover and let rise in a warm place until doubled, about 1 hour.
2. Punch dough down. Turn out onto a lightly floured surface; divide in half. Divide each portion into thirds. Shape each piece into a 15-in. rope.
3. Place 3 ropes on a greased baking sheet and braid; pinch ends to seal and tuck ends under. Repeat with remaining dough. Cover and let rise until doubled, about 1 hour.
4. Preheat oven to 350°. Beat egg and cold water; brush over braids. Sprinkle with sesame or poppy seeds if desired. Bake until golden brown, 30-40 minutes. Remove to wire racks to cool.
1 piece 139 cal., 5g fat (1g sat. fat), 29mg chol., 233mg sod., 20g carb. (2g sugars, 1g fiber), 4g pro.

Challah Tips

How do I make my challah round? To create a round loaf, first create the braid, then wrap it around itself in a coil and tuck the end under. Make the individual ropes a little longer so the braid is long enough to shape into a full coil.

How should I store challah? Once the loaf is completely cool, store it in an airtight container at room temperature. It will keep fresh for a few days. Or, wrap it tightly in foil or freezer paper and freeze it for up to 6 months.

What can I make with leftover challah? If you haven't yet tried French toast or bread pudding made with challah, you're in for a treat! The egg in the bread gives these dishes a rich, custardy texture. You can also use challah in any recipe that calls for brioche.

Best Ever Banana Bread

Whenever I pass a display of bananas in the grocery store, I can almost smell the wonderful aroma of this bread. It really is good!
—Gert Kaiser, Kenosha, WI

Prep: 15 min.
Bake: 1¼ hours + cooling
Makes: 1 loaf (16 pieces)

1¾ cups all-purpose flour
1½ cups sugar
1 tsp. baking soda
½ tsp. salt
2 large eggs, room temperature
2 medium ripe bananas, mashed (1 cup)
½ cup canola oil
¼ cup plus 1 Tbsp. buttermilk
1 tsp. vanilla extract
1 cup chopped walnuts, optional

1. Preheat oven to 350°. In a large bowl, stir together flour, sugar, baking soda and salt. In another bowl, combine eggs, bananas, oil, buttermilk and vanilla; add to the flour mixture, stirring just until combined. If desired, fold in nuts.
2. Pour into greased or parchment-lined 9x5-in. loaf pan. Bake until a toothpick comes out clean, 1¼ to 1½ hours. Cool in pan for 15 minutes before removing to a wire rack to cool completely.
1 piece 257 cal., 13g fat (1g sat. fat), 23mg chol., 171mg sod., 34g carb. (21g sugars, 1g fiber), 4g pro.

"I have been trying all sorts of banana bread recipes and this by far is the absolute best. The only change I make is to cut the sugar in half; bananas are already so sweet. Works perfectly every time."

—Anita's, tasteofhome.com

Soft Buttermilk Dinner Rolls

Warm, buttery dinner rolls are absolutely irresistible. I save time and use a stand mixer to make my dough.
—Jennifer Patterson, Shoshone, ID

Prep: 40 min. + rising
Bake: 20 min. + cooling
Makes: 20 servings

1 pkg. (¼ oz.) active dry yeast
¼ cup warm water (110° to 115°)
1 cup warm buttermilk (110° to 115°)
½ cup plus 1 Tbsp. softened butter, divided
1 large egg, room temperature
⅓ cup sugar
1 tsp. salt
4 cups bread flour

1. Dissolve yeast in warm water until foamy. In a large bowl, combine 1 cup buttermilk, ½ cup butter, egg, sugar, salt and yeast mixture. Add 3 cups flour; beat on medium until smooth, 1 minute. Add the remaining flour, ¼ cup at a time, to form a soft dough.

2. Turn out dough onto a lightly floured surface; knead until smooth and elastic, 6-8 minutes. Place in a greased bowl, turning once to grease the top. Cover and let rise in a warm place until doubled, about 1 hour.
3. Punch down dough. Turn out onto a lightly floured surface; divide and shape into 20 balls. Place in a greased 13x9-in. pan. Cover with a kitchen towel; let rise in a warm place until almost doubled, about 45 minutes.
4. Preheat oven to 350°. Melt the remaining 1 Tbsp. butter; brush over rolls. Bake until golden brown, 20-25 minutes. Cool in pan for 20 minutes. Remove to a wire rack; serve warm.
Note To substitute for each cup of buttermilk, use 1 Tbsp. white vinegar or lemon juice plus enough milk to measure 1 cup. Stir, then let stand 5 min. Or, use 1 cup plain yogurt or 1¾ tsp. cream of tartar plus 1 cup milk.
1 roll 167 cal., 6g fat (4g sat. fat), 24mg chol., 187mg sod., 24g carb. (4g sugars, 1g fiber), 4g pro.

Homemade Bagels

Instead of going to a baker, surprise your family with homemade bagels. For variation and flavor, sprinkle the tops with cinnamon sugar instead of sesame and poppy seeds.
—Rebecca Phillips, Burlington, CT

Prep: 30 min. + rising
Bake: 20 min. • **Makes:** 1 dozen

- 1 tsp. active dry yeast
- 1¼ cups warm 2% milk (110° to 115°)
- ½ cup butter, softened
- 2 Tbsp. sugar
- 1 tsp. salt
- 1 large egg yolk, room temperature
- 3¾ to 4¼ cups all-purpose flour
  Sesame or poppy seeds, optional

1. In a large bowl, dissolve yeast in warm milk. Add butter, sugar, salt and egg yolk; mix well. Stir in enough flour to form a soft dough.
2. Turn onto a floured surface; knead until smooth and elastic, 6-8 minutes. Place in a greased bowl, turning once to grease top. Cover and let rise in a warm place until doubled, about 1 hour.
3. Punch dough down. Shape into 12 balls. Push thumb through centers to form a 1½-in. hole. Stretch and shape to form an even ring. Place on a floured surface. Cover and let rest for 10 minutes; flatten bagels slightly.
4. Fill a Dutch oven two-thirds full with water; bring to a boil. Drop bagels, 2 at a time, into boiling water. Cook for 45 seconds; turn and cook 45 seconds longer. Remove with a slotted spoon; drain well on paper towels.
5. Sprinkle with sesame or poppy seeds if desired. Place 2 in. apart on greased baking sheets. Bake at 400° until golden brown, 20-25 minutes. Remove from pans to wire racks to cool.
1 bagel 237 cal., 9g fat (5g sat. fat), 38mg chol., 271mg sod., 33g carb. (3g sugars, 1g fiber), 5g pro.

Cinnamon Swirl Bread

Your family will be impressed with the soft texture and appealing swirls of cinnamon in these buttery loaves.
—Diane Armstrong, Elm Grove, WI

Prep: 25 min. + rising
Bake: 30 min.
Makes: 2 loaves (16 pieces each)

- 2 pkg. (¼ oz. each) active dry yeast
- ⅓ cup warm water (110° to 115°)
- 1 cup warm 2% milk (110° to 115°)
- 1 cup sugar, divided
- 2 large eggs, room temperature
- 6 Tbsp. butter, softened
- 1½ tsp. salt
- 5½ to 6 cups all-purpose flour
- 2 Tbsp. ground cinnamon

1. In a large bowl, dissolve yeast in warm water. Add milk, ½ cup sugar, eggs, butter, salt and 3 cups flour; beat on medium speed until smooth. Stir in enough remaining flour to form a soft dough.
2. Turn out dough onto a floured surface; knead until smooth and elastic, 6-8 minutes. Place in a greased bowl; turn once to grease the top. Cover; let rise in a warm place until doubled, about 1 hour.
3. Mix cinnamon and remaining ½ cup sugar. Punch down dough. Turn out onto a lightly floured surface; divide in half. Roll out each portion into an 18x8-in. rectangle; sprinkle each with about ¼ cup cinnamon sugar to within ½ in. of edges. Roll up jelly-roll style, starting with a short side; pinch seam to seal. Place in 2 greased 9x5-in. loaf pans, seam side down. Cover; let rise in a warm place until doubled, about 1½ hours.
4. Bake at 350° until golden brown, 30-35 minutes. Remove from pans to wire racks to cool.
1 piece 132 cal., 3g fat (2g sat. fat), 20mg chol., 141mg sod., 23g carb. (7g sugars, 1g fiber), 3g pro.

Contest-Winning New England
Clam Chowder, Page 98

Cozy
Soups

Parsnip & Celery Root Bisque

With its smooth texture and earthy vegetable flavors, this soup makes a simple yet elegant first course. Try chives and pomegranate seeds on top.
—Merry Graham, Newhall, CA

Prep: 25 min. • **Cook:** 45 min.
Makes: 8 servings (2 qt.)

2   Tbsp. olive oil
2   medium leeks (white portion only), chopped (about 2 cups)
1½ lbs. parsnips, peeled and chopped (about 4 cups)
1   medium celery root, peeled and cubed (about 1½ cups)
4   garlic cloves, minced
6   cups chicken stock
1½ tsp. salt
¾   tsp. coarsely ground pepper
1   cup heavy whipping cream
2   Tbsp. minced fresh parsley
2   tsp. lemon juice
2   Tbsp. minced fresh chives
    Pomegranate seeds, optional

1. In a large saucepan, heat oil over medium-high heat; saute leeks for 3 minutes. Add parsnips and celery root; cook and stir 4 minutes. Add garlic, cook and stir 1 minute. Stir in stock, salt and pepper; bring to a boil. Reduce heat; simmer, covered, until the vegetables are tender, 25-30 minutes.
2. Puree soup using an immersion blender. Or, cool slightly and puree soup in batches in a blender; return to pan. Stir in cream, parsley and lemon juice; heat through. Serve with chives and pomegranate seeds if desired.
1 cup 248 cal., 15g fat (7g sat. fat), 34mg chol., 904mg sod., 25g carb. (8g sugars, 5g fiber), 6g pro.

Did You Know?
Celery root, or celeriac, is the root of a celery plant—but not the variety used in most cooking. Celery root is denser than celery, with a potato-like texture and an earthier flavor.

Buffalo Chicken Chili

This chili is rich in the best way. The cream cheese, blue cheese and tangy hot sauce join forces for a dinner recipe everyone will love.
—Peggy Woodward, Shullsburg, WI

Prep: 10 min. • **Cook:** 5½ hours
Makes: 6 servings (about 2 qt.)

1   can (15½ oz.) navy beans, rinsed and drained
1   can (14½ oz.) chicken broth
1   can (14½ oz.) fire-roasted diced tomatoes
1   can (8 oz.) tomato sauce
½   cup Buffalo wing sauce
½   tsp. onion powder
½   tsp. garlic powder
1   lb. boneless skinless chicken breast halves
1   pkg. (8 oz.) cream cheese, cubed and softened
    Optional: Crumbled blue cheese, chopped celery and chopped green onions

1. In a 4- or 5-qt. slow cooker, combine the first 7 ingredients. Add chicken. Cover and cook on low until chicken is tender, 5-6 hours.
2. Remove chicken; shred with 2 forks. Return to slow cooker. Stir in cream cheese. Cover and cook on low until cheese is melted, about 30 minutes. Stir until blended. Serve with toppings as desired.
Note Leftovers won't freeze well due to the cream cheese, which can curdle when frozen.
1¼ cups 337 cal., 16g fat (8g sat. fat), 80mg chol., 1586mg sod., 25g carb. (5g sugars, 5g fiber), 25g pro.

Ramen Corn Chowder

This tastes so good, as if it simmered for hours, but it's ready in 15 minutes. I thought the original recipe was lacking in flavor, so I jazzed it up with extra corn and bacon bits.

—Darlene Brenden, Salem, OR

Takes: 15 min. • **Makes:** 4 servings

- 2   cups water
- 1   pkg. (3 oz.) chicken ramen noodles
- 1   can (15¼ oz.) whole kernel corn, drained
- 1   can (14¾ oz.) cream-style corn
- 1   cup 2% milk
- 1   tsp. dried minced onion
- ¼   tsp. curry powder
- ¾   cup shredded cheddar cheese
- ⅓   cup cubed cooked bacon
- 1   Tbsp. minced fresh parsley
- 1   Tbsp. minced chives

1. In a small saucepan, bring water to a boil. Break noodles into large pieces. Add noodles and contents of seasoning packet to water. Reduce heat to medium. Cook, uncovered, for 2-3 minutes or until noodles are tender.
2. Stir in the corn, cream-style corn, milk, onion and curry powder; heat through. Stir in the cheese, bacon, parsley and chives until blended. If desired, top with additional bacon, chives or cheddar.
1 cup 333 cal., 9g fat (5g sat. fat), 17mg chol., 1209mg sod., 49g carb. (13g sugars, 4g fiber), 13g pro.

"Delish—easy peasy on a cold afternoon—15 minutes and a warm belly! I added jalapenos for spice and if you don't have curry, use 1 tsp. of cumin and ⅛ tsp. of allspice to replace it."

—Jennifer9326, tasteofhome.com

Hearty Homemade Chicken Noodle Soup

This satisfying soup with a hint of cayenne is brimming with vegetables, chicken and noodles. The recipe came from my father-in-law, but I made some adjustments to give it my own spin.

—Norma Reynolds, Overland Park, KS

Prep: 20 min. • **Cook:** 5½ hours
Makes: 12 servings (3 qt.)

- 12   fresh baby carrots, cut into ½-in. pieces
- 4   celery ribs, cut into ½-in. pieces
- ¾   cup finely chopped onion
- 1   Tbsp. minced fresh parsley
- ½   tsp. pepper
- ¼   tsp. cayenne pepper
- 1½   tsp. mustard seed
- 2   garlic cloves, peeled and halved
- 1¼   lbs. boneless skinless chicken breast halves
- 1¼   lbs. boneless skinless chicken thighs
- 4   cans (14½ oz. each) chicken broth
- 1   pkg. (9 oz.) refrigerated linguine

Optional: Coarsely ground pepper and additional minced fresh parsley

1. In a 5-qt. slow cooker, combine the first 6 ingredients. Place mustard seed and garlic on a double thickness of cheesecloth; bring up corners of cloth and tie with kitchen string to form a bag. Place in slow cooker. Add chicken and broth. Cover and cook on low until meat is tender, 5-6 hours.
2. Discard spice bag. Remove chicken; cool slightly. Stir linguine into soup; cover and cook on high until the pasta is tender, about 30 minutes longer. Cut chicken into pieces and return to soup; heat through. If desired, sprinkle with coarsely ground pepper and additional parsley.
1 cup 199 cal., 6g fat (2g sat. fat), 73mg chol., 663mg sod., 14g carb. (2g sugars, 1g fiber), 22g pro.
Diabetic exchanges 3 lean meat, 1 starch.

Chicken Matzo Ball Soup

The keys to this amazing chicken matzo ball soup are slow-cooking it and using boxed matzo ball mix. Some people swear by seltzer, but it's not necessary—the mix makes perfect, fluffy matzo balls every time. Add chicken fat (schmaltz) for extra-authentic flavor. The matzo balls will taste as if they came straight from Grandma's kitchen.

—Shannon Sarna, South Orange, NJ

Prep: 30 min. + chilling
Cook: 1½ hours
Makes: 26 servings (6½ qt.)

- 1   broiler/fryer chicken (3 to 4 lbs.)
- 1   lb. chicken wings
- 6   qt. water
- 3   large carrots, chopped
- 2   medium parsnips, peeled and chopped
- 1   medium turnip, peeled and chopped
- 1   large onion, chopped
- 1   bunch fresh dill sprigs
- 1   bunch fresh parsley sprigs
- 1½ tsp. whole peppercorns
- 3   tsp. salt

Matzo Balls
- 1   pkg. (5 oz.) matzo ball mix
- 4   large eggs
- ¼   cup safflower oil
- ¼   cup rendered chicken fat
- 2   Tbsp. snipped fresh dill
- 2   Tbsp. minced fresh parsley
- 10 cups water

1. Place chicken and wings in a stockpot; add water, vegetables, herbs and seasonings. Slowly bring to a boil. Reduce heat; simmer, covered, 1-2 hours.
2. Remove chicken and wings and cool. Strain broth through a cheesecloth-lined colander; reserve vegetables. Skim off fat.

Remove meat from bones and cut into bite-sized pieces; discard bones. Return broth, vegetables and meat to pot. If using immediately, skim off fat. Or, cool broth, then refrigerate 8 hours or overnight; remove fat from surface before using. (Broth may be refrigerated up to 3 days or frozen 4-6 months.)
3. Meanwhile, in a large bowl, beat matzo ball mix, eggs, oil, chicken fat, dill and parsley until combined. Cover and refrigerate for at least 30 minutes.
4. In another stockpot, bring water to a boil. Drop rounded Tbsp. of matzo ball dough into boiling water. Reduce heat; cover and simmer until a toothpick inserted into a matzo ball comes out clean (do not lift cover while simmering), 20-25 minutes.
5. Carefully remove matzo balls from water with a slotted spoon; place 1 matzo ball in each soup bowl. Add soup.

1 cup 167 cal., 10g fat (2g sat. fat), 60mg chol., 523mg sod., 8g carb. (1g sugars, 1g fiber), 11g pro.

Storing Matzo Balls

Store the matzo balls separately from the soup in a covered container—this prevents them from absorbing too much liquid and falling apart. Reheat the balls in the soup on the stovetop or in the microwave. If you're freezing them, you can freeze them right in the soup, or freeze separately for easy meal prep.

Hearty Black Bean Soup

Cumin and chili powder give spark to this thick, hearty soup. If you have leftover meat—smoked sausage, browned ground beef or roast—toss it in for the last 30 minutes of cooking.
—Amy Chop, Oak Grove, LA

Prep: 10 min. • **Cook:** 9 hours
Makes: 8 servings (2 qt.)

- 3 medium carrots, halved and thinly sliced
- 2 celery ribs, thinly sliced
- 1 medium onion, chopped
- 4 garlic cloves, minced
- 1 can (30 oz.) black beans, rinsed and drained
- 2 cans (14½ oz. each) reduced-sodium chicken broth or vegetable broth
- 1 can (15 oz.) crushed tomatoes
- 1½ tsp. dried basil
- ½ tsp. dried oregano
- ½ tsp. ground cumin
- ½ tsp. chili powder
- ½ tsp. hot pepper sauce
  Hot cooked rice

In a 3-qt. slow cooker, combine the first 12 ingredients. Cover and cook on low until vegetables are tender, 9-11 hours. Serve with rice.

1 cup 129 cal., 0 fat (0 sat. fat), 0 chol., 627mg sod., 24g carb. (6g sugars, 6g fiber), 8g pro. **Diabetic exchanges** 1½ starch, 1 lean meat.

Northwest Salmon Chowder

I've lived on a farm in the Yakima Valley all my life. I have a big garden, and by the end of fall, my shelves are full of canned fruits and vegetables. This recipe uses some of the root vegetables I grow—along with the salmon that is so plentiful here.
—Josephine Parton, Granger, WA

Prep: 10 min. • **Cook:** 1 hour
Makes: 8 servings (2 qt.)

- ½ cup each chopped celery, onion and green pepper
- 1 garlic clove, minced
- 3 Tbsp. butter
- 1 can (14½ oz.) chicken broth
- 1 cup uncooked diced peeled potatoes
- 1 cup shredded carrots
- 1½ tsp. salt
- ½ tsp. pepper
- ¾ tsp. dill weed
- 1 can (14¾ oz.) cream-style corn
- 2 cups half-and-half cream
- 2 cups fully cooked salmon chunks or 1 can salmon, drained, bones and skin removed (14¾ oz.)
  Optional: Crumbled cooked bacon, minced chives and cracked black pepper

1. In a large saucepan, saute celery, onion, green pepper and garlic in butter until vegetables are tender. Add broth, potatoes, carrots, salt, pepper and dill; bring to a boil.
2. Reduce heat; cover and simmer until the root vegetables are nearly tender, 40 minutes. Stir in corn, cream and salmon. Simmer for 15 minutes or until heated through. If desired, garnish with bacon, chives and cracked black pepper.
1 cup 273 cal., 15g fat (8g sat. fat), 83mg chol., 1060mg sod., 18g carb. (5g sugars, 2g fiber), 16g pro.

Tasty Taco Soup

This popular soup offers a bright assortment of colors and flavors. Garnish with shredded cheese, sour cream or sliced jalapenos if you like.
—Jennifer Villarreal, Texas City, TX

Takes: 30 min.
Makes: 8 servings (about 2 qt.)

- 1½ lbs. ground beef
- 1 envelope taco seasoning
- 2 cans (15¼ oz. each) whole kernel corn, undrained
- 2 cans (15 oz. each) Ranch Style beans (pinto beans in seasoned tomato sauce)
- 2 cans (14½ oz. each) diced tomatoes, undrained
  Tortilla chips and shredded cheddar cheese

1. In a Dutch oven, cook beef over medium heat until no longer pink; drain. Stir in the taco seasoning, corn, beans and tomatoes. Cover and cook 15 minutes or until heated through, stirring occasionally.
2. Place tortilla chips in soup bowls; ladle soup over top. Sprinkle with cheese.
1 cup 380 cal., 13g fat (5g sat. fat), 53mg chol., 1395mg sod., 38g carb. (9g sugars, 9g fiber), 23g pro.

"Easy to make and yummy to eat! It is more like a chili, but regardless of texture is still very tasty. What a wonderful recipe to have on hand for cool spring evenings!"

—apschwartz, tasteofhome.com

Ham & Lentil Soup

This is a combination of two soup recipes I came across and adapted. I often serve it for Sunday dinner, making enough so there are leftovers for my husband's lunch thermos. He's a bricklayer and regularly works outside during winter.
—Andi Haug, Hendrum, MN

Prep: 5 min. • **Cook:** 2 hours 10 min.
Makes: 12 servings (3 qt.)

- 1   meaty ham bone
- 6   cups water
- 1¼ cups dried lentils, rinsed
- 1   can (28 oz.) diced tomatoes, undrained
- 2   to 3 carrots, sliced
- 2   celery ribs, sliced
- ¼   cup chopped green onions
- ½   tsp. salt
- ½   tsp. garlic powder
- ½   tsp. dried oregano
- ⅛   tsp. pepper
- 12 oz. bulk pork sausage, cooked and drained
- 2   Tbsp. chopped fresh parsley

1. In a Dutch oven, bring ham bone and water to a boil. Reduce heat; cover and simmer for 1½ hours.
2. Remove ham bone. To broth, add the lentils, tomatoes, carrots, celery, onions and seasonings; bring to a boil. Reduce heat; cover and simmer until lentils and vegetables are tender, 30-40 minutes.
3. Meanwhile, remove ham from bone; coarsely chop. Add the ham, sausage and parsley to soup; heat through.
1 cup 188 cal., 7g fat (2g sat. fat), 29mg chol., 672mg sod., 18g carb. (3g sugars, 4g fiber), 14g pro.

Bacon-Potato Corn Chowder

I was raised on a farm, and a warm soup with homey ingredients, like this one, was always a treat after a chilly day outside. My hearty chowder nourishes the family.
—Katie Lillo, Big Lake, MN

Takes: 30 min. • **Makes:** 6 servings

- ½   lb. bacon strips, chopped
- ¼   cup chopped onion
- 1½ lbs. Yukon Gold potatoes (about 5 medium), peeled and cubed
- 1   can (14¾ oz.) cream-style corn
- 1   can (12 oz.) evaporated milk
- ¼   tsp. salt
- ¼   tsp. pepper

1. In a large skillet, cook bacon over medium heat until crisp, stirring occasionally. Remove with a slotted spoon; drain on paper towels. Discard drippings, reserving 1½ tsp. in pan. Add onion to the drippings; cook and stir over medium-high heat until tender.
2. Meanwhile, place potatoes in a large saucepan; add water to cover. Bring to a boil over high heat. Reduce heat to medium; cook, uncovered, 10-15 minutes or until tender. Drain, reserving 1 cup of the potato water.
3. Add corn, milk, salt, pepper, potatoes and the reserved potato water to saucepan; heat through. Stir in bacon and onion.
1 cup 335 cal., 13g fat (6g sat. fat), 37mg chol., 592mg sod., 44g carb. (10g sugars, 3g fiber), 12g pro.

Thicken It Up!

To make your soup thicker, puree some of the potatoes with the potato water in a blender, or mash some to release the starches. If you prefer, you can make a slurry of water and cornstarch, then stir it into the chowder and simmer for a few minutes until thickened.

Shrimp Gumbo

A crisp green salad and crusty French bread complete this gumbo meal. I always have hot sauce available when I serve this. I've found instant microwave rice packages make the process a little easier.

—Jo Ann Graham, Ovilla, TX

Prep: 30 min. • **Cook:** 1 hour
Makes: 11 servings (2¾ qt.)

- ¼ cup all-purpose flour
- ¼ cup canola oil
- 3 celery ribs, chopped
- 1 medium green pepper, chopped
- 1 medium onion, chopped
- 4 cups chicken broth
- 3 garlic cloves, minced
- 1 tsp. salt
- 1 tsp. pepper
- ½ tsp. cayenne pepper
- 2 lbs. uncooked shrimp (26-30 per lb.), peeled and deveined
- 1 pkg. (16 oz.) frozen sliced okra
- 4 green onions, sliced
- 1 medium tomato, chopped
- 1½ tsp. gumbo file powder
  Hot cooked rice

1. In a Dutch oven over medium heat, cook and stir flour and oil until caramel-colored, stirring occasionally, about 12 minutes (do not burn). Add the celery, green pepper and onion; cook and stir until tender, 5-6 minutes. Stir in the broth, garlic, salt, pepper and cayenne; bring to a boil. Reduce heat; cover and simmer for 30 minutes.
2. Stir in the shrimp, okra, green onions and tomato. Return to a boil. Reduce heat; cover and simmer until shrimp turn pink, about 10 minutes. Stir in file powder. Serve with rice.

1 cup 159 cal., 7g fat (1g sat. fat), 102mg chol., 681mg sod., 9g carb. (3g sugars, 2g fiber), 15g pro.
Diabetic exchanges 2 lean meat, 1 vegetable, 1 fat.

About File Powder

Gumbo file powder, used to thicken and flavor Creole recipes, is available in spice shops. If you don't want to use gumbo file powder, combine 2 Tbsp. each cornstarch and water until smooth. Gradually stir into gumbo. Bring to a boil; cook and stir for 2 minutes or until thickened.

Alphabet Soup

I'm a teenager and love to make this fun chicken soup for my family. It makes me so happy when they tell me how much they like it!
—Sarah Mackey, New Smyrna Beach, FL

Takes: 25 min.
Makes: 10 servings (2½ qt.)

- 3 medium carrots, chopped
- 2 celery ribs, chopped
- ¾ cup chopped sweet onion
- 1 Tbsp. olive oil
- 2 qt. chicken broth
- 3 cups shredded cooked chicken breast
- ¼ tsp. dried thyme
- 1½ cups uncooked alphabet pasta
- 3 Tbsp. minced fresh parsley

In a Dutch oven, saute carrots, celery and onion in oil until tender, 3-5 minutes. Stir in broth, chicken and thyme. Bring to a boil. Stir in pasta. Reduce heat; simmer, uncovered, until the pasta is tender, about 10 minutes. Stir in parsley.
1 cup 163 cal., 4g fat (1g sat. fat), 26mg chol., 828mg sod., 20g carb. (3g sugars, 2g fiber), 12g pro.

The Best Ever Tomato Soup

Creamy, rich and bursting with brightness, this soup is the ultimate sidekick to a grilled cheese sandwich.
—Josh Rink, Milwaukee, WI

Prep: 20 minutes
Cook: 30 minutes
Makes: 16 servings (4 qt.)

- 3 Tbsp. olive oil
- 3 Tbsp. butter
- ¼ to ½ tsp. crushed red pepper flakes
- 3 large carrots, peeled and chopped
- 1 large onion, chopped
- 2 garlic cloves, minced
- 2 tsp. dried basil
- 3 cans (28 oz. each) whole peeled tomatoes, undrained
- 1 container (32 oz.) chicken stock
- 2 Tbsp. tomato paste
- 3 tsp. sugar
- 1 tsp. salt
- ½ tsp. pepper
- 1 cup heavy whipping cream, optional

Optional: Thinly sliced fresh basil leaves and grated Parmesan cheese

1. In a 6-qt. stockpot or Dutch oven, heat oil, butter and pepper flakes over medium heat until butter is melted. Add carrots and onion; cook, uncovered, over medium heat, stirring frequently, until vegetables are softened, 8-10 minutes. Add garlic and basil; cook and stir 1 minute longer. Stir in tomatoes, chicken stock, tomato paste, sugar, salt and pepper; mix well. Bring to a boil. Reduce heat; simmer, uncovered, to let flavors blend, 20-25 minutes.
2. Remove pot from heat. Using a blender, puree soup in batches until smooth. If desired, slowly stir in heavy cream, stirring continuously to incorporate. Return pot to stove to heat through. Top with fresh basil and Parmesan cheese if desired.
1 cup 104 cal., 5g fat (2g sat. fat), 6mg chol., 572mg sod., 15g carb. (10g sugars, 2g fiber), 3g pro.
Diabetic exchanges 1 starch, 1 fat.

Tex-Mex Chili

Need to satisfy big, hearty appetites? Look no further than a chili brimming with beef stew meat, plenty of beans and tasty spices.
—Eric Hayes, Antioch, CA

Prep: 20 min. • **Cook:** 6 hours
Makes: 12 servings (about 4 qt.)

- 3   lbs. beef stew meat
- 1   Tbsp. canola oil
- 3   garlic cloves, minced
- 3   cans (16 oz. each) kidney beans, rinsed and drained
- 3   cans (15 oz. each) tomato sauce
- 1   can (14½ oz.) diced tomatoes, undrained
- 1   cup water
- 1   can (6 oz.) tomato paste
- ¾   cup salsa verde
- 1   envelope chili seasoning
- 2   tsp. dried minced onion
- 1   tsp. chili powder
- ½   tsp. crushed red pepper flakes
- ½   tsp. ground cumin
- ½   tsp. cayenne pepper

Optional: Shredded cheddar cheese, minced fresh cilantro, sour cream, sliced jalapeno or Fresno peppers and additional salsa verde

1. In a large skillet, brown beef in oil in batches. Add garlic; cook 1 minute longer. Transfer to a 6-qt. slow cooker.
2. Stir in beans, tomato sauce, tomatoes, water, tomato paste, salsa verde and seasonings. Cover and cook on low until meat is tender, 6-8 hours. Garnish each serving with toppings as desired.
Freeze option Before adding toppings, cool chili. Freeze chili in freezer containers. To use, partially thaw in refrigerator overnight. Heat through in a saucepan, stirring occasionally; add a little broth or water if necessary. Garnish with toppings as desired.
1⅓ cups 334 cal., 9g fat (3g sat. fat), 70mg chol., 1030mg sod., 31g carb. (7g sugars, 8g fiber), 32g pro.
Diabetic exchanges 3 lean meat, 1 starch, 1 vegetable.

Hearty Cheese Soup

This rich, creamy soup is a stick-to-the-ribs pleaser. Chunky and cheesy, it's simply wonderful during cold winter months. If your family prefers the flavors of cheeseburger soup, substitute lean ground beef for the ground turkey.
—Cathy Smith, Amarillo, TX

Prep: 20 min. • **Cook:** 30 min.
Makes: 10 servings

- 1   lb. lean ground turkey
- ¾   cup chopped onion
- 4   cups diced peeled potatoes
- 4   cups reduced-sodium chicken broth
- ¾   cup shredded carrots
- ¾   cup diced celery
- 1   tsp. salt
- 1   tsp. dried basil
- 1   tsp. dried parsley flakes
- ½   tsp. pepper
- ¼   cup all-purpose flour
- 1½ cups fat-free milk
- 6   oz. reduced-fat Velveeta, cubed
- ¼   cup reduced-fat sour cream

1. In a large saucepan, cook turkey and onion over medium heat until meat is no longer pink, breaking it into crumbles; drain. Add the potatoes, broth, carrots, celery, salt, basil, parsley and pepper. Bring to a boil. Reduce heat; cover and simmer for 8-10 minutes or until the vegetables are tender.
2. In a small bowl, combine flour and milk until smooth; stir into soup. Bring to a boil; cook and stir for 1-2 minutes or until thickened. Reduce heat to low; add cheese. Cook and stir until the cheese is melted. Remove from the heat; stir in sour cream.

1 cup 208 cal., 6g fat (3g sat. fat), 46mg chol., 833mg sod., 22g carb. (6g sugars, 2g fiber), 16g pro.
Diabetic exchanges 2 lean meat, 1 starch, 1 vegetable.

Sausage & Kale Soup

This is my family's absolute favorite soup, and I can have it on the table in less than 45 minutes—which makes it one of my favorites too. I usually double the recipe so the flavors can blend, making the soup even better the next day.
—Dawn Rohn, Riverton, WY

Prep: 15 min. • **Cook:** 25 min.
Makes: 14 servings (3½ qt.)

- 1 lb. smoked kielbasa or Polish sausage, cut into ¼-in. slices
- 3 medium Yukon Gold or red potatoes, chopped
- 2 medium onions, chopped
- 2 Tbsp. olive oil
- 1 bunch kale, trimmed and torn
- 4 garlic cloves, minced
- ¼ tsp. pepper
- ¼ tsp. salt
- 2 bay leaves
- 1 can (14½ oz.) diced tomatoes, undrained
- 1 can (15 oz.) garbanzo beans or chickpeas, rinsed and drained
- 1 carton (32 oz.) chicken broth

1. In a Dutch oven over medium-low heat, cook sausage, potatoes and onions in oil for 5 minutes or until the sausage is heated through, stirring occasionally. Add kale; cover and cook for 2-3 minutes or until kale is wilted. Add garlic; cook 1 minute longer.

2. Add the remaining ingredients. Bring to a boil. Reduce heat; cover and simmer for 9-12 minutes or until potatoes are tender. Discard bay leaves.

1 cup 187 cal., 11g fat (3g sat. fat), 22mg chol., 706mg sod., 16g carb. (3g sugars, 3g fiber), 7g pro.

Loaded Baked Potato Soup

The only thing that beats this comforting potato soup is the fact that it simmers on its own all day.
—Barbara Bleigh, Colonial Height, VA

Prep: 35 min. • **Cook:** 6 hours
Makes: 10 servings

- 2 large onions, chopped
- 3 Tbsp. butter
- 2 Tbsp. all-purpose flour
- 2 cups water, divided
- 4 cups chicken broth
- 2 medium potatoes, peeled and diced
- 1½ cups mashed potato flakes
- ½ lb. sliced bacon, cooked and crumbled
- ¾ tsp. pepper
- ½ tsp. salt
- ½ tsp. dried basil
- ⅛ tsp. dried thyme
- 1 cup half-and-half cream
- ½ cup shredded cheddar cheese
- 2 green onions, sliced

1. In a large skillet, saute onions in butter until tender. Stir in flour. Gradually stir in 1 cup water. Bring to a boil; cook and stir for 2 minutes or until thickened. Transfer to a 5-qt. slow cooker.

2. Add broth, potatoes, potato flakes, bacon, pepper, salt, basil, thyme and the remaining 1 cup water. Cover and cook on low until potatoes are tender, 6-8 hours. Stir in cream; heat through. Garnish with cheese and green onions.

1 cup 212 cal., 11g fat (6g sat. fat), 35mg chol., 723mg sod., 20g carb. (3g sugars, 2g fiber), 7g pro.

"Great slow cooker soup! Very easy to put together and perfect for a chilly evening. We garnished it with cheese, green onions and a dollop of sour cream. Delicious! Will make this one often this winter!"

—Debglass11, tasteofhome.com

Creamy Vegetable Chowder

This rich soup has it all. You can lower the fat content by using turkey bacon and skim milk. It's delicious either way.
—Suzanna VandeBrake, Peyton, CO

Prep: 30 min. • **Cook:** 1 hour
Makes: 12 servings (3 qt.)

- ¾ lb. sliced bacon, chopped
- 2 large onions, chopped
- 2 medium carrots, chopped
- 2 celery ribs, chopped
- 2 medium parsnips, chopped
- 2 small turnips, chopped
- ¾ cup all-purpose flour
- ½ tsp. salt
- ½ tsp. cayenne pepper
- 2 cartons (32 oz. each) chicken broth
- 1 medium sweet potato, peeled and chopped
- 3 small red potatoes, chopped
- 2 bay leaves
- 1 Tbsp. Worcestershire sauce
- ¼ tsp. hot pepper sauce
- 1 cup half-and-half cream
- ½ cup minced fresh parsley

1. In a Dutch oven over medium heat, cook bacon until crisp, then remove to paper towels. Drain pot, reserving 3 Tbsp. drippings. Add onions, carrots, celery, parsnips and turnips. Cook and stir until fragrant, 6-8 minutes.
2. Sprinkle vegetables with flour, salt and cayenne; stir until blended. Gradually add broth. Bring to a boil; cook and stir until thickened, 2 minutes. Add sweet potato, potatoes, bay leaves, Worcestershire sauce and pepper sauce.
3. Reduce heat; cover and simmer until potatoes are tender, 15-20 minutes. Stir in cream and parsley; heat through. Discard bay leaves.
1 cup 205 cal., 10g fat (4g sat. fat), 24mg chol., 956mg sod., 21g carb. (6g sugars, 3g fiber), 6g pro.

Old-Fashioned Split Pea Soup with Ham Bone

Not only is this old-fashioned favorite a snap to make but it's economical too. Carrots, celery and onion accent the subtle flavor of the split peas, while a ham bone adds a meaty touch. It's sure to chase away autumn's chill.
—Laurie Todd, Columbus, MS

Prep: 15 min. + standing
Cook: 2½ hours
Makes: 10 servings (about 2½ qt.)

- 1 pkg. (16 oz.) dried green split peas
- 1 meaty ham bone
- 1 large onion, chopped
- 1 tsp. salt
- ½ tsp. pepper
- ½ tsp. dried thyme
- 1 bay leaf
- 1 cup chopped carrot
- 1 cup chopped celery

1. Sort peas and rinse with cold water. Place peas in a Dutch oven; add water to cover by 2 in. Bring to a boil; boil for 2 minutes. Remove from heat; cover and let stand or until peas are softened, 1-4 hours. Drain and rinse peas; discard liquid.
2. Return peas to Dutch oven. Add 2½ qts. water, ham bone, onion, salt, pepper, thyme and bay leaf. Bring to a boil. Reduce heat; cover and simmer for 1½ hours, stirring occasionally.
3. Remove the ham bone; when cool enough to handle, remove meat from bone. Discard bone; dice meat and return to soup. Add carrot and celery. Simmer, uncovered, 45-60 minutes or until soup reaches desired thickness and vegetables are tender. Discard bay leaf.
1 cup 202 cal., 3g fat (1g sat. fat), 11mg chol., 267mg sod., 31g carb. (6g sugars, 12g fiber), 14g pro.
Diabetic exchanges 2 starch, 1 lean meat.

Classic French Onion Soup

Enjoy my signature soup the way my granddaughter Becky does: I make it for her in a French onion soup bowl complete with garlic croutons and gobs of melted Swiss cheese on top.
—Lou Sansevero, Ferron, UT

Prep: 20 min. • **Cook:** 2 hours
Makes: 12 servings (2¼ qt.)

- 5   Tbsp. olive oil, divided
- 1   Tbsp. butter
- 8   cups thinly sliced onions (about 3 lbs.)
- 3   garlic cloves, minced
- ½   cup port wine or dry sherry
- 2   cartons (32 oz. each) beef broth
- ½   tsp. pepper
- ¼   tsp. salt
- 24 slices French bread baguette (½ in. thick)
- 2   large garlic cloves, peeled and halved
- ¾   cup shredded Gruyere or Swiss cheese

1. In a Dutch oven, heat 2 Tbsp. oil and butter over medium heat. Add onions; cook and stir until softened, 10-13 minutes. Reduce heat to medium-low; cook, stirring occasionally, until deep golden brown, 30-40 minutes. Add minced garlic; cook 2 minutes longer.

2. Stir in wine. Bring to a boil; cook until liquid is reduced by half. Add broth, pepper and salt; return to a boil. Reduce heat. Simmer, covered, stirring occasionally, for 1 hour.

3. Meanwhile, preheat oven to 400°. Place baguette slices on a baking sheet; brush both sides with remaining 3 Tbsp. oil. Bake until toasted, 3-5 minutes on each side. Rub toasts with halved garlic.

4. To serve, ladle soup into twelve 8-oz. broiler-safe bowls or ramekins on baking sheets; place 2 toasts in each. Top with cheese. Broil 4 in. from heat until cheese is melted.

¾ cup soup with 2 pieces bread and 1 Tbsp. cheese 195 cal., 10g fat (3g sat. fat), 9mg chol., 765mg sod., 21g carb. (4g sugars, 2g fiber), 6g pro.

French Onion Soup Tips

- It's best to use sweet onions for this soup; they complement the savory beef broth the best. If you need a substitute, use yellow onions.

- After the onions, beef broth is truly the backbone ingredient in French onion soup, so using a good quality broth is key. Store-bought is fine, or consider making your own.

- Store leftover soup in an airtight container in the refrigerator for up to 3 days, or freeze for up to 6 months. Either way, store the cheese and bread separately. To reheat, gently bring the soup to a simmer on the stovetop and top with bread and cheese according to the recipe.

Contest-Winning New England Clam Chowder

This is the best New England clam chowder recipe ever! In the Pacific Northwest, we dig our own razor clams and I grind them for the chowder. Since these aren't readily available, the canned clams are perfectly acceptable.
—Sandy Larson, Port Angeles, WA

Prep: 20 min. • **Cook:** 35 min.
Makes: 5 servings

- 4   center-cut bacon strips
- 2   celery ribs, chopped
- 1   large onion, chopped
- 1   garlic clove, minced
- 3   small potatoes, peeled and cubed
- 1   cup water
- 1   bottle (8 oz.) clam juice
- 3   tsp. reduced-sodium chicken bouillon granules
- ¼   tsp. white pepper
- ¼   tsp. dried thyme
- ⅓   cup all-purpose flour
- 2   cups fat-free half-and-half, divided
- 2   cans (6½ oz. each) chopped clams, undrained

1. In a Dutch oven, cook bacon over medium heat until crisp. Remove to paper towels to drain. Saute celery and onion in the drippings until tender. Add garlic; cook 1 minute longer. Stir in potatoes, water, clam juice, bouillon, pepper and thyme. Bring to a boil. Reduce heat; simmer, uncovered, until the potatoes are tender, 15-20 minutes.
2. In a small bowl, combine flour and 1 cup half-and-half until smooth. Gradually stir into the soup. Bring to a boil; cook and stir until thickened, 1-2 minutes.

3. Stir in clams and the remaining 1 cup half-and-half; heat through (do not boil). Crumble the cooked bacon; sprinkle over each serving.
1⅓ cups 280 cal., 5g fat (1g sat. fat), 36mg chol., 805mg sod., 42g carb. (9g sugars, 3g fiber), 15g pro.
Diabetic exchanges 2½ starch, 1 lean meat.

Did You Know?

White pepper comes from fully ripened peppercorns that have had their skins removed. It has a milder flavor than black pepper and is helpful in dishes where you might not want black flecks to show. You can substitute black pepper (perhaps using a bit less than called for).

Loaded Broccoli-Cheese Potato Chowder

For anyone who loves baked potatoes or broccoli cheese soup, this is the best of both worlds. If you have bacon lovers in your house, offer crumbled cooked bacon as a topping. Then everyone is happy, carnivore or not!
—Vivi Taylor, Middleburg, FL

Prep: 15 min. • **Cook:** 6 hours 10 min.
Makes: 8 servings (2 qt.)

  1 pkg. (20 oz.) refrigerated
     O'Brien hash brown potatoes
  1 garlic clove, minced
  2 cups reduced-fat sour cream
  ¼ cup all-purpose flour
  ½ tsp. pepper
  ⅛ tsp. ground nutmeg
  3 cups vegetable stock
  1 pkg. (12 oz.) frozen broccoli
     florets, thawed
  4 cups shredded cheddar cheese
  ½ cup finely chopped green
     onions

1. Combine hash browns and garlic in a 5- or 6-qt. slow cooker. In a large bowl, whisk sour cream, flour, pepper and nutmeg until smooth; stir in stock. Pour into slow cooker; stir to combine. Cook, covered, on low until hash browns are tender, 6-8 hours.
2. Add broccoli and 3 cups cheese; cover and cook until cheese is melted, about 10 minutes longer. Serve with green onions and the remaining 1 cup cheese.
1 cup 386 cal., 23g fat (13g sat. fat), 62mg chol., 921mg sod., 26g carb. (6g sugars, 2g fiber), 20g pro.

Black Bean & Pumpkin Chili

My family is crazy about this slow-cooker chili because it uses ingredients you don't usually find in chili. Pumpkin is the unexpected element that makes this dish so special. Cook up a big batch and freeze some for later; it tastes even better reheated.
—Deborah Vliet, Holland, MI

Prep: 20 min. • **Cook:** 4 hours
Makes: 10 servings (2½ qt.)

   2   Tbsp. olive oil
   1   medium onion, chopped
   1   medium sweet yellow pepper,
       chopped
   3   garlic cloves, minced
   2   cans (15 oz. each) black beans,
       rinsed and drained
   1   can (15 oz.) solid-pack pumpkin
   1   can (14½ oz.) diced tomatoes,
       undrained
   3   cups chicken broth
  2½   cups cubed cooked turkey
   2   tsp. dried parsley flakes
   2   tsp. chili powder
  1½   tsp. ground cumin
  1½   tsp. dried oregano
   ½   tsp. salt
       Optional: Cubed avocado and
       thinly sliced green onions

1. In a large skillet, heat oil over medium-high heat. Add onion and pepper; cook and stir until tender. Add garlic; cook 1 minute longer.
2. Transfer to a 5-qt. slow cooker; stir in the next 10 ingredients. Cook, covered, on low 4-5 hours. If desired, top with avocado and green onions.
1 cup 192 cal., 5g fat (1g sat. fat), 28mg chol., 658mg sod., 21g carb. (5g sugars, 7g fiber), 16g pro.
Diabetic exchanges 2 lean meat, 1½ starch, ½ fat.

Contest-Winning Pepperoni Pizza Chili

Pizza and chili together in one dish—what could be better? Fill folks up at halftime when you dish up big bowlfuls of this chili.

—Jennifer Gelormino, Pittsburgh, PA

Prep: 20 min. • **Cook:** 30 min.
Makes: 12 servings (3 qt.)

- 2 lbs. ground beef
- 1 lb. bulk hot Italian sausage
- 1 large onion, chopped
- 1 large green pepper, chopped
- 4 garlic cloves, minced
- 1 jar (16 oz.) salsa
- 1 can (16 oz.) hot chili beans, undrained
- 1 can (16 oz.) kidney beans, rinsed and drained
- 1 can (12 oz.) pizza sauce
- 1 pkg. (8 oz.) sliced pepperoni, halved
- 1 cup water
- 2 tsp. chili powder
- ½ tsp. salt
- ½ tsp. pepper
- 3 cups shredded part-skim mozzarella cheese

1. In a Dutch oven, cook the beef, sausage, onion, green pepper and garlic over medium heat until the meat is no longer pink; drain.
2. Stir in salsa, beans, pizza sauce, pepperoni, water, chili powder, salt and pepper. Bring to a boil. Reduce heat; cover and simmer until heated through, about 20 minutes. Sprinkle servings with cheese.
Freeze option Before adding cheese, cool chili. Freeze chili in freezer containers. To use, partially thaw in refrigerator overnight. Heat through in a saucepan, stirring occasionally and adding a little water if necessary. Sprinkle each serving with cheese.
1 cup chili with ¼ cup cheese 464 cal., 28g fat (11g sat. fat), 94mg chol., 1240mg sod., 21g carb. (6g sugars, 5g fiber), 33g pro.

"As the name states, this IS a contest-winning chili! I won a contest against 12 other chilis by a landslide."

—Charlie443, tasteofhome.com

Navy Bean Vegetable Soup

My family really likes bean soup, so I came up with this enticing version. The leftovers are, dare I say, even better the next day!

—Eleanor Mielke, Mitchell, SD

Prep: 35 min. + soaking
Cook: 9 hours
Makes: 12 servings (3 qt.)

- 1½ cups dried navy beans
- 8 cups water
- 4 medium carrots, thinly sliced
- 2 celery ribs, chopped
- 1 medium onion, chopped
- 2 cups cubed fully cooked ham
- 1 envelope vegetable recipe mix (Knorr)
- 1 envelope onion soup mix
- 1 bay leaf
- ½ tsp. pepper

1. Rinse and sort beans. Place in a large saucepan; add water to cover by 2 in. Let soak, covered, overnight. Drain and rinse beans; discard liquid.
2. Return beans to saucepan; add water to cover by 2 in. Bring to a boil. Boil 15 minutes. Drain and rinse beans; discard liquid.
3. Transfer beans to a 5-qt. slow cooker. Add 8 cups water. Stir in remaining ingredients. Cover and cook on low until beans are tender, 9-10 hours. Discard bay leaf.
1 cup 157 cal., 2g fat (1g sat. fat), 12mg chol., 763mg sod., 24g carb. (4g sugars, 8g fiber), 11g pro.

Cozy Soups **101**

Easy Chicken
Casserole, Page 121

Casseroles & Oven Entrees

Beef & Potato Moussaka

My son—who is now 27—brought home this recipe when he had a sixth-grade assignment about Greece. It earned high marks when we made it for his class. Traditional moussaka is usually made with eggplant; this one uses potatoes instead.

—Jean Puffer, Chilliwack, BC

Prep: 25 min.
Bake: 1 hour + standing
Makes: 6 servings

- 1 lb. ground beef
- 1 medium onion, chopped
- 1 garlic clove, minced
- ¾ cup water
- 1 can (6 oz.) tomato paste
- 3 Tbsp. minced fresh parsley
- 1 tsp. salt
- ½ tsp. dried mint, optional
- ¼ tsp. ground cinnamon
- ¼ tsp. pepper

Parmesan Sauce

- ¼ cup butter, cubed
- ¼ cup all-purpose flour
- 2 cups whole milk
- 4 large eggs, lightly beaten
- ½ cup grated Parmesan cheese
- ½ tsp. salt
- 5 medium potatoes, peeled and thinly sliced

1. Preheat oven to 350°. In a large skillet, cook beef and onion over medium heat until meat is no longer pink, 7-9 minutes, breaking into crumbles. Add garlic; cook 1 minute longer. Drain. Stir in water, tomato paste, parsley, salt, mint if desired, cinnamon and pepper.
2. For sauce, melt butter in a saucepan over medium heat. Stir in flour until smooth; gradually add milk. Bring to a boil; cook and stir for 2 minutes or until thickened. Remove from the heat. Stir a small amount of the hot mixture into eggs; return all to the pan, stirring constantly. Add cheese and salt.

3. Place half the potato slices in a greased shallow 3-qt. baking dish. Top with half the cheese sauce and all the meat mixture. Arrange the remaining potatoes over the meat mixture; top with the remaining cheese sauce.
4. Bake, uncovered, until a thermometer reads 160°, about 1 hour. Let stand for 10 minutes before serving.
1 serving 488 cal., 24g fat (12g sat. fat), 205mg chol., 918mg sod., 40g carb. (9g sugars, 3g fiber), 27g pro.

Bake it Now

We don't recommend preparing this moussaka recipe in advance to bake later. If you're short on time, cook as directed, cool the moussaka and then refrigerate until you're ready to eat. Reheat in the oven until warmed through.

Cheddar-Topped Barbecue Meat Loaf

My family loves the bold barbecue flavor of this tender meat loaf. I love that it's such an easy recipe to prepare in the slow cooker.
—David Snodgrass, Columbia, MO

Prep: 20 min. • **Cook:** 3¼ hours
Makes: 8 servings

- 3 large eggs, lightly beaten
- ¾ cup old-fashioned oats
- 1 large green or sweet red pepper, chopped (about 1½ cups)
- 1 small onion, finely chopped
- 1 envelope onion soup mix
- 3 garlic cloves, minced
- ½ tsp. salt
- ¼ tsp. pepper
- 2 lbs. lean ground beef (90% lean)
- 1 cup ketchup
- 2 Tbsp. brown sugar
- 1 Tbsp. barbecue seasoning
- 1 tsp. ground mustard
- 1 cup shredded cheddar cheese

1. Cut three 18x3-in. strips of heavy-duty foil; crisscross them so they resemble spokes of a wheel. Place strips on bottom and up sides of a 3-qt. slow cooker. Coat strips with cooking spray.
2. In a large bowl, combine eggs, oats, pepper, onion, onion soup mix, garlic, salt and pepper. Add beef; mix lightly but thoroughly. Shape into a 7-in. round loaf. Place loaf in center of strips in slow cooker. Cook, covered, on low for 3-4 hours or until a thermometer reads at least 160°.
3. In a small bowl, mix ketchup, brown sugar, barbecue seasoning and mustard; pour over meat loaf and sprinkle with cheese. Cook, covered, on low until cheese is melted, about 15 minutes longer. Let stand for 5 minutes. Using foil strips as handles, remove meat loaf to a platter.

1 piece 356 cal., 17g fat (7g sat. fat), 154mg chol., 1358mg sod., 22g carb. (13g sugars, 2g fiber), 29g pro.

Mexican Chicken Manicotti

Our family enjoys trying different ethnic cuisines. This Italian specialty has a little Mexican zip. Be careful not to overcook the manicotti. If the filled shells happen to break, just place them in the pan break-side down.
—Keely Jankunas, Corvallis, MT

Prep: 25 min. • **Bake:** 40 min.
Makes: 7 servings

- 1 pkg. (8 oz.) manicotti shells
- 2 cups cubed cooked chicken
- 2 cups shredded Monterey Jack cheese, divided
- 1½ cups shredded cheddar cheese
- 1 cup sour cream
- 1 small onion, diced, divided
- 1 can (4 oz.) chopped green chiles, divided

Sauce
- 1 can (10¾ oz.) condensed cream of chicken soup, undiluted
- 1 cup salsa
- ⅔ cup whole milk

1. Cook manicotti according to package directions. Meanwhile, in a large bowl, combine the chicken, 1½ cups Monterey Jack cheese, cheddar cheese, sour cream, half of the onion and 6 Tbsp. chiles.
2. For sauce, combine soup, salsa, milk and the remaining onion and chiles. Spread ½ cup in a greased 13x9-in. baking dish.
3. Drain manicotti and rinse in cold water; stuff each with about ¼ cupful chicken mixture. Arrange over sauce in baking dish. Pour remaining sauce over shells.
4. Cover and bake at 350° for 30 minutes. Uncover; sprinkle with remaining ½ cup Monterey Jack cheese. Bake 10 minutes longer or until cheese is melted.

1 serving 535 cal., 29g fat (17g sat. fat), 118mg chol., 937mg sod., 32g carb. (6g sugars, 3g fiber), 32g pro.

Texas-Style Lasagna

With its spicy flavor, this dish is a real crowd-pleaser. It goes wonderfully with side servings of picante sauce, guacamole and tortilla chips.

Effie Dish, Fort Worth, TX

Prep: 40 min.
Bake: 30 min. + standing
Makes: 12 servings

1½ lbs. ground beef
1 tsp. seasoned salt
1 pkg. (1¼ oz.) taco seasoning
1 can (14½ oz.) diced tomatoes, undrained
1 can (15 oz.) tomato sauce
1 can (4 oz.) chopped green chiles
2 cups 4% cottage cheese
2 large eggs, lightly beaten
12 corn tortillas (6 in.), torn
3½ to 4 cups shredded Monterey Jack cheese

Optional: Crushed tortilla chips, salsa and cubed avocado

1. In a large skillet, cook beef over medium until no longer pink, 6-8 minutes, breaking into crumbles; drain. Add seasoned salt, taco seasoning, tomatoes, tomato sauce and chiles. Reduce heat; simmer, uncovered, for 15-20 minutes. In a small bowl, combine cottage cheese and eggs.
2. In a greased 13x9-in. baking dish, layer half of each of the following: meat sauce, tortillas, the cottage cheese mixture and Monterey Jack cheese. Repeat layers.
3. Bake, uncovered, at 350° for 30 minutes or until bubbly. Let stand 10 minutes before serving. Garnish with toppings if desired.
1 piece 349 cal., 18g fat (10g sat. fat), 101mg chol., 1041mg sod., 20g carb. (3g sugars, 2g fiber), 26g pro.

Cornmeal Oven-Fried Chicken

This chicken dish perks up the dinner table. Its flavorful cornmeal and bread-crumb coating is a good variation from the usual.

—Deborah Williams, Peoria, AZ

Prep: 20 min. • **Bake:** 40 min.
Makes: 6 servings

- ½ cup dry bread crumbs
- ½ cup cornmeal
- ⅓ cup grated Parmesan cheese
- ¼ cup minced fresh parsley or 4 tsp. dried parsley flakes
- ¾ tsp. garlic powder
- ½ tsp. salt
- ½ tsp. onion powder
- ½ tsp. dried thyme
- ½ tsp. pepper
- ½ cup buttermilk
- 1 broiler/fryer chicken (3 to 4 lbs.), cut up and skin removed
- 1 Tbsp. butter, melted

1. Preheat oven to 375°. In a large shallow dish, combine the first 9 ingredients. Place buttermilk in a shallow bowl. Dip chicken in the buttermilk, then in the bread crumb mixture, a few pieces at a time, and turn to coat.

2. Place in a 13x9-in. baking pan coated with cooking spray. Bake for 10 minutes; drizzle with butter. Bake until juices run clear, 30-40 minutes longer.

Note To substitute for each cup of buttermilk, use 1 Tbsp. white vinegar or lemon juice plus enough milk to measure 1 cup. Stir; let stand 5 min. Or, use 1 cup plain yogurt or 1¾ tsp. cream of tartar plus 1 cup milk.

3 oz. cooked chicken 249 cal., 9g fat (3g sat. fat), 82mg chol., 331mg sod., 13g carb. (2g sugars, 1g fiber), 27g pro. **Diabetic exchanges** 3 lean meat, 1 starch, ½ fat.

Roasted Chicken with Rosemary

Herbs, garlic and butter give this hearty meal-in-one a classic flavor. It's a lot like pot roast, only it uses chicken instead of beef.
—Isabel Zienkosky, Salt Lake City, UT

Prep: 20 min.
Bake: 2 hours + standing
Makes: 9 servings

- ½   cup butter, cubed
- 4   Tbsp. minced fresh rosemary or 2 Tbsp. dried rosemary, crushed
- 2   Tbsp. minced fresh parsley
- 1   tsp. salt
- ½   tsp. pepper
- 3   garlic cloves, minced
- 1   whole roasting chicken (5 to 6 lbs.)
- 6   small red potatoes, halved
- 6   medium carrots, halved lengthwise and cut into 2-in. pieces
- 2   medium onions, quartered

1. In a small saucepan, melt butter; stir in the seasonings and garlic. Place chicken breast side up on a rack in a shallow roasting pan; tie drumsticks together with kitchen string. Spoon half the butter mixture over the chicken. Place potatoes, carrots and onions around chicken. Drizzle remaining butter mixture over vegetables.
2. Bake at 350° for 1½ hours. Baste with cooking juices; bake 30-60 minutes longer, basting occasionally, until a thermometer inserted in thickest part of thigh reads 170°-175°. (Cover loosely with foil if chicken browns too quickly.)
3. Let stand 10-15 minutes, tented with foil if necessary, before carving. Serve with vegetables.
1 serving 449 cal., 28g fat (11g sat. fat), 126mg chol., 479mg sod., 16g carb. (5g sugars, 3g fiber), 33g pro.

Corn Dog Casserole

Reminiscent of traditional corn dogs, this fun main dish really hits the spot. It tastes especially good right from the oven.
—Marcy Suzanne Olipane, Belleville, IL

Prep: 25 min. • **Bake:** 30 min.
Makes: 10 servings

- 2   cups thinly sliced celery
- 2   Tbsp. butter
- 1½   cups sliced green onions
- 1½   lbs. hot dogs
- 2   large eggs
- 1½   cups 2% milk
- 2   tsp. rubbed sage
- ¼   tsp. pepper
- 2   pkg. (8½ oz. each) cornbread/muffin mix
- 2   cups shredded sharp cheddar cheese, divided

1. In a small skillet, saute celery in butter for 5 minutes. Add green onion; saute until the vegetables are tender, 5 minutes longer. Place in a large bowl.
2. Preheat oven to 400°. Cut hot dogs into ½-in. slices. In the same skillet, saute hot dog slices until lightly browned, about 5 minutes; add to vegetables. Reserve 1 cup.
3. In a large bowl, whisk eggs, milk, sage and pepper. Add the remaining hot dog mixture. Stir in cornbread mixes. Add 1½ cups cheese. Spread into a shallow 3-qt. or 13x9-in. baking dish. Top with reserved hot dog mixture and remaining cheese.
4. Bake, uncovered, until golden brown, about 30 minutes.
1 cup 578 cal., 38g fat (16g sat. fat), 108mg chol., 1307mg sod., 40g carb. (13g sugars, 4g fiber), 19g pro.

So-Tender Swiss Steak

When I was little, my mother's Swiss steak was the dinner I requested the most. Now it's a favorite in my house too.
—Linda McGinty, Parma, OH

Prep: 30 min. • **Bake:** 2 hours
Makes: 8 servings

- ¼ cup all-purpose flour
- ½ tsp. salt
- ¼ tsp. pepper
- 2 lbs. beef top round steak, cut into serving-size pieces
- 2 Tbsp. canola oil
- 1 medium onion, thinly sliced
- 2 cups water
- 2 Tbsp. Worcestershire sauce

Gravy
- ¼ cup all-purpose flour
- ¼ tsp. salt
- ⅛ tsp. pepper
- 1¼ cups beef broth or water
  Optional: Hot cooked noodles or mashed potatoes

1. Preheat oven to 325°. In a large shallow dish, combine flour, salt and pepper. Pound steak with a mallet to tenderize. Add the steak, a few pieces at a time, and toss to coat.

2. In an ovenproof Dutch oven, brown steak in oil on both sides. Arrange onion slices between layers of meat. Add water and Worcestershire sauce.

3. Bake, covered, until the meat is very tender, 2 to 2½ hours. Remove meat to a serving platter and keep warm.

4. For gravy, in a small bowl, combine flour, salt, pepper and broth until smooth; stir into pan juices. Bring to a boil over medium heat; cook and stir 2 minutes or until thickened. If desired, serve steak and gravy with noodles or mashed potatoes.

4 oz. cooked beef 213 cal., 7g fat (2g sat. fat), 64mg chol., 424mg sod., 9g carb. (1g sugars, 1g fiber), 27g pro.

Tasty Onion Chicken

French-fried onions are the secret to a yummy, crunchy coating that keeps chicken juicy and tender. This entree is perfect with green beans and buttermilk biscuits.
—Jennifer Hoeft, Thorndale, TX

Takes: 30 min. • **Makes:** 4 servings

- ½ cup butter, melted
- 1 Tbsp. Worcestershire sauce
- 1 tsp. ground mustard
- 1 can (2.8 oz.) French-fried onions, crushed
- 4 boneless skinless chicken breast halves (4 oz. each)

1. Preheat oven to 400°. In a shallow bowl, combine butter, Worcestershire sauce and mustard. Place onions in another shallow bowl. Dip chicken in the butter mixture, then coat with onions.

2. Place the chicken in a greased 11x7-in. baking dish; drizzle with remaining butter mixture. Bake, uncovered, for 20-25 minutes or until a thermometer reads 165°.

1 chicken breast half 460 cal., 36g fat (18g sat. fat), 124mg chol., 449mg sod., 10g carb. (0 sugars, 0 fiber), 23g pro.

"Very easy and tasty. We will definitely make this again and again. My husband and I used the leftovers to top our salads the next day."

—ChocolateMudCake,
   tasteofhome.com

Turkey Potpies

With golden brown crust and scrumptious filling, these comforting potpies will warm you down to your toes. Because the recipe makes two, you can eat one now and freeze the other for later. They bake and cut beautifully.
—Laurie Jensen, Cadillac, MI

Prep: 40 min.
Bake: 40 min. + standing
Makes: 2 pies (6 servings each)

2 medium potatoes, peeled and cut into 1-in. pieces
3 medium carrots, cut into 1-in. slices
1 medium onion, chopped
1 celery rib, diced
2 Tbsp. butter
1 Tbsp. olive oil
6 Tbsp. all-purpose flour
3 cups chicken broth
4 cups cubed cooked turkey
⅔ cup frozen peas
½ cup plus 1 Tbsp. heavy whipping cream, divided
1 Tbsp. minced fresh parsley
1 tsp. garlic salt
¼ tsp. pepper
2 sheets refrigerated pie crust
1 large egg

1. Preheat oven to 375°. In a Dutch oven, saute potatoes, carrots, onion and celery in butter and oil until tender. Stir in flour until blended; gradually add broth. Bring to a boil; cook and stir for 2 minutes or until thickened. Stir in turkey, peas, ½ cup cream, parsley, garlic salt and pepper.
2. Spoon into 2 ungreased 9-in. pie plates. Unroll crusts; place over the filling. Trim crusts and seal to edge of pie plates. Cut out a decorative center or cut slits in crusts. In a small bowl, whisk egg and remaining 1 Tbsp. cream; brush over crusts.

3. Bake until golden brown, 40-45 minutes. Let stand for 10 minutes before cutting.
Freeze option Cover and freeze unbaked potpies up to 3 months. To use, remove from freezer 30 minutes before baking (do not thaw). Preheat oven to 425°. Place pie on a baking sheet; cover edge loosely with foil. Bake 30 minutes. Reduce oven setting to 350°; remove foil. Bake until golden brown and a thermometer inserted in center reads 165°, 55-60 minutes longer.
1 serving 287 cal., 15g fat (7g sat. fat), 78mg chol., 542mg sod., 21g carb. (3g sugars, 2g fiber), 17g pro.

Turkey Potpie Tips

Can I use other kinds of vegetables in this recipe?
You can try different root vegetables such as sweet potatoes or turnips in this pot pie. If you're short on time or looking for an easy shortcut, you can opt for your favorite frozen vegetable mix.

What can I do if the crust is getting too brown before the potpies are done? If you're worried your crust might burn, simply lay a loose piece of foil over the pot pie for the remainder of the baking time. You can also make a pie crust shield to prevent burning—and reuse it for baking other pies at home, too!

Ham Loaf

I copied this recipe exactly the way Grandma has written it in her worn cookbook. The only difference today is that I can't get home-smoked ham like those Grandpa used to cure in his old-fashioned smokehouse. But that never matters to hungry folks at the table—Grandma's recipe is still a winner every time!
—Esther Mishler, Hollsopple, PA

Prep: 15 min. • **Bake:** 70 min.
Makes: 8 servings

- 2 large eggs
- 1 cup 2% milk
- 1 cup dry bread crumbs
- ¼ tsp. pepper
- 1½ lb. ground fully cooked ham
- ½ lb. ground pork

Glaze

- ⅓ cup packed brown sugar
- ¼ cup cider vinegar
- ½ tsp. ground mustard
- 2 Tbsp. water

1. Preheat oven to 350°. In a large bowl, beat the eggs; add milk, bread crumbs and pepper. Add ham and pork; mix well. Transfer to a 9x5-in. loaf pan. Bake for 30 minutes.
2. Meanwhile, combine the glaze ingredients; spoon over loaf. Bake until a thermometer inserted in the loaf reads 145°, 40 minutes longer, basting occasionally with glaze.
1 piece 393 cal., 23g fat (8g sat. fat), 115mg chol., 1241mg sod., 21g carb. (11g sugars, 1g fiber), 25g pro.

Make 'em Mini

To make mini loaves, divide the meat mixture among the cups of a muffin tin. Fill any empty cups with water. Bake as directed; check for doneness after 30 minutes.

Chicken & Swiss Stuffing Bake

I love to cook but just don't have much time. This casserole is both comforting and fast, which makes it my favorite kind of recipe. I like to serve it with a green salad.
—Jena Coffey, Sunset Hills, MO

Prep: 20 min. • **Bake:** 25 min.
Makes: 8 servings

- 1 can (10¾ oz.) condensed cream of mushroom soup, undiluted
- 1 cup 2% milk
- 1 pkg. (6 oz.) stuffing mix
- 2 cups cubed cooked chicken breast
- 2 cups fresh broccoli florets, cooked
- 2 celery ribs, finely chopped
- 1½ cups shredded Swiss cheese, divided

1. In a large bowl, combine soup and milk until blended. Add the stuffing mix with the contents of seasoning packet, chicken, broccoli, celery and 1 cup cheese. Transfer to a greased 13x9-in. baking dish.
2. Bake, uncovered, at 375° for 20 minutes or until heated through. Sprinkle with the remaining cheese; bake until the cheese is melted, 5 minutes longer.
Freeze option Sprinkle remaining cheese over unbaked casserole. Cover and freeze. To use, partially thaw in refrigerator overnight. Remove from refrigerator 30 minutes before baking. Bake casserole as directed, increasing time as necessary to heat through and for a thermometer inserted in center to read 165°.
1 cup 247 cal., 7g fat (4g sat. fat), 42mg chol., 658mg sod., 24g carb. (0 sugars, 3g fiber), 22g pro.

Mini Scallop Casseroles

Tiny and tender bay scallops take center stage in these miniature dishes. They're reminiscent of pot pies, creamy and packed with flavorful veggies in every bite.

—Vivian Manary, Nepean, ON

Prep: 30 min. • **Bake:** 20 min.
Makes: 4 servings

- 3 celery ribs, chopped
- 1 cup sliced fresh mushrooms
- 1 medium green pepper, chopped
- 1 small onion, chopped
- 2 Tbsp. butter
- ⅓ cup all-purpose flour
- ¼ tsp. salt
- ¼ tsp. pepper
- 2 cups fat-free milk
- 1 lb. bay scallops

Topping
- 1 cup soft bread crumbs
- 1 Tbsp. butter, melted
- ¼ cup shredded cheddar cheese

1. In a large skillet, saute celery, mushrooms, green pepper and onion in butter until tender. Stir in flour, salt and pepper until blended; gradually add milk. Bring to a boil; cook and stir for 2 minutes or until thickened.

2. Reduce heat; add scallops. Cook, stirring occasionally, 3-4 minutes or until the scallops are firm and opaque.

3. Preheat oven to 350°. Divide the mixture among four 10-oz. ramekins or custard cups. For the topping, in a small bowl, combine crumbs and butter; sprinkle over scallop mixture.

4. Bake, uncovered, until bubbly, 15-20 minutes. Sprinkle with cheese; bake 5 minutes longer or until the cheese is melted.

1 serving 332 cal., 12g fat (7g sat. fat), 70mg chol., 588mg sod., 27g carb. (9g sugars, 2g fiber), 28g pro.

Pizza Tater Tot Casserole

For a new spin on a classic casserole, try my easy version. For a fun twist, add your family's favorite pizza toppings!
—Sharon Skildum, Maple Grove, MN

Prep: 10 min. • **Bake:** 35 min.
Makes: 8 servings

> 1½ lbs. ground beef
> 1 medium green pepper, chopped, optional
> 1 medium onion, chopped
> ½ lb. sliced fresh mushrooms
> 1 can (15 oz.) pizza sauce
> 1 tsp. dried basil
> 3 cups shredded part-skim mozzarella cheese
> 1 pkg. (32 oz.) frozen Tater Tots
> 1 cup shredded cheddar cheese

1. Preheat oven to 400°. In a large skillet, cook the beef, green pepper if desired, onion and mushrooms over medium heat until the meat is no longer pink, breaking meat into crumbles; drain. Add pizza sauce and basil.
2. Transfer to a greased 3-qt. or 13x9-in. baking dish. Top with mozzarella cheese and potatoes. Bake, uncovered, until the potatoes are lightly browned, 30-35 minutes.
3. Sprinkle with cheddar cheese; bake until the cheese is melted, about 5 minutes.
1 serving 572 cal., 32g fat (13g sat. fat), 96mg chol., 1081mg sod., 41g carb. (7g sugars, 5g fiber), 36g pro.

"This was easy to make and full of flavors. The family loved it!"

—Medic 716, tasteofhome.com

Mexican Casserole

Trying to use what I had on hand one day, I came up with this recipe. Choose your favorite taco seasoning and salsa to make the casserole as spicy or as mild as you like.
—David Mills, Indianapolis, IN

Prep: 20 min. • **Bake:** 40 min.
Makes: 6 servings

- 1½ lbs. ground beef
- 1 envelope taco seasoning
- ¾ cup water
- 1 can (16 oz.) refried beans
- ½ cup salsa
- 6 flour tortillas (6 in.)
- 2 cups frozen corn, thawed
- 2 cups shredded cheddar cheese
  Optional: Shredded lettuce, chopped tomatoes, sliced ripe olives and sour cream

1. Preheat oven to 350°. In a large skillet over medium heat, cook beef over until no longer pink, 7-9 minutes, crumbling the meat; drain. Stir in taco seasoning and water. Bring to a boil. Reduce heat; simmer, uncovered, 5 minutes.
2. Meanwhile, in a microwave-safe bowl, combine beans and salsa. Cover and microwave 1-2 minutes or until spreadable.
3. Place 3 tortillas in a greased round 2½-qt. baking dish. Layer with half each of the beef, bean mixture, corn and cheese; repeat the layers.
4. Bake, uncovered, until the cheese is melted, 40-45 minutes. Let stand for 5 minutes. If desired, serve with lettuce, tomatoes, olives and sour cream.

1¼ cups 602 cal., 31g fat (14g sat. fat), 107mg chol., 1404mg sod., 43g carb. (3g sugars, 5g fiber), 36g pro.

Little Cheddar Meat Loaves

These tiny loaves are great when you are craving meat loaf but don't want to wait for a full-sized loaf to bake. My husband and I just love these served with au gratin or fried potatoes.
—Paula Petersen, Granite City, IL

Takes: 30 min. • **Makes:** 2 servings

- 1 large egg, lightly beaten
- ⅓ cup quick-cooking oats
- 2 Tbsp. ketchup
- 1 Tbsp. dried minced onion
- ½ lb. lean ground beef (90% lean)

Topping
- 4 tsp. ketchup
- 4 Tbsp. shredded cheddar cheese

1. In a large bowl, combine egg, oats, ketchup and onion. Crumble beef over the oats mixture; mix well. Coat 4 muffin cups with cooking spray; fill three-fourths full with meat mixture. Spread ketchup over loaves.
2. Bake at 400° for 15 minutes. Sprinkle with cheese. Bake until no pink remains and a thermometer reads 160°, about 5 minutes longer. Let stand for 5 minutes before removing from muffin cups.
2 mini meat loaves 343 cal., 16g fat (7g sat. fat), 190mg chol., 463mg sod., 18g carb. (4g sugars, 2g fiber), 30g pro.

Easy Chicken Casserole

This may be a basic chicken casserole, but I never bring home leftovers when I take it to a potluck. The stick-to-your-ribs dish has broad appeal; I especially like that the crumb topping adds a bit of crunch to each serving.

—Faye Hintz, Springfield, MO

Prep: 15 min. • **Bake:** 30 min.
Makes: 10 servings

8 cups cubed cooked chicken
2 cans (10½ oz. each) condensed cream of chicken soup, undiluted
1 cup sour cream
1 cup crushed Ritz crackers (about 25 crackers)
2 Tbsp. butter, melted
1 tsp. celery seed
   Optional: Minced fresh parsley

1. Preheat oven to 350°. Combine chicken, soup and sour cream; spread into a greased 13x9-in. baking dish. Combine cracker crumbs, butter and celery seed; sprinkle over the chicken mixture.
2. Bake, uncovered, until bubbly, 30-35 minutes. If desired, garnish with parsley.
1 cup 386 cal., 21g fat (8g sat. fat), 116mg chol., 629mg sod., 12g carb. (2g sugars, 1g fiber), 35g pro.

The Raw Deal

If you're starting with raw chicken, cook it first in a skillet over medium heat until it reaches 165° and is fully cooked through—then make the casserole. The casserole's baking time isn't long enough to cook the chicken without burning the sauce and topping.

Roadside Diner Cheeseburger Quiche

Here is an unforgettable quiche that tastes just like its burger counterpart. Easy and appealing, it's perfect for guests and fun for the whole family.

  Barbara J. Miller, Oakdale, MN

Prep: 20 min.
Bake: 50 min. + standing
Makes: 8 servings

1 sheet refrigerated pie crust
¾ lb. ground beef
2 plum tomatoes, seeded and chopped
1 medium onion, chopped
½ cup dill pickle relish
½ cup crumbled cooked bacon
5 large eggs
1 cup heavy whipping cream
½ cup 2% milk
2 tsp. prepared mustard
1 tsp. hot pepper sauce
½ tsp. salt
¼ tsp. pepper
1½ cups shredded cheddar cheese
½ cup shredded Parmesan cheese

Optional: Mayonnaise, additional pickle relish, crumbled cooked bacon, chopped onion and chopped tomato

1. Preheat oven to 375°. Unroll crust into a 9-in. deep-dish pie plate; flute edges.
In a large skillet, cook beef over medium heat until no longer pink, breaking it into crumbles; drain. Stir in tomatoes, onion, relish and bacon. Transfer to prepared crust.
2. In a large bowl, whisk the eggs, cream, milk, mustard, pepper sauce, salt and pepper. Pour over beef mixture. Sprinkle with cheeses.
3. Bake until a knife inserted in the center comes out clean, 50-60 minutes. If necessary, cover edges with foil during the last 15 minutes to prevent overbrowning. Let stand for 10 minutes before cutting. Garnish with optional ingredients as desired.
1 piece 502 cal., 35g fat (19g sat. fat), 236mg chol., 954mg sod., 24g carb. (8g sugars, 1g fiber), 23g pro.

Au Gratin Ham Potpie

We first had Aunt Dolly's potpie at a family get-together. We loved it and were so happy she shared the recipe. Now we make it almost every time we bake a ham.

—Mary Zinsmeister, Slinger, WI

Prep: 15 min. • **Bake:** 40 min.
Makes: 6 servings

- 1 pkg. (4.9 oz.) au gratin potatoes
- 1½ cups boiling water
- 2 cups frozen peas and carrots
- 1½ cups cubed fully cooked ham
- 1 can (10¾ oz.) condensed cream of chicken soup, undiluted
- 1 can (4 oz.) mushroom stems and pieces, drained
- ½ cup 2% milk
- ½ cup sour cream
- 1 jar (2 oz.) diced pimientos, drained
- 1 sheet refrigerated pie crust

1. Preheat oven to 400°. In a large bowl, combine potatoes, contents of the sauce mix and water. Stir in peas and carrots, ham, soup, mushrooms, milk, sour cream and pimientos. Transfer to an ungreased 2-qt. round baking dish.
2. Unroll crust; roll out to fit top of dish. Place over potato mixture; flute edges and cut slits in crust. Bake until golden brown, 40-45 minutes. Let stand for 5 minutes before serving.

1 piece 434 cal., 20g fat (9g sat. fat), 45mg chol., 1548mg sod., 47g carb. (7g sugars, 3g fiber), 14g pro.

"So yummy and had to double recipe to feed my family of five because my young kids love it so much!"

—aubrie06, tasteofhome.com

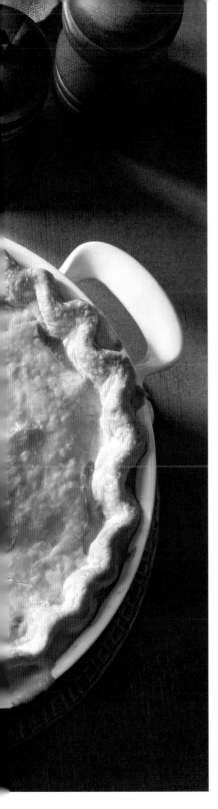

Roast Chicken with Oyster Stuffing

The aroma of this roasted chicken is almost as wonderful as its flavor, and the oyster stuffing is to die for. If you're not crazy about turkey dinners, try this instead for a lovely holiday meal.

—Joann Jensen, Lowell, IN

Prep: 35 min.
Bake: 2 hours + standing
Makes: 6 servings (4 cups stuffing)

- 1   can (8 oz.) whole oysters
- 1   celery rib, chopped
- 1   small onion, chopped
- ¼   cup butter, cubed
- 2   Tbsp. minced fresh parsley
- ½   tsp. Italian seasoning
- 3   cups cubed bread, lightly toasted
- 1   roasting chicken (6 to 7 lbs.)
- ¼   cup butter, melted
- 1   to 2 tsp. paprika

1. Drain oysters, reserving liquid; coarsely chop oysters. Set aside. In a small skillet, saute celery and onion in butter until tender. Stir in parsley and Italian seasoning. Place bread cubes in a large bowl; add the butter mixture, oysters and ¼ cup reserved oyster liquid.
2. Just before baking, loosely stuff chicken with stuffing. Place breast side up on a rack in a large roasting pan; tie drumsticks together. Combine melted butter and paprika; spoon over chicken.
3. Bake, uncovered, at 350° for 2 to 2½ hours or until a thermometer reads 165° when inserted in center of stuffing and thigh reaches at least 170°, basting occasionally with pan drippings. (Cover loosely with foil if chicken browns too quickly.)
4. Cover chicken and let stand for 10 minutes before removing stuffing and carving. Skim fat and thicken pan juices if desired.

1 serving 738 cal., 48g fat (19g sat. fat), 239mg chol., 447mg sod., 12g carb. (1g sugars, 1g fiber), 61g pro.

Pizza Lover's Pie

Love pizza? Then you'll love the tasty spin this recipe puts on it. Plus, it's easy to tailor for picky eaters.

—Carol Gillespie, Chambersburg, PA

Prep: 20 min. • **Bake:** 20 min.
Makes: 8 servings

- ¼   lb. bulk pork sausage
- ½   cup chopped green pepper
- ¼   cup chopped onion
- 1   loaf (1 lb.) frozen bread dough, thawed and halved
- 2   cups shredded part-skim mozzarella cheese
- ½   cup grated Parmesan cheese
- 1   can (8 oz.) pizza sauce
- 8   slices pepperoni
- 1   can (4 oz.) mushroom stems and pieces, drained
- ¼   tsp. dried oregano

1. Preheat oven to 400°. In a large skillet, cook sausage, green pepper and onion over medium heat until sausage is no longer pink, breaking it into crumbles; drain.
2. Roll out half the dough into a 12-in. circle. Transfer to a greased 9-in. deep-dish pie plate. Layer with half each of the following: mozzarella, Parmesan and pizza sauce. Top with the sausage mixture, pepperoni, mushrooms and ⅛ tsp. oregano.
3. Roll out remaining dough to fit top of pie. Place over filling; seal edges. Layer with remaining pizza sauce, cheeses and oregano. Bake until golden brown, 18-22 minutes.
1 piece 305 cal., 12g fat (5g sat. fat), 27mg chol., 743mg sod., 32g carb. (5g sugars, 3g fiber), 17g pro.
Diabetic exchanges 2 starch, 2 medium-fat meat.

Taco Lasagna

If you like foods with southwestern flair, this just might become a new favorite. Loaded with cheese, meat and beans, the layered casserole comes together in a snap. There are never any leftovers when I take this dish to potlucks.
—Terri Keenan, Tuscaloosa, AL

Prep: 20 min. • **Bake:** 25 min.
Makes: 9 servings

- 1   lb. ground beef
- ½   cup chopped green pepper
- ½   cup chopped onion
- ⅔   cup water
- 1   envelope taco seasoning
- 1   can (15 oz.) black beans, rinsed and drained
- 1   can (14½ oz.) Mexican diced tomatoes, undrained
- 6   flour tortillas (8 in.)
- 1   can (16 oz.) refried beans
- 3   cups shredded Mexican cheese blend

1. Preheat oven to 350°. In a large skillet, cook the beef, green pepper and onion over medium heat, breaking meat into crumbles, until beef is no longer pink; drain. Add water and taco seasoning; bring to a boil. Reduce heat; simmer, uncovered, for 2 minutes. Stir in black beans and tomatoes. Simmer, uncovered, for 10 minutes.
2. Place 2 tortillas in a greased 13x9-in. baking dish. Spread with half the refried beans and half the beef mixture; sprinkle with 1 cup cheese. Repeat layers. Top with the remaining tortillas and cheese.
3. Bake, covered, 25-30 minutes or until heated through and cheese is melted.
1 piece 454 cal., 21g fat (9g sat. fat), 65mg chol., 1138mg sod., 39g carb. (3g sugars, 5g fiber), 25g pro.

Crispy Fish & Chips

A British pub classic turns crown jewel when you add horseradish, panko and Worcestershire and bake it in the oven. You can also try it with a white fish like cod or haddock.
—Linda Schend, Kenosha, WI

Takes: 30 min. • **Makes:** 4 servings

- 4   cups frozen steak fries
- 4   salmon fillets (6 oz. each)
- 1   to 2 Tbsp. prepared horseradish
- 1   Tbsp. grated Parmesan cheese
- 1   Tbsp. Worcestershire sauce
- 1   tsp. Dijon mustard
- ¼   tsp. salt
- ½   cup panko bread crumbs
       Cooking spray

1. Preheat oven to 450°. Arrange steak fries in a single layer on a baking sheet. Bake on the lowest oven rack until light golden brown, 18-20 minutes.
2. Meanwhile, place the salmon fillets on a foil-lined baking sheet coated with cooking spray. In a small bowl, mix horseradish, cheese, Worcestershire sauce, mustard and salt; stir in panko. Press mixture onto fillets. Spritz tops with cooking spray.
3. Bake salmon on middle oven rack 8-10 minutes or until fish just begins to flake easily with a fork. Serve with fries.
1 fillet with ¾ cup fries 416 cal., 19g fat (4g sat. fat), 86mg chol., 698mg sod., 26g carb. (2g sugars, 2g fiber), 32g pro. **Diabetic exchanges** 5 lean meat, 1½ starch.

Spanakopita

This Mediterranean dish is always a crowd-pleaser! Phyllo dough can be tricky to work with, so I always make sure the dough is only briefly thawed before using it. Usually, I take it out of the freezer and let it sit on the counter while I prep the spinach mixture. Make sure you squeeze the spinach well before adding it to the filling—any excess liquid will release during baking and make the bottom pastry wet and soggy... and there's no way to fix it.

—Lora Moncure, Portland, ME

Prep: 40 min.
Bake: 45 min. + cooling
Makes: 12 servings

1   Tbsp. plus 1 cup olive oil, divided
1   large onion, finely chopped
3   garlic cloves, minced
2   pkg. (10 oz. each) frozen chopped spinach, thawed and squeezed dry
½   pkg. (16 oz.) frozen phyllo dough, thawed
2   large eggs, lightly beaten
2   cups (8 oz. each) crumbled feta cheese
3   Tbsp. chopped fresh parsley
1   Tbsp. snipped fresh dill
2   tsp. chopped fresh mint, optional
½   tsp. salt
¼   tsp. pepper

1. Preheat oven to 350°. In a large skillet, heat 1 Tbsp. oil over medium heat; add onion. Cook and stir until tender, 3-5 minutes. Add garlic; cook and stir 1 minute longer. Stir in spinach. Remove from the heat; let cool 5 minutes.
2. In a large bowl, combine eggs, feta, parsley, dill, mint if desired, salt and pepper. Stir in spinach mixture.

3. Brush a 13x9-in. baking dish with some of the remaining 1 cup oil. Unroll phyllo dough. Layer 8 sheets of phyllo in prepared dish, brushing each with oil, pressing edges of dough up sides of pan if necessary. (Keep remaining phyllo covered with a damp towel to prevent it from drying out.)
4. Spread spinach mixture over phyllo layers. Top with remaining phyllo sheets, brushing each with oil. Cut into 12 rectangles through top layer of phyllo only. Bake until golden brown, 45-50 minutes. Let stand 5 minutes before cutting.
1 piece 273 cal., 20g fat (4g sat. fat), 41mg chol., 410mg sod., 16g carb. (2g sugars, 3g fiber), 8g pro.

Spanakopita Tips

Can I use fresh spinach for this recipe? We use frozen spinach here for ease, but you can use fresh. Cook the spinach in a large skillet with olive oil until it wilts and releases its liquid. When it's cool enough to handle, squeeze out the excess liquid. Then, proceed with the recipe as directed.

Can I use puff pastry? You could make this recipe with puff pastry or crescent roll dough, but it wouldn't be the same. Authentic Greek spanakopita is made with phyllo dough.

What should I serve with spanakopita? This makes a great side to Mediterranean dishes like lamb chops. It's also a fantastic vegetarian main dish when paired with a Greek salad, a side of hummus and pita bread.

Peppery Roast Beef

With its spicy coating and creamy horseradish sauce, this tender roast is sure to be the star of any meal, whether it's a sit-down dinner or serve-yourself potluck.

—Maureen Brand, Somers, IA

Prep: 15 min.
Bake: 2½ hours + standing
Makes: 12 servings

- 1   Tbsp. olive oil
- 1   Tbsp. seasoned pepper
- 2   garlic cloves, minced
- ½   tsp. dried thyme
- ¼   tsp. salt
- 1   boneless beef eye round or top round roast (4 to 5 lbs.)

Horseradish Sauce
- 1   cup sour cream
- 2   Tbsp. lemon juice
- 2   Tbsp. milk
- 2   Tbsp. prepared horseradish
- 1   Tbsp. Dijon mustard
- ¼   tsp. salt
- ⅛   tsp. pepper

1. Preheat oven to 325°. In a small bowl, combine the oil, seasoned pepper, garlic, thyme and salt; rub over the roast. Place fat side up on a rack in a shallow roasting pan.
2. Bake, uncovered, 2½ to 3 hours or until meat reaches desired doneness (for medium-rare, a thermometer should read 135°; medium, 140°; medium-well, 145°). Let stand 10 minutes before slicing.
3. In a small bowl, combine the sauce ingredients. Serve with roast.
4 oz. cooked beef with about 1 Tbsp. sauce 228 cal., 10g fat (4g sat. fat), 83mg chol., 211mg sod., 3g carb. (1g sugars, 0 fiber), 30g pro.

Apple Cider Chicken & Dumplings

I came up with this recipe one fall when I had an abundance of apple cider. Adding some to a down-home classic was such a delectable decision.
—Margaret Sumner-Wichmann, Questa, NM

Prep: 10 min. • **Bake:** 65 min.
Makes: 4 servings

- 8 bone-in chicken thighs (3 lbs.), skin removed
- 2 Tbsp. butter
- 1 medium red onion, chopped
- 1 celery rib, chopped
- 2 Tbsp. minced fresh parsley
  Salt and pepper to taste
- 3 Tbsp. all-purpose flour
- 3 cups chicken broth
- 1 cup apple cider or juice

Dumplings
- 2 cups all-purpose flour
- 1 Tbsp. baking powder
- ½ tsp. salt
- 1 Tbsp. cold butter
- 1 large egg, room temperature, lightly beaten
- ⅔ cup 2% milk

1. Preheat oven to 350°. In a Dutch oven, brown chicken in butter; remove and set aside. In the same pot, combine onion, celery, parsley, salt and pepper; cook and stir until the vegetables are tender. Sprinkle with flour and mix well. Add broth and cider. Bring to a boil, cook and stir until thickened, about 2 minutes. Add chicken. Cover and bake for 45-50 minutes. Increase heat to 425°.

2. Meanwhile, for dumplings, combine flour, baking powder and salt; cut in butter until crumbly. Combine egg and milk; stir into the dry ingredients just until moistened. Drop batter into 12 mounds onto hot chicken mixture.

3. Bake, uncovered, for 10 minutes. Cover and bake until a toothpick inserted into a dumpling comes out clean, about 10 minutes longer.

1 serving 721 cal., 27g fat (11g sat. fat), 220mg chol., 1548mg sod., 65g carb. (12g sugars, 3g fiber), 50g pro.

Tuna Noodle Casserole

Families are sure to love the creamy texture and comforting taste of this traditional tuna casserole that goes together in a jiffy. I serve it with a green salad and warm rolls for a nutritious supper.

—Ruby Wells, Cynthiana, KY

Prep: 20 min. • **Bake:** 30 min.
Makes: 4 servings

- 1   can (10¾ oz.) reduced-fat reduced-sodium condensed cream of celery soup, undiluted
- ½   cup fat-free milk
- 2   cups yolk-free noodles, cooked
- 1   cup frozen peas, thawed
- 1   can (5 oz.) light water-packed tuna, drained and flaked
- 1   jar (2 oz.) diced pimientos, drained
- 2   Tbsp. dry bread crumbs
- 1   Tbsp. butter, melted

1. Preheat oven to 400°. In a large bowl, combine soup and milk until smooth. Add the noodles, peas, tuna and pimientos; mix well.
2. Pour into a 1½-qt. baking dish coated with cooking spray. Bake, uncovered, 25 minutes or until heated through. Toss bread crumbs and butter; sprinkle over the top. Bake until golden brown, about 5 minutes longer.

1 cup 238 cal., 5g fat (2g sat. fat), 27mg chol., 475mg sod., 32g carb. (6g sugars, 4g fiber), 15g pro.
Diabetic exchanges 2 starch, 2 lean meat, ½ fat.

"This recipe brought a tear. In the early '60s I lived with my grandmother and it was her favorite dish. Without her it will never be quite the same, but it's still very good."

—Peg255, tasteofhome.com

Pinwheel Steak Potpie

On cool nights, nothing hits the spot like a steaming homemade potpie—especially one you can get on the table fast. The pinwheel crust on top has become my signature.

—Kristin Shaw, Castleton, NY

Prep: 25 min. • **Bake:** 20 min.
Makes: 6 servings

- 2   Tbsp. butter
- 1¼   lbs. beef top sirloin steak, cut into ½-in. cubes
- ¼   tsp. pepper
- 1   pkg. (16 oz.) frozen vegetables for stew
- 2   Tbsp. water
- ½   tsp. dried thyme
- 1   jar (12 oz.) mushroom or beef gravy
- 1   tube (8 oz.) refrigerated crescent rolls

1. Preheat oven to 375°. In a 10-in. cast-iron or other ovenproof skillet, heat butter over medium-high heat. Brown beef in batches; remove from pan. Sprinkle with pepper; keep warm.
2. In the same skillet, combine vegetables, water and thyme; stir in gravy. Bring to a boil. Reduce heat; simmer, uncovered, until vegetables are thawed. Stir in the beef; remove from heat.
3. Unroll crescent dough and separate into 8 triangles. Starting from the wide end of each triangle, roll up a third of the length and place over beef mixture with pointed ends toward the center.
4. Bake, uncovered, until golden brown, 16-18 minutes.

1 serving 365 cal., 18g fat (6g sat. fat), 67mg chol., 716mg sod., 29g carb. (4g sugars, 1g fiber), 22g pro.

Slow-Cooker Chicken
Potpie, Page 140

Stovetop, Slow Cooker & Other Mains

Easy Slow-Cooker Tamale Dinner

Here is a quick and easy dinner that's very satisfying. No need to fool with corn husks here! My parents and friends often request this for dinner.
—Laurel Lawshae, Round Rock, TX

Prep: 20 min. · **Cook:** 4 hours
Makes: 4 servings

- 1 lb. ground turkey
- 1 large egg, lightly beaten
- 1½ cups 2% milk
- ¾ cup yellow cornmeal
- 1 can (14½ oz.) diced tomatoes, undrained
- 1 cup frozen corn, thawed
- 4 tsp. chili powder
- 2 tsp. ground cumin
- 1 tsp. salt
- 1 tsp. garlic powder
- 1 tsp. onion powder
   Shredded cheddar cheese, sour cream and salsa
   Chopped green onions, optional

1. In a small skillet, cook turkey over medium heat until no longer pink, 6-8 minutes, breaking into crumbles; drain. In a large bowl, combine egg, milk and cornmeal until smooth. Add tomatoes, corn, seasonings and turkey.

2. Transfer to a greased 3-qt. slow cooker. Cook, covered, on low until edges are brown, 4-5 hours. Serve with cheese, sour cream and salsa. If desired, sprinkle with green onions.

1 serving 402 cal., 13g fat (4g sat. fat), 129mg chol., 960mg sod., 43g carb. (9g sugars, 5g fiber), 31g pro.

Which Grease?

To grease a slow cooker insert, use a light coating of cooking spray, butter or vegetable oil—enough to make it nonstick, but not to make the food greasy.

Bistro Mac & Cheese

I like mac and cheese with a salad and crusty bread. It's a satisfying meal that feels upscale but will fit just about any budget. And because the Gorgonzola is so mild in this dish, even the kiddos will go for it.
—Charlotte Giltner, Mesa, AZ

Takes: 25 min. • **Makes:** 8 servings

- 1 pkg. (16 oz.) uncooked elbow macaroni
- 5 Tbsp. butter, divided
- 3 Tbsp. all-purpose flour
- 2½ cups 2% milk
- 1 tsp. salt
- ½ tsp. onion powder
- ½ tsp. pepper
- ¼ tsp. garlic powder
- 1 cup shredded part-skim mozzarella cheese
- 1 cup shredded cheddar cheese
- ½ cup crumbled Gorgonzola cheese
- 3 oz. cream cheese, softened
- ½ cup sour cream
- ½ cup seasoned panko bread crumbs
  Minced fresh parsley, optional

1. Cook macaroni according to the package directions; drain. Meanwhile, in a Dutch oven, melt 3 Tbsp. butter over low heat. Stir in flour until smooth; gradually whisk in milk and seasonings. Bring to a boil, stirring constantly; cook and stir 2 minutes or until thickened.
2. Reduce heat; stir in cheeses until melted. Stir in sour cream. Add macaroni; toss to coat.
3. In a small skillet, heat remaining 2 Tbsp. butter over medium heat. Add bread crumbs; cook and stir until golden brown. Sprinkle over top. If desired, sprinkle with parsley.
1 cup 468 cal., 22g fat (14g sat. fat), 68mg chol., 649mg sod., 49g carb. (7g sugars, 2g fiber), 20g pro.

Prosciutto-Pepper Pork Chops

Here's a dish that's easy, fast and, most importantly, delicious. Serve these cheesy chops with a green salad for a light and satisfying meal.
—Donna Prisco, Randolph, NJ

Takes. 20 min. • **Makes:** 4 servings

- 4   boneless pork loin chops (4 oz. each)
- ⅛ tsp. garlic powder
- ⅛ tsp. pepper
- 2   tsp. canola oil
- 4   thin slices prosciutto or deli ham
- ½ cup julienned roasted sweet red peppers
- 2   slices reduced-fat provolone cheese, cut in half

1. Sprinkle pork chops with garlic powder and pepper. In a large nonstick skillet, cook the chops in oil over medium heat until a thermometer inserted in the pork reads 145°, 4-5 minutes on each side.
2. Top each pork chop with prosciutto, red peppers and cheese. Cover and cook for 1-2 minutes or until cheese is melted. Let stand 5 minutes before serving.
1 pork chop 237 cal., 12g fat (4g sat. fat), 72mg chol., 483mg sod., 1g carb. (1g sugars, 0 fiber), 28g pro.
Diabetic exchanges 4 lean meat, ½ fat.

Tacos in a Bowl

This easy skillet dish offers a tasty use for leftover taco meat. Garnish it with sour cream and salsa for added southwestern flavor.
—Sue Schoening, Sheboygan, WI

Takes: 25 min. • **Makes:** 2 servings

- ½ lb. lean ground beef (90% lean)
- 2   Tbsp. finely chopped onion
- ¾ cup canned diced tomatoes, drained
- 2   Tbsp. taco seasoning
- 1   cup water
- 1   pkg. (3 oz.) ramen noodles
- ¼ cup shredded cheddar or Mexican cheese blend
     Crushed tortilla chips, optional

1. In a small skillet, cook beef and onion over medium heat until meat is no longer pink, 6-8 minutes, breaking beef into crumbles; drain.
2. Stir in tomatoes, taco seasoning and water. Bring to a boil. Add ramen noodles (discard seasoning packet or save for another use). Cook and stir until the noodles are tender, 3-5 minutes.
3. Spoon into serving bowls; sprinkle with cheese and, if desired, tortilla chips.
1 cup 480 cal., 21g fat (10g sat. fat), 85mg chol., 1279mg sod., 40g carb. (3g sugars, 2g fiber), 30g pro.

Quick Shrimp Creole

My mother made shrimp Creole when I was growing up, so I've carried on the family tradition. For extra kick, pass the Louisiana hot sauce.
—Gina Norton, Wonder Lake, IL

Takes: 30 min. • **Makes:** 6 servings

- 3 cups uncooked instant brown rice
- 3 Tbsp. canola oil
- 2 medium onions, halved and sliced
- 1 medium sweet red pepper, coarsely chopped
- 1 medium green pepper, coarsely chopped
- ½ cup chopped celery
- 2 Tbsp. all-purpose flour
- 1 tsp. dried oregano
- ¾ tsp. pepper
- ½ tsp. salt
- 1 can (14½ oz.) diced tomatoes, undrained
- 1 can (8 oz.) tomato sauce
- 1 lb. uncooked shrimp (31-40 per lb.), peeled and deveined
  Louisiana-style hot sauce, optional

1. Cook rice according to package directions. Meanwhile, in a large skillet, heat oil over medium-high heat. Add onions, peppers and celery; cook and stir 6-8 minutes or until tender.

2. Stir in flour, oregano, pepper and salt until blended. Stir in tomatoes and tomato sauce. Bring to a boil, stirring constantly; cook and stir until thickened. Reduce heat; simmer, covered, 5-8 minutes or until flavors are blended, stirring occasionally.

3. Add shrimp; cook, covered, 4-5 minutes longer or until shrimp turn pink, stirring occasionally. Serve with rice and, if desired, hot sauce.

1 cup shrimp mixture with ⅔ cup rice 356 cal., 10g fat (1g sat. fat), 92mg chol., 588mg sod., 48g carb. (6g sugars, 5g fiber), 19g pro. **Diabetic exchanges** 2½ starch, 2 lean meat, 1½ fat, 1 vegetable.

"I made this for Mardi Gras. This recipe is really, really good. I did add some broth during cooking because it was drying out. Since my hot sauce is rather wimpy, I added ½ tsp. cayenne. This will be the shrimp creole recipe I use from now on. Thanks for sharing it."
—beekeeper100, tasteofhome.com

Fried Chicken & Waffles

Chicken and waffles as a culinary tradition has origins in both Pennsylvania Dutch cuisine and soul food, with some variations. This version features fried chicken in a flavorful coating that is crispy outside, tender inside, and a spongy, chewy waffle with some crisp ridges.
—*Taste of Home* Test Kitchen

Prep: 40 min. • **Cook:** 40 min.
Makes: 8 servings

- 1¾ cups all-purpose flour
- 1 Tbsp. dried thyme
- 1 Tbsp. paprika
- 2 tsp. salt
- 2 tsp. garlic powder
- 1 tsp. pepper
- 1 large egg
- ⅓ cup 2% milk
- 2 Tbsp. lemon juice
- 3- to 4-lb. broiler/fryer chicken, cut up
- Oil for deep-fat frying

Waffles

- 2 cups all-purpose flour
- 1 Tbsp. sugar
- 2 tsp. baking powder
- ½ tsp. salt
- 3 large eggs, separated
- 2 cups 2% milk
- ¼ cup canola oil
- Maple syrup

1. In a shallow bowl, mix the first 6 ingredients. In a separate shallow bowl, whisk egg, milk and lemon juice until blended. Dip chicken in the flour mixture to coat all sides; shake off excess. Dip in the egg mixture, then again in flour mixture.
2. In an electric skillet or deep fryer, heat oil to 375°. Fry chicken, a few pieces at a time, until the skin is golden brown and the juices run clear, 6-10 minutes on each side. Drain on paper towels, keep warm.

3. For the waffles, in a bowl, combine flour, sugar, baking powder and salt. Combine egg yolks, milk and oil; stir into the dry ingredients just until moistened. In a small bowl, beat egg whites until stiff peaks form; fold into the batter. Bake in a preheated waffle maker according to manufacturer's directions. Place chicken on waffles; drizzle with maple syrup.

4 oz. cooked chicken with 1 waffle 668 cal., 40g fat (7g sat. fat), 162mg chol., 691mg sod., 40g carb. (5g sugars, 2g fiber), 34g pro.

Fried Chicken & Waffles Tips

How do I know when fried chicken is done? In general, chicken is done if the juices run clear when pierced. To be extra certain, you should test the internal temperature of the thickest part of the chicken. Chicken is safe to eat when it reaches an internal temperature of 165°, though we prefer the taste and texture of dark meat cooked to 170 to 175°.

Which are the best chicken parts to use? Any chicken that tastes good fried will work here—so, you can use any part you like! Boneless chicken does make it easy to eat with a knife and fork, along with the waffle. Boneless thighs are juicy and tender, but you can also use wings or chicken strips.

Slow-Cooker Chicken Potpie

This slow cooker version of a comfort food favorite takes just minutes of prep. No need to even make a crust, just bake refrigerated biscuits to top portions of the tasty chicken-vegetable mixture.
—*Taste of Home* Test Kitchen

Prep: 15 min. • **Cook:** 5 hours.
Makes: 8 servings

- 2 lbs. boneless skinless chicken breasts, cubed
- 1 can (10½ oz.) condensed cream of chicken soup, undiluted
- 1 cup 2% milk
- 2 medium potatoes, peeled and cubed
- 1 medium onion, chopped
- 1 celery rib, sliced
- 1½ tsp. garlic powder
- 1 tsp. poultry seasoning
- 1 tsp. salt
- ½ tsp. pepper
- 2½ cups frozen mixed vegetables (about 12 oz.), thawed
- 1 tube (16.3 oz.) large refrigerated buttermilk biscuits

1. Combine the first 10 ingredients in a greased 4- or 5-qt. slow cooker. Cook, covered, on low until chicken is no longer pink, 4½ to 5 hours.
2. Stir in mixed vegetables; cook 30 minutes longer.
3. Meanwhile, bake biscuits according to package directions. Spoon chicken mixture into bowls; top with biscuits.

1 cup stew with 1 biscuit 420 cal., 13g fat (4g sat. fat), 68mg chol., 914mg sod., 47g carb. (8g sugars, 4g fiber), 30g pro.

Garlic-Butter Steak

This quick and easy skillet entree is definitely restaurant quality and sure to become a staple at your house!
—Lily Julow, Lawrenceville, GA

Takes: 20 min. • **Makes:** 2 servings

- 2 Tbsp. butter, softened, divided
- 1 tsp. minced fresh parsley
- ½ tsp. minced garlic
- ¼ tsp. reduced-sodium soy sauce
- 1 beef flat iron steak or boneless top sirloin steak (¾ lb.)
- ⅛ tsp. salt
- ⅛ tsp. pepper

1. Mix 1 Tbsp. butter with parsley, garlic and soy sauce.
2. Sprinkle steak with salt and pepper. In a large skillet, heat remaining 1 Tbsp. butter over medium heat. Add steak; cook until meat reaches desired doneness (for medium-rare, a thermometer should read 135°; medium, 140°; medium-well, 145°), 4-7 minutes per side. Serve with garlic butter.

4 oz. cooked beef with 2 tsp. garlic butter 316 cal., 20g fat (10g sat. fat), 124mg chol., 337mg sod., 0 carb. (0 sugars, 0 fiber), 32g pro.

Hawaiian Pork Chops

For a great meal when friends drop in, I recommend one of my husband's sweet-and-sour favorites. This tastes just like Hawaiian pizza, and I usually have all the ingredients on hand.
—Michelle Cavalier, Hampton, VA

Takes: 30 min. • **Makes:** 4 servings

- 4 boneless pork loin chops (¾ in. thick and 4 oz. each)
- ¼ tsp. salt
- ¼ tsp. pepper
- 3 tsp. canola oil, divided
- ⅓ cup chopped green pepper
- ⅓ cup thinly sliced onion
- 1 can (14½ oz.) reduced-sodium beef broth
- 1 can (8 oz.) unsweetened pineapple chunks, undrained
- ¼ cup ketchup
- 2 Tbsp. brown sugar
- 1 Tbsp. cider vinegar
- 2 Tbsp. cornstarch
- 3 Tbsp. cold water
  Hot cooked rice, optional

1. Sprinkle pork chops with salt and pepper. Heat 2 tsp. oil in a large nonstick skillet over medium heat. Cook pork chops until lightly browned, 3-4 minutes on each side. Remove and keep warm.

2. In the same skillet, saute green pepper and onion in remaining 1 tsp. oil until almost tender, about 2 minutes. Stir in broth, pineapple, ketchup, brown sugar and vinegar. Bring to a boil. Return pork to the pan. Reduce heat; cover and simmer until a thermometer inserted in pork reads 145°, 5-7 minutes. Remove and keep warm.

3. Combine cornstarch and water until smooth; stir into skillet. Bring to a boil; cook and stir until thickened, 1-2 minutes. Serve with pork and, if desired, rice.

1 pork chop with ¾ cup sauce 250 cal., 7g fat (2g sat. fat), 57mg chol., 554mg sod., 24g carb. (16g sugars, 1g fiber), 23g pro. **Diabetic exchanges** 3 lean meat, ½ starch, ½ fruit, ½ fat.

Ramen Chicken Stir Fry

A frozen pasta-vegetable blend and ramen noodles make this dish a cinch to toss together. This filling meal is so easy to fix that teenagers can make it themselves.
—Lois McAtee, Oceanside, CA

Takes: 25 min. • **Makes:** 4 servings

- 1 lb. boneless skinless chicken breasts, cut into strips
- 2 Tbsp. vegetable oil
- 1½ cups water
- 2 garlic cloves, minced
- 2 pkg. (3 oz. each) chicken ramen noodles
- 1 pkg. (16 oz.) frozen stir-fry vegetable blend
- 1 sweet red pepper, julienned
- 2 Tbsp. soy sauce
  Sliced green onions, optional

In a large skillet or wok, stir-fry the chicken in oil. Add water and garlic; bring to a boil. Add noodles and the contents of the seasoning packets, vegetables, red pepper and soy sauce. Cover and simmer until noodles and vegetables are tender, 7-9 minutes. If desired, garnish with green onions.

1 cup 453 cal., 17g fat (5g sat. fat), 63mg chol., 1361mg sod., 43g carb. (6g sugars, 5g fiber), 31g pro.

Need More Spice?

Add ¼ tsp. hot pepper flakes (or more to taste) when adding the noodles and seasoning packets to the stir-fry. Or you could let each diner customize their heat level by serving Sriracha or another type of hot sauce on the side.

Burgundy Beef

When my adult children are coming over for dinner, this is their most-requested dish. All three of them, and their significant others, love this dish.
—Urilla Cheverie, Andover, MA

Prep: 10 min. • **Cook:** 8¼ hours
Makes: 10 servings

    4   lbs. beef top sirloin steak,
        cut into 1-in. cubes
    3   large onions, sliced
    1   cup water
    1   cup burgundy wine or
        beef broth
    1   cup ketchup
    ¼   cup quick-cooking tapioca
    ¼   cup packed brown sugar
    ¼   cup Worcestershire sauce
    4   tsp. paprika
    1½ tsp. salt
    1   tsp. minced garlic
    1   tsp. ground mustard
    2   Tbsp. cornstarch
    3   Tbsp. cold water
        Hot cooked noodles

1. In a 5-qt. slow cooker, combine the first 12 ingredients. Cook, covered, on low until meat is tender, 8-9 hours.
2. Combine cornstarch and water until smooth; stir into slow cooker. Cook, covered, on high until gravy is thickened, about 15 minutes. Serve with noodles.
1 cup 347 cal., 8g fat (3g sat. fat), 74mg chol., 811mg sod., 24g carb. (15g sugars, 1g fiber), 40g pro.

"I made this for my mother's birthday dinner and everyone loved it. I used a Pinot Noir and Amish noodles. Delicious!"
—katlaydee3, tasteofhome.com

Porcupine Meatballs

These well-seasoned meatballs in a rich tomato sauce are one of my mom's best main dishes. I used to love this meal when I was growing up. I made it at home for our children, and now my daughters make it for their families.
—Darlis Wilfer, West Bend, WI

Prep: 20 min. • **Cook:** 1 hour
Makes: 4 servings

    ½   cup uncooked long grain rice
    ½   cup water
    ⅓   cup chopped onion
    1   tsp. salt
    ½   tsp. celery salt
    ⅛   tsp. pepper
    ⅛   tsp. garlic powder
    1   lb. ground beef
    2   Tbsp. canola oil
    1   can (15 oz.) tomato sauce
    1   cup water
    2   Tbsp. brown sugar
    2   tsp. Worcestershire sauce

1. In a bowl, combine the first 7 ingredients. Add beef and mix well. Shape into 1½-in. balls. In a large skillet, brown meatballs in oil; drain.
2. Combine tomato sauce, water, brown sugar and Worcestershire sauce; pour over meatballs. Reduce heat; cover and simmer for 1 hour.
1 serving 421 cal., 21g fat (6g sat. fat), 70mg chol., 1317mg sod., 34g carb. (9g sugars, 2g fiber), 24g pro.

Melt-in-Your-Mouth Sausages

My family loves this recipe. It's such a good all-around dish, either for sandwiches like these or sliced and served over spaghetti.
—Ilean Schultheiss, Cohocton, NY

Prep: 10 min. • **Cook:** 4 hours
Makes: 8 servings

- 8 Italian sausage links (2 lbs.)
- 1 jar (26 oz.) meatless spaghetti sauce
- ½ cup water
- 1 can (6 oz.) tomato paste
- 1 large green pepper, thinly sliced
- 1 large onion, thinly sliced
- 1 Tbsp. grated Parmesan cheese
- 1 tsp. dried parsley flakes
- 8 brat buns, split
   Additional Parmesan cheese, optional

1. Place sausages in a large skillet; cover with water. Bring to a boil. Reduce heat. Cover and simmer for 10 minutes or until a thermometer reads 160°; drain well.
2. Meanwhile, in a 3-qt. slow cooker, combine the spaghetti sauce, water, tomato paste, pepper, onion, cheese and parsley. Add sausages. Cover and cook on low 4-5 hours or until vegetables are tender. Serve in buns. Sprinkle with additional cheese if desired.

1 sandwich 557 cal., 29g fat (9g sat. fat), 62mg chol., 1510mg sod., 51g carb. (14g sugars, 4g fiber), 24g pro.

Shrimp & Noodle Bowls

It'll look as if you got takeout, but this dish comes from your kitchen. Convenience items reduce the prep time.
—Mary Bergfeld, Eugene, OR

Takes: 25 min. • **Makes:** 6 servings

- 8 oz. uncooked angel hair pasta
- 1 lb. cooked small shrimp
- 2 cups broccoli coleslaw mix
- 6 green onions, thinly sliced
- ½ cup minced fresh cilantro
- ⅔ cup reduced-fat sesame ginger salad dressing

1. Cook pasta according to package directions; drain and rinse in cold water.
2. Transfer pasta to a large bowl. Add shrimp, coleslaw mix, green onions and cilantro. Drizzle with dressing; toss to coat. Cover and refrigerate until serving.

1⅓ cups 260 cal., 3g fat (0 sat. fat), 147mg chol., 523mg sod., 36g carb. (6g sugars, 2g fiber), 22g pro.
Diabetic exchanges 2 starch, 2 lean meat, 1 vegetable.

Blue Plate Beef Patties

A friend and I discovered this recipe together and both consider it a staple menu item. I fix the moist, mild-tasting patties often for family and friends. We love them with mashed potatoes, rice or noodles and the gravy, which gets great flavor from fresh mushrooms.

—Phyllis Miller, Danville, IN

Takes: 20 min. • **Makes:** 4 servings

- 1 large egg, room temperature
- 2 green onions with tops, sliced
- ¼ cup seasoned bread crumbs
- 1 Tbsp. prepared mustard
- 1½ lbs. ground beef
- 1 jar (12 oz.) beef gravy
- ½ cup water
- 2 to 3 tsp. prepared horseradish
- ½ lb. fresh mushrooms, sliced
   Minced fresh parsley, optional

1. In a large bowl, beat the egg; stir in onions, bread crumbs and mustard. Add beef and mix lightly but thoroughly. Shape into four ½-in.-thick patties.

2. In an ungreased skillet, cook patties until meat is no longer pink, 4-5 minutes on each side; drain.

3. In a small bowl, combine gravy, water and horseradish; add mushrooms. Pour over patties. Cook, uncovered, until mushrooms are tender and heated through, about 5 minutes. If desired, sprinkle with parsley.

1 serving 438 cal., 24g fat (9g sat. fat), 170mg chol., 825mg sod., 14g carb. (2g sugars, 1g fiber), 41g pro.

"This is delicious! Easy to make, it has a wonderful flavor. A great family dinner and for casual company."

—karenella, tasteofhome.com

Green Chile Beef Burritos

I love recipes like this one, that are wholly satisfying while being leaner in fat and calories. The meat is so tender and delicious.
—Shirley Davidson, Thornton, CO

Prep: 20 min. • **Cook:** 8 hours
Makes: 2 dozen

- 2 beef sirloin tip roasts (3 lbs. each)
- 4 cans (4 oz. each) chopped green chiles
- 1 medium onion, chopped
- 3 medium jalapeno peppers, seeded and chopped
- 3 garlic cloves, sliced
- 3 tsp. chili powder
- 1½ tsp. ground cumin
- 1 tsp. salt-free seasoning blend, optional
- 1 cup reduced-sodium beef broth
- 24 fat-free flour tortillas (8 in.), warmed
  Optional. Chopped tomatoes, shredded lettuce and shredded reduced-fat cheddar cheese

1. Trim fat from roasts; cut meat into large chunks. Place in a 5- or 6-qt. slow cooker. Top with chiles, onion, jalapenos, garlic, chili powder, cumin and, if desired, seasoning blend. Pour broth over all. Cover and cook on low until meat is tender, 8-9 hours.

2. Remove beef; cool slightly. Shred with 2 forks. Cool the cooking liquid slightly; skim off fat. In a blender, cover and process cooking liquid in small batches until smooth.

3. Return liquid and beef to slow cooker; heat through. Place ⅓ cup beef mixture on each tortilla. Top with tomatoes, lettuce and cheese as desired. Fold in ends and sides of tortillas.

Note Wear disposable gloves when cutting hot peppers; the oils can burn skin. Avoid touching your face.

1 burrito 262 cal., 5g fat (2g sat. fat), 72mg chol., 376mg sod., 26g carb. (0 sugars, 2g fiber), 26g pro.
Diabetic exchanges 3 lean meat, 2 starch.

Lemon-Batter Fish

Fishing is a popular recreational activity where we live, so folks are always looking for ways to prepare their catches. My husband ranks this as one of his favorites.
—Jackie Hannahs, Cedar Springs, MI

Takes: 25 min. • **Makes:** 6 servings

- 1½ cups all-purpose flour, divided
- 1 tsp. baking powder
- ¾ tsp. salt
- ½ tsp. sugar
- 1 large egg, lightly beaten
- ⅔ cup water
- ⅔ cup lemon juice, divided
- 2 lbs. perch or walleye fillets, cut into serving-sized pieces
  Oil for frying
  Lemon wedges, optional

1. Combine 1 cup flour, baking powder, salt and sugar. In another bowl, combine egg, water and ⅓ cup lemon juice; stir into the dry ingredients until smooth.
2. Place the remaining ⅓ cup lemon juice and the remaining ½ cup flour in separate shallow bowls. Dip fillets in the lemon juice, then flour, then coat with the egg mixture.
3. In a large skillet, heat 1 in. oil over medium-high heat. Fry fillets until golden brown and the fish flakes easily with a fork, 2-3 minutes on each side. Drain on paper towels. If desired, serve with lemon wedges.
5 oz. cooked fish 384 cal., 17g fat (2g sat. fat), 167mg chol., 481mg sod., 22g carb. (1g sugars, 1g fiber), 33g pro.
Lime-Batter Fish Substitute lime juice for the lemon juice.

"Forget about restaurant fish and chips...stay home and make this yourself! The lemon flavor is delicious and the batter is so light and tasty!"
—olsons514, tasteofhome.com

Pizza Spaghetti

The idea for this recipe came to me when I saw someone dip a slice of pizza into a pasta dish. My wife and kids love it, and so do my friends!
—Robert Smith, Las Vegas, NV

Prep: 20 min. • **Cook:** 30 min.
Makes: 6 servings

- ½ lb. lean ground beef (90% lean)
- ½ lb. Italian turkey sausage links, casings removed
- ½ cup chopped sweet onion
- 4 cans (8 oz. each) no-salt-added tomato sauce
- 3 oz. sliced turkey pepperoni
- 1 Tbsp. sugar
- 2 tsp. minced fresh parsley or ½ tsp. dried parsley flakes
- 2 tsp. minced fresh basil or ½ tsp. dried basil
- 9 oz. uncooked whole wheat spaghetti
- 3 Tbsp. grated Parmesan cheese

1. In a large nonstick skillet, cook beef and sausage with onion over medium-high heat until no longer pink, 5-7 minutes, breaking meat into crumbles. Stir in tomato sauce, pepperoni, sugar and herbs; bring to a boil. Reduce heat; simmer, uncovered, until thickened, 20-25 minutes.
2. Meanwhile, in a 6-qt. stockpot, cook spaghetti according to the package directions; drain and return to pot. Toss with sauce. Sprinkle individual servings with cheese.
1⅓ cups 354 cal., 9g fat (3g sat. fat), 57mg chol., 512mg sod., 45g carb. (11g sugars, 7g fiber), 25g pro.
Diabetic exchanges 3 starch, 3 lean meat.

Turkey a la King

This is a smart way to use up leftover turkey. You might want to make a double batch!
—Mary Gaylord, Balsam Lake, WI

Takes: 25 min. • **Makes:** 6 servings

1 medium onion, chopped
¾ cup sliced celery
¼ cup diced green pepper
¼ cup butter, cubed
¼ cup all-purpose flour
1 tsp. sugar
1½ cups chicken broth
¼ cup half-and-half cream
3 cups cubed cooked turkey or chicken
1 can (4 oz.) sliced mushrooms, drained
6 slices bread, toasted

1. In a large skillet, saute onion, celery and green pepper in butter until tender. Stir in flour and sugar until a paste forms.
2. Gradually stir in broth. Bring to a boil; boil until thickened, about 1 minute. Reduce heat. Add cream, turkey and mushrooms; heat through. Serve with toast.
1 serving 297 cal., 13g fat (7g sat. fat), 98mg chol., 591mg sod., 21g carb. (4g sugars, 2g fiber), 24g pro.

Slow-Cooked Hungarian Goulash

You will love how easily this slow-cooked version of a beloved ethnic dish comes together. My son shared the recipe with me many years ago.
—Jackie Kohn, Duluth, MN

Prep: 15 min. • **Cook:** 8 hours
Makes: 8 servings

2 lbs. beef top round steak, cut into 1-in. cubes
1 cup chopped onion
2 Tbsp. all-purpose flour
1½ tsp. paprika
1 tsp. garlic salt
½ tsp. pepper
1 can (14½ oz.) diced tomatoes, undrained
1 bay leaf
1 cup sour cream
   Hot cooked egg noodles
   Minced fresh parsley, optional

1. Place beef and onion in a 3-qt. slow cooker. Combine flour, paprika, garlic salt and pepper; sprinkle over the beef and stir to coat. Stir in the tomatoes; add bay leaf. Cover and cook on low until the meat is tender, 8-10 hours.
2. Discard bay leaf. Just before serving, stir in sour cream; heat through. Serve with noodles. Garnish with parsley if desired.
Freeze option Before adding sour cream, cool stew. Freeze stew in freezer containers. To use, partially thaw in refrigerator overnight. Heat through in a saucepan, stirring occasionally; add broth if necessary. Remove from heat; stir in sour cream.
1 cup 224 cal., 8g fat (5g sat. fat), 83mg chol., 339mg sod., 7g carb. (4g sugars, 1g fiber), 27g pro.

Apricot Ham Steak

Ham is a versatile main menu item that's a standby with all country cooks. One of the best and easiest ways to serve ham slices is topped with a slightly sweet glaze, like this apricot version.
—Scott Woodward, Shullsburg, WI

Takes: 10 min. • **Makes:** 4 servings

- 2 Tbsp. butter, divided
- 4 fully cooked boneless ham steaks (5 oz. each)
- ½ cup apricot preserves
- 1 Tbsp. cider vinegar
- ¼ tsp. ground ginger
  Dash salt

1. In a large skillet, heat 1 Tbsp. butter over medium heat. Cook ham on both sides until lightly browned and heated through. Remove from pan; keep warm.
2. Add the remaining 1 Tbsp. butter and the remaining ingredients to pan; cook and stir over medium heat until blended and heated through. Serve over ham.
1 ham steak 299 cal., 11g fat (5g sat. fat), 88mg chol., 1899mg sod., 26g carb. (17g sugars, 0 fiber), 26g pro.
Grilled Apricot Ham Steaks
Melt 1 Tbsp. butter and brush over ham steaks. Grill, covered, over medium heat until lightly browned, 3-5 minutes on each side. Prepare sauce and serve as directed.

Sloppy Joe Sandwiches

You'll love this quick, easy and economical dish. Brown sugar adds a touch of sweetness, both for traditional sandwiches on buns or as a down-home topping for rice, biscuits or baked potatoes.
—Laurie Hauser, Rochester, NY

Takes: 30 min. • **Makes:** 4 servings

- 1 lb. ground beef
- 1 cup ketchup
- ¼ cup water
- 2 Tbsp. brown sugar
- 2 tsp. Worcestershire sauce
- 2 tsp. prepared mustard
- ½ tsp. garlic powder
- ½ tsp. onion powder
- ½ tsp. salt
- 4 hamburger buns, split

In a large skillet, cook beef over medium heat until no longer pink; drain. Stir in the ketchup, water, brown sugar, Worcestershire sauce, mustard, garlic powder, onion powder and salt. Bring to a boil. Reduce heat; cover and simmer for 15-20 minutes. Serve on buns.
1 sandwich 439 cal., 16g fat (6g sat. fat), 75mg chol., 1360mg sod., 46g carb. (17g sugars, 2g fiber), 27g pro.

Too Saucy?

If your Sloppy Joe mixture is too thin, it's an easy fix. Just take the cover off and continue simmering to let the liquid evaporate until it reaches a good consistency for sandwiches.

Salmon Cakes

Salmon was a special treat for us on Sundays when we were growing up. We ate these cakes fast as Mama could fry them—she couldn't get them off the griddle fast enough!
—Imogene Hutton, Brownwood, TX

Takes: 30 min. • **Makes:** 3 servings

- 2 large eggs
- ¼ cup heavy whipping cream
- ¼ cup cornmeal
- 2 Tbsp. sliced green onions
- 2 Tbsp. all-purpose flour
- ¼ tsp. baking powder
  Dash pepper
- ½ tsp. salt, optional
- 1 can (14¾ oz.) salmon, drained, bones and skin removed
- 1 to 2 Tbsp. butter

1. In a small bowl, beat eggs. Stir in cream, cornmeal, green onions, flour, baking powder, pepper and, if desired, salt. Flake salmon into bowl; blend gently.

2. Melt butter in a large nonstick skillet or griddle over medium heat. Drop salmon mixture by ⅓ cupfuls onto skillet. Fry in batches until lightly browned, about 5 minutes on each side. Serve warm.

Note Heavy whipping cream ranges from 36-40% butterfat and doubles in volume when whipped. It is often labeled as either heavy cream or whipping cream.

2 patties 451 cal., 25g fat (10g sat. fat), 267mg chol., 694mg sod., 16g carb. (1g sugars, 1g fiber), 39g pro.

Polynesian Roast Beef

This marvelous recipe from my sister has been a family favorite for years. Pineapple and peppers are a perfect contrast to the rich and savory beef.
—Annette Mosbarger, Peyton, CO

Prep: 15 min. • **Cook:** 7 hours
Makes: 10 servings

- 1 beef top round roast (3¼ lbs.)
- 2 Tbsp. browning sauce, optional
- ¼ cup all-purpose flour
- 1 tsp. salt
- ¼ tsp. pepper
- 1 medium onion, sliced
- 1 can (8 oz.) unsweetened sliced pineapple
- ¼ cup packed brown sugar
- 2 Tbsp. cornstarch
- ¼ tsp. ground ginger
- ½ cup beef broth
- ¼ cup reduced-sodium soy sauce
- ½ tsp. minced garlic
- 1 medium green pepper, sliced

1. Cut roast in half; brush with browning sauce if desired. Combine flour, salt and pepper; rub over the meat. Place onion in a 3-qt. slow cooker; top with roast.
2. Drain pineapple, reserving juice; refrigerate the pineapple slices. In a small bowl, combine brown sugar, cornstarch and ginger; whisk in broth, soy sauce, garlic and the reserved pineapple juice until smooth. Pour over the meat. Cook, covered, on low for 6-8 hours.
3. Add pineapple and green pepper. Cook until the meat is tender, 1 hour longer.

4 oz. cooked beef 253 cal., 5g fat (2g sat. fat), 82mg chol., 560mg sod., 16g carb. (10g sugars, 1g fiber), 34g pro.

Meatless Chili Mac

I came across this recipe in a newspaper years ago. It's been a hit at our house ever since. It's fast and flavorful, and it appeals to all ages.
—Cindy Ragan, North Huntingdon, PA

Prep: 15 min. • **Cook:** 25 min.
Makes: 8 servings

- 1 large onion, chopped
- 1 medium green pepper, chopped
- 1 Tbsp. olive oil
- 1 garlic clove, minced
- 2 cups water
- 1½ cups uncooked elbow macaroni
- 1 can (16 oz.) mild chili beans, undrained
- 1 can (15½ oz.) great northern beans, rinsed and drained
- 1 can (14½ oz.) diced tomatoes, undrained
- 1 can (8 oz.) tomato sauce
- 4 tsp. chili powder
- 1 tsp. ground cumin
- ½ tsp. salt
- ½ cup fat-free sour cream

1. In a Dutch oven, saute onion and green pepper in oil until tender. Add garlic; cook 1 minute longer. Stir in the water, macaroni, beans, tomatoes, tomato sauce, chili powder, cumin and salt.

2. Bring to a boil. Reduce heat; cover and simmer until macaroni is tender, 15-20 minutes. Top each serving with 1 Tbsp. sour cream.

1¼ cups 206 cal., 3g fat (1g sat. fat), 1mg chol., 651mg sod., 37g carb. (6g sugars, 9g fiber), 10g pro.
Diabetic exchanges 2 starch, 1 vegetable,1 lean meat.

Turkey Scallopini

Quick-cooking turkey breast slices make it easy to prepare a satisfying meal in minutes. I've also flattened boneless skinless chicken breast halves in place of the turkey.
—Karen Adams, Cleveland, TN

Takes: 20 min. • **Makes:** 4 servings

 1   pkg. (17.6 oz.) turkey breast cutlets
 ¼   cup all-purpose flour
 ⅛   tsp. salt
 ⅛   tsp. pepper
 1   large egg
 2   Tbsp. water
 1   cup soft bread crumbs
 ½   cup grated Parmesan cheese
 ¼   cup butter, cubed
      Minced fresh parsley

1. Flatten turkey to ¼-in. thickness. In a shallow bowl, combine flour, salt and pepper. In another bowl, beat egg and water. In a third shallow bowl, combine bread crumbs and cheese.

2. Dredge turkey in the flour mixture, then dip in the egg mixture and coat with crumbs. Let stand for 5 minutes.

3. Melt butter in a large skillet over medium-high heat; cook turkey for 2-3 minutes on each side or until the meat is no longer pink and the coating is golden brown. Sprinkle with parsley.

Note To make soft bread crumbs, tear bread into pieces and place in a food processor or blender. Cover and pulse until crumbs form. One slice of bread yields ½ to ¾ cup crumbs.

4 oz. cooked turkey 358 cal., 17g fat (10g sat. fat), 169mg chol., 463mg sod., 12g carb. (1g sugars, 0 fiber), 38g pro.

Chicken Scallopini Substitute 4 boneless skinless chicken breast halves for the turkey; flatten to ¼-in. thickness and proceed as directed.

Pork Chops with Sauerkraut

I pair tender pork chops with tangy sauerkraut in this filling main dish. It's so quick and easy to put together, and it leaves everyone satisfied.
—Stephanie Miller, Omaha, NE

Prep: 15 min. • **Cook:** 3 hours
Makes: 4 servings

- 2 Tbsp. canola oil
- 4 bone-in center-cut pork loin chops (8 oz. each)
- 1 jar (32 oz.) sauerkraut, undrained
- ¾ cup packed brown sugar
- 1 medium green pepper, sliced
- 1 medium onion, sliced

1. Heat oil in a large skillet over medium heat; brown pork chops, 3-4 minutes on each side. Drain.
2. In a 5-qt. slow cooker, combine sauerkraut and brown sugar. Top with the pork chops, green pepper and onion.
3. Cook, covered, on low until meat is tender, 3-4 hours. Serve with a slotted spoon.
1 serving 599 cal., 26g fat (8g sat. fat), 111mg chol., 1589mg sod., 54g carb. (46g sugars, 7g fiber), 39g pro.

Why Pre-Cook?

Searing the pork chops before adding them to the slow cooker will ensure the meat stays tender—and will also amp up the flavor, too. Just be sure to follow the timing of the recipe to prevent overcooking.

Maple Mustard Chicken

My husband loves this chicken dish. It calls for only five ingredients, and we try to have them all on hand for a delicious and cozy dinner anytime.
—Jennifer Seidel, Midland, MI

Prep: 5 min. • **Cook:** 3 hours
Makes: 6 servings

- 6 boneless skinless chicken breast halves (6 oz. each)
- ½ cup maple syrup
- ⅓ cup stone-ground mustard
- 2 Tbsp. quick-cooking tapioca
   Hot cooked brown rice

Place chicken in a 3-qt. slow cooker. In a small bowl, combine syrup, mustard and tapioca; pour over the chicken. Cook, covered, on low until tender, 3-4 hours. Serve with rice.
Freeze option Cool chicken in sauce. Freeze in freezer containers. To use, partially thaw in refrigerator overnight. Heat through slowly in a covered skillet until a thermometer inserted in chicken reads 165°, stirring occasionally; add broth or water if necessary.
1 chicken breast half 289 cal., 4g fat (1g sat. fat), 94mg chol., 296mg sod., 24g carb. (17g sugars, 2g fiber), 35g pro.

Country Ham & Potatoes

Browned potatoes are a simple but perfect side for country ham. Not only do the potatoes pick up the flavor of the ham, but they look beautiful! Just add veggies or a salad and dinner's done.

—Helen Bridges, Washington, VA

Takes: 30 min. • **Makes:** 6 servings

2   lbs. fully cooked sliced ham (about ½ in. thick)
2   to 3 Tbsp. butter
1½ lbs. potatoes, peeled, quartered and cooked
    Snipped fresh parsley

In a large heavy skillet, brown ham over medium-high heat in butter on both sides until heated through. Move ham to 1 side of the skillet; brown potatoes in drippings until tender. Sprinkle potatoes with parsley.
1 serving 261 cal., 9g fat (5g sat. fat), 64mg chol., 1337mg sod., 21g carb. (1g sugars, 1g fiber), 28g pro.

Slow-Cooker Lasagna

No-cook lasagna noodles take the work out of this traditional favorite adapted for the slow cooker. Because it's so easy to assemble, it's great for workdays as well as weekends. We like it accompanied by Parmesan bread or garlic cheese toast.

—Lisa Micheletti, Collierville, TN

Prep: 25 min. • **Cook:** 4 hours
Makes: 8 servings

1   lb. ground beef
1   large onion, chopped
2   garlic cloves, minced
1   can (29 oz.) tomato sauce
1   cup water
1   can (6 oz.) tomato paste
1   tsp. salt
1   tsp. dried oregano
1   pkg. (8 oz.) no-cook lasagna noodles
4   cups shredded part-skim mozzarella cheese
1½ cups 4% cottage cheese
½   cup grated Parmesan cheese

1. In a skillet over medium heat, cook beef and onion until meat is no longer pink, breaking beef into crumbles. Add garlic; cook 1 minute longer. Drain. Stir in tomato sauce, water, tomato paste, salt and oregano.
2. Spread a fourth of the meat sauce in an ungreased 5-qt. slow cooker. Arrange a third of the noodles over sauce (break to fit if necessary). Combine cheeses; spoon a third of the mixture over noodles. Repeat layers twice. Top with the remaining meat sauce.
3. Cover and cook on low until noodles are tender, 4-5 hours.
1 piece 510 cal., 23g fat (11g sat. fat), 89mg chol., 1464mg sod., 39g carb. (9g sugars, 4g fiber), 38g pro.

"Always a hit. I like to make a double batch and use half ricotta and half cottage cheese. My husband likes me to add ground Italian sausage."

—peacharmadillo, tasteofhome.com

Meat Loaf in a Mug

Here's a quick, delicious single serving of meat loaf. This smart take on a classic gives you traditional meat loaf flavor with hardly any cleanup—and no leftovers!
—Ruby Matt, Garnavillo, IA

Takes: 15 min. • **Makes:** 1 serving

- 2 Tbsp. 2% milk
- 1 Tbsp. ketchup
- 2 Tbsp. quick-cooking oats
- 1 tsp. onion soup mix
- ¼ lb. lean ground beef

1. In a small bowl, combine milk, ketchup, oats and soup mix. Crumble beef over mixture and mix lightly but thoroughly. Pat into a microwave-safe mug or custard cup coated with cooking spray.
2. Cover and microwave on high for 3 minutes or until meat is no longer pink and a thermometer reads 160°; drain. Let stand for 3 minutes. If desired, serve with additional ketchup.

1 serving 316 cal., 14g fat (5g sat. fat), 100mg chol., 471mg sod., 14g carb. (6g sugars, 1g fiber), 33g pro.

Open-Faced Turkey Sandwich

Turkey with gravy makes divine comfort food that reminds me of old-time diners on the East Coast. Happily, my gravy is not from a can!
—Christine Schwester, Divide, CO

Takes: 25 min. • **Makes:** 6 servings

- ⅓ cup butter, cubed
- 1 small onion, chopped
- ⅓ cup all-purpose flour
- 2 tsp. minced fresh parsley
- ¼ tsp. pepper
- ⅛ tsp. garlic powder
- ⅛ tsp. dried thyme
- 3 cups reduced-sodium chicken broth
- 1¼ lbs. sliced deli turkey
- 12 slices white bread

1. In a large cast-iron or other heavy skillet, heat butter over medium heat. Add onion; cook and stir until tender, 4-5 minutes. Stir in flour, parsley and seasonings until blended; gradually whisk in broth. Bring to a boil, stirring constantly; cook and stir until slightly thickened, 1-2 minutes.
2. Add turkey, 1 slice at a time; heat through. Serve over bread.
2 open-faced sandwiches 361 cal., 14g fat (7g sat. fat), 60mg chol., 1462mg sod., 33g carb. (4g sugars, 2g fiber), 25g pro.

Slow-Cooker Beef Stew

When there's a chill in the air, I love to make my slow-cooked stew. It's loaded with tender chunks of beef, potatoes and carrots.
—Earnestine Wilson, Waco, TX

Prep: 25 min. • **Cook:** 7 hours
Makes: 8 servings (2 qt.)

1½ lbs. potatoes, peeled and cubed
6 medium carrots, cut into 1-in. lengths
1 medium onion, coarsely chopped
3 celery ribs, coarsely chopped
3 Tbsp. all-purpose flour
1½ lbs. beef stew meat, cut into 1-in. cubes
3 Tbsp. canola oil
1 can (14½ oz.) diced tomatoes, undrained
1 can (14½ oz.) beef broth
1 tsp. ground mustard
½ tsp. salt
½ tsp. pepper
½ tsp. dried thyme
½ tsp. browning sauce, optional
 Minced fresh thyme, optional

1. Layer the potatoes, carrots, onion and celery in a 5-qt. slow cooker. Place flour in a large shallow dish. Add stew meat; turn to coat evenly. In a large skillet, brown meat in oil in batches. Place over vegetables.
2. In a large bowl, combine tomatoes, broth, mustard, salt, pepper, thyme and, if desired, browning sauce. Pour over beef. Cover and cook on low until the meat and vegetables are tender, 7-8 hours. If desired, sprinkle with fresh thyme before serving.
1 cup 272 cal., 12g fat (3g sat. fat), 53mg chol., 541mg sod., 23g carb. (6g sugars, 4g fiber), 19g pro.
Diabetic exchanges 2 lean meat, 1½ starch, 1 fat.

Tropical BBQ Chicken

Here is my favorite slow-cooker recipe. The delicious, slightly spicy sauce will win you over, too!
—Yvonne McKim, Vancouver, WA

Prep: 15 min. • **Cook:** 3 hours
Makes: 2 servings

- 2 chicken leg quarters (8 oz. each), skin removed
- 3 Tbsp. ketchup
- 2 Tbsp. orange juice
- 1 Tbsp. brown sugar
- 1 Tbsp. red wine vinegar
- 1 Tbsp. olive oil
- 1 tsp. minced fresh parsley
- ½ tsp. Worcestershire sauce
- ¼ tsp. garlic salt
- ⅛ tsp. pepper
- 2 tsp. cornstarch
- 1 Tbsp. cold water

1. With a sharp knife, cut leg quarters at the joints if desired; place in a 1½-qt. slow cooker. In a small bowl, combine ketchup, orange juice, brown sugar, vinegar, oil, parsley, Worcestershire sauce, garlic salt and pepper; pour over the chicken.
2. Cook, covered, on low until meat is tender, 3-4 hours.
3. Remove chicken to a serving platter; keep warm. Skim fat from cooking juices; transfer ½ cup to a small saucepan. Bring liquid to a boil. Combine cornstarch and water until smooth. Gradually stir into the pan. Return to a boil; cook and stir until thickened, about 2 minutes. Serve with chicken. If desired, top with additional fresh parsley.
1 serving 301 cal., 14g fat (3g sat. fat), 83mg chol., 601mg sod., 18g carb. (14g sugars, 0 fiber), 25g pro.

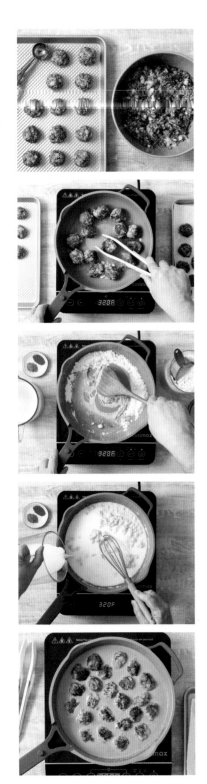

Mom's Swedish Meatballs

Mom fixed these meatballs for all sorts of family dinners, potluck suppers and PTA meetings. After smelling the aromas of browning meat and caramelized onions, everyone will be ready to eat.
—Marybeth Mank, Mesquite, TX

Prep: 30 min. • **Cook:** 40 min.
Makes: 6 servings

- ¾ cup seasoned bread crumbs
- 1 medium onion, chopped
- 2 large eggs, lightly beaten
- ⅓ cup minced fresh parsley
- 1 tsp. coarsely ground pepper
- ¾ tsp. salt
- 2 lbs. ground beef

Gravy
- ½ cup all-purpose flour
- 2¾ cups 2% milk
- 2 cans (10½ oz. each) condensed beef consomme, undiluted
- 1 Tbsp. Worcestershire sauce
- 1 tsp. coarsely ground pepper
- ¾ tsp. salt
   Optional: ¼ tsp. each ground allspice and ground nutmeg

Noodles
- 1 pkg. (16 oz.) egg noodles
- ¼ cup butter, cubed
- ¼ cup minced fresh parsley

1. In a large bowl, combine the first 6 ingredients. Add beef; mix lightly but thoroughly. Shape into 1½-in. meatballs (about 36). In a large skillet over medium heat, brown meatballs in batches. Using a slotted spoon, remove to paper towels to drain, reserving drippings in pan.
2. For gravy, stir flour into drippings; cook over medium-high heat until light brown (do not burn). Gradually whisk in milk until smooth. Stir in consomme, Worcestershire sauce, pepper, salt and allspice and nutmeg if desired.

Bring to a boil over medium-high heat; cook and stir until thickened, about 2 minutes.
3. Reduce heat to medium-low; return meatballs to pan. Cook, uncovered, until meatballs are cooked through, 15-20 minutes longer, stirring occasionally.
4. Meanwhile, cook noodles according to package directions. Drain; toss with butter. Serve with the meatball mixture; sprinkle with parsley.

6 meatballs with 1¾ cups noodles and about ⅓ cup gravy 834 cal., 33g fat (14g sat. fat), 248mg chol., 1711mg sod., 81g carb. (10g sugars, 4g fiber), 50g pro.

Swedish Meatballs Tips

What else can I serve with Swedish meatballs?
Swedish meatballs are delicious with mashed potatoes or a crisp cucumber salad. We also suggest doubling this recipe and keeping the meatballs warm in a slow cooker for the ultimate party appetizer.

How can I make the Swedish meatballs sauce creamier?
For a richer sauce, use half-and-half or heavy cream instead of milk. Alternatively, you can adjust the richness of individual servings by adding a few dollops of full-fat sour cream or plain Greek yogurt to the top of each plate just before serving.

Mac & Cheese

Slow-cooked mac and cheese—the words alone are enough to make mouths water. This is comfort food at its best: rich and extra cheesy.
—Shelby Molina, Whitewater, WI

Prep: 25 min. • **Cook:** 2½ hours
Makes: 9 servings

- 2 cups uncooked elbow macaroni
- 1 can (12 oz.) evaporated milk
- 1½ cups whole milk
- 2 large eggs
- ¼ cup butter, melted
- 1 tsp. salt
- 2½ cups shredded cheddar cheese
- 2½ cups shredded sharp cheddar cheese, divided

1. Cook macaroni according to package directions; drain and rinse in cold water. In a large bowl, combine evaporated milk, whole milk, eggs, butter and salt. Stir in cheddar cheese, 2 cups sharp cheddar cheese and macaroni.
2. Transfer to a greased 3-qt. slow cooker. Cook, covered, on low until center is set, 2½ to 3 hours, stirring once. Sprinkle with the remaining ½ cup sharp cheddar cheese.
¾ cup 415 cal., 28g fat (20g sat. fat), 143mg chol., 745mg sod., 20g carb. (6g sugars, 1g fiber), 21g pro.

"Made this for a tailgating party, and it received many great reviews—had a number of people say, 'Don't lose that recipe!' Definitely a hit in my family."

—katmarie, tasteofhome.com

Baja Pork Tacos

This delicious recipe is my copycat version of the most excellent Mexican food we ever had in Flagstaff, Arizona. The original recipe used beef instead of pork, but this comes mighty close to the same taste.
—Ariella Winn, Mesquite, TX

Prep: 10 min. • **Cook:** 8 hours
Makes: 12 servings

- 1 boneless pork sirloin roast (3 lbs.)
- 5 cans (4 oz. each) chopped green chiles
- 2 Tbsp. reduced-sodium taco seasoning
- 3 tsp. ground cumin
- 24 corn tortillas (6 in.), warmed
- 3 cups shredded lettuce
- 1½ cups shredded part-skim mozzarella cheese

1. Cut roast in half; place in a 3- or 4-qt. slow cooker. Mix chiles, taco seasoning and cumin; spoon over pork. Cook, covered, on low until the meat is tender, 8-10 hours.
2. Remove pork; cool slightly. Skim fat from cooking juices. Shred meat with 2 forks. Return to slow cooker; heat through. Serve in tortillas with lettuce and cheese.
Freeze option Place the cooled pork mixture in freezer containers; freeze up to 3 months. To use, partially thaw in the refrigerator overnight. Heat through in a covered saucepan, stirring gently; add broth if necessary.
2 tacos 320 cal., 11g fat (4g sat. fat), 77mg chol., 434mg sod., 26g carb. (1g sugars, 4g fiber), 30g pro.
Diabetic exchanges 3 medium-fat meat, 2 starch.

Slow-Cooker Boeuf Bourguignon

I'd wanted to make beef Burgundy ever since I got one of Julia Child's cookbooks, but I wanted to fix it in a slow cooker. My version of the popular beef stew is still rich, hearty and delicious, but without the need to watch it on the stovetop or in the oven.
—Crystal Jo Bruns, Iliff, CO

Prep: 30 min. + marinating
Cook: 8 hours • **Makes:** 12 servings

- 3 lbs. beef stew meat
- 1¾ cups dry red wine
- 3 Tbsp. olive oil
- 3 Tbsp. dried minced onion
- 2 Tbsp. dried parsley flakes
- 1 bay leaf
- 1 tsp. dried thyme
- ¼ tsp. pepper
- 8 bacon strips, chopped
- 1 lb. whole fresh mushrooms, quartered
- 24 pearl onions, peeled (about 2 cups)
- 2 garlic cloves, minced
- ⅓ cup all-purpose flour
- 1 tsp. salt
  Hot cooked whole wheat egg noodles, optional

1. Place beef in a large resealable bowl; add wine, oil and seasonings. Turn to coat. Cover; refrigerate overnight.
2. In a large skillet, cook bacon over medium heat until crisp, stirring occasionally. Remove with a slotted spoon; drain on paper towels. Discard drippings, reserving 1 Tbsp. in pan.
3. Add mushrooms and onions to bacon drippings; cook and stir over medium-high heat until tender. Add garlic; cook 1 minute longer.

4. Drain beef, reserving marinade; transfer beef to a 4- or 5-qt. slow cooker. Sprinkle with flour and salt; toss to coat. Top with the bacon and mushroom mixture. Add the reserved marinade.
5. Cook, covered, on low until beef is tender, 8-10 hours. Remove bay leaf. If desired, serve stew with noodles.

⅔ **cup beef mixture** 289 cal., 15g fat (5g sat. fat), 77mg chol., 350mg sod., 8g carb. (2g sugars, 1g fiber), 25g pro.
Diabetic exchanges 3 lean meat, 1½ fat, 1 vegetable.

Slow-Cooker Boeuf Bourguignon Tips

What cut of meat is best for boeuf bourguignon? Use a tougher cut with good marbling, such as beef chuck, rump roast, stewing beef, beef shoulder or beef brisket. In general, you can use any cut you'd find in a slow-cooker beef recipe. These well-used muscles contain a lot of connective tissue, which breaks down into rich collagen during the slow cooking process, resulting in perfectly tender bites of beef.

What kind of red wine should I use? The best type of wine for boeuf bourguignon is a good-quality Burgundy, like pinot noir. Other red wines, such as cabernet sauvignon or merlot can be suitable, so long as they contain rich elements to enhance the depth and complexity of the dish.

Slow-Cooked Meat Loaf for Two

My husband and I both work late, so it's great to come home to a classic homemade meat loaf. With mashed potatoes and veggies on the side, it reminds me of a supper my mom would make.
—Ginger Cortese, Hollsopple, PA

Prep: 15 min. • **Cook:** 5 hours
Makes: 2 servings

- 1 can (10¾ oz.) condensed cream of celery soup, undiluted
- 1¼ cups water
- 1 large egg
- ¼ cup dry bread crumbs
- 2 Tbsp. grated Parmesan cheese
- 1½ tsp. dried parsley flakes
- ½ tsp. garlic powder
- ¼ tsp. onion powder
- ⅛ tsp. salt, optional
- ⅛ tsp. pepper
- ½ lb. lean ground beef (90% lean)
  Hot mashed potatoes, optional

1. In a small bowl, combine soup and water until blended. Pour half the soup mixture into a 1½-qt. slow cooker. Cover and refrigerate the remaining soup mixture.
2. In a small bowl, combine egg, bread crumbs, cheese, parsley, garlic powder, onion powder, salt if desired and pepper. Crumble beef over the mixture and mix well.
3. Shape into a loaf; place in slow cooker. Cook, covered, on low for 5-6 hours or until meat is no longer pink and a thermometer reads 160°.
4. For gravy, place the reserved soup mixture in a small saucepan; cook over low heat until heated through. Serve meat loaf and gravy with mashed potatoes if desired.
1 piece 407 cal., 22g fat (7g sat. fat), 174mg chol., 1099mg sod., 23g carb. (2g sugars, 5g fiber), 30g pro.

Sweet Tea Barbecued Chicken

Marinades sometimes use coffee or espresso, and that inspired me to try tea and apple juice to perk up this sauce.
—Kelly Williams, Forked River, NJ

Prep: 15 min. • **Cook:** 1 hour
Makes: 8 servings

- 1 cup unsweetened apple juice
- 1 cup water
- 2 tsp. seafood seasoning
- 1 tsp. paprika
- 1 tsp. garlic powder
- 1 tsp. coarsely ground pepper
- 1 chicken (4 to 5 lbs.), cut up
- 1 cup barbecue sauce
- ½ cup sweet tea

1. Preheat oven to 350°. Pour apple juice and water into a large shallow roasting pan. Mix the seafood seasoning, paprika, garlic powder and pepper; rub over chicken. Place chicken in roasting pan.
2. Bake, covered, 50-60 minutes or until juices run clear and a thermometer reads 170° to 175°. Transfer chicken to a foil-lined 15x10x1-in. baking pan.
3. Whisk barbecue sauce and sweet tea; brush some mixture over the chicken.
4. Place chicken on greased grill rack; grill over medium heat 3-4 minutes per side, occasionally brushing with the remaining sauce.
1 piece 374 cal., 17g fat (5g sat. fat), 104mg chol., 608mg sod., 19g carb. (16g sugars, 1g fiber), 33g pro.

"Great BBQ chicken. Slow baking the chicken first made it juicy and tender. Finished it off on the grill with a North Carolina sauce with the sweet tea. Wonderful Memorial Day dish!"
—cbybee, tasteofhome.com

Skillet Lasagna

My husband loves my simple stovetop lasagna. Loaded with beef and two types of cheese, this easy version makes a super supper.
—Lucinda Walker, Somerset, PA

Prep: 25 min.
Cook: 40 min. + standing
Makes: 8 servings

- 1½ lbs. lean ground beef (90% lean)
- 1 small onion, chopped
- 1 medium green pepper, chopped
- 1 jar (24 oz.) spaghetti sauce with mushrooms
- 1 tsp. dried oregano
- 1 tsp. dried basil
- 6 lasagna noodles, cooked and rinsed
- 3 cups shredded mozzarella cheese
- ½ cup grated Parmesan cheese
  Torn fresh basil leaves, optional

1. In a Dutch oven, brown beef, onion and pepper, breaking beef into crumbles; drain if necessary. Stir in spaghetti sauce, oregano and basil. Simmer, uncovered, 10-15 minutes.
2. Spread ¼ cup of the meat sauce in a 10-in. cast-iron or other heavy skillet. Top with 3 noodles, cutting to fit as needed. Layer with half the remaining sauce and half the mozzarella and Parmesan cheeses. Top with the remaining noodles, meat sauce and Parmesan.
3. Cover and cook on medium heat for 3 minutes. Reduce heat to low; cook for 35 minutes. Sprinkle with the remaining mozzarella and let stand for 10 minutes with cover ajar. If desired, sprinkle with torn fresh basil leaves.
1 piece 395 cal., 18g fat (9g sat. fat), 78mg chol., 842mg sod., 29g carb. (10g sugars, 3g fiber), 31g pro.

Ham & Jack Pudgy Pie

Pepper jack cheese spices up these warm, melty sandwiches.
—Terri McKitrick, Delafield, WI

Takes: 10 min. • **Makes:** 1 serving

- 2 slices sourdough bread
- 2 Tbsp. diced fully cooked ham
- 2 Tbsp. canned sliced mushrooms
- 3 Tbsp. shredded pepper jack cheese
- 1 Tbsp. salsa

1. Place 1 slice bread in a greased sandwich iron. Top with ham, mushrooms, cheese, salsa and remaining bread slice. Close iron.
2. Cook over a hot campfire until golden brown and cheese is melted, 3-6 minutes, turning occasionally.
1 sandwich 268 cal., 9g fat (4g sat. fat), 33mg chol., 823mg sod., 32g carb. (4g sugars, 2g fiber), 15g pro.
Diabetic exchanges 2 starch, 2 medium-fat meat.

"Had to try them just because the name of them amused me. I used slab ham, sautéed mushrooms and Pico de Gallo. Everyone loved them! Thanks for such a fun name for a twist on grilled cheese."

—NaomieMoore, tasteofhome.com

Pork Chops with Cranberry Pan Sauce

Moist and tender pork chops are treated to a sweet, light cranberry glaze in this weeknight-friendly entree. It's one of my husband's favorites and quite suitable for company, too.
—Stephanie Homme, Baton Rouge, LA

Takes: 30 min. • **Makes:** 6 servings

- 6 boneless pork loin chops (4 oz. each)
- ¾ tsp. salt
- ¼ tsp. coarsely ground pepper
- 2 tsp. cornstarch
- 1 cup cranberry-apple juice
- 2 tsp. honey
- ¾ cup dried cranberries
- 1 Tbsp. minced fresh tarragon
- 1 Tbsp. minced fresh parsley
- 3 cups hot cooked brown rice

1. Sprinkle pork chops with salt and pepper. In a large skillet coated with cooking spray, brown chops over medium heat, 3-5 minutes per side. Remove from pan.
2. In same pan, mix cornstarch, juice and honey until smooth; stir in cranberries and herbs. Bring to a boil, stirring to loosen browned bits from pan; cook until thickened and bubbly, about 2 minutes.
3. Add pork chops. Reduce heat; simmer, covered, for 4-5 minutes or until a thermometer inserted in the pork reads 145°. Let stand 5 minutes before serving. Serve with rice.
1 pork chop with ½ cup rice 374 cal., 8g fat (3g sat. fat), 55mg chol., 333mg sod., 52g carb. (23g sugars, 3g fiber), 25g pro.

Grampa's German-Style Pot Roast

Grampa was of German heritage and loved the Old World recipes his mother gave him. I made a few changes so I could prepare this dish in a slow cooker and give it a slightly updated flavor.

—Nancy Heishman, Las Vegas, NV

Prep: 20 min.
Cook: 6 hours + standing
Makes: 8 servings

- 4 thick-sliced bacon strips
- 1 lb. baby Yukon Gold potatoes
- 4 medium carrots, sliced
- 1 can (14 oz.) sauerkraut, rinsed and well drained
- ¾ cup chopped dill pickles
- 1 tsp. smoked paprika
- 1 tsp. ground allspice
- ½ tsp. kosher salt
- ½ tsp. pepper
- 1 boneless beef chuck roast (3 lbs.)
- 2 pkg. (14.4 oz. each) frozen pearl onions, thawed
- 4 garlic cloves, minced
- ½ cup stout beer or beef broth
- ⅓ cup Dusseldorf mustard
- ½ cup sour cream
- ½ cup minced fresh parsley

1. In a large skillet, cook bacon over medium heat until crisp. Remove bacon to paper towels to drain, reserving drippings in pan.
2. Meanwhile, place potatoes, carrots, sauerkraut and pickles in a 7-qt. slow cooker.
3. Mix paprika, allspice, salt and pepper; rub over roast. Brown roast in bacon drippings over medium heat. Transfer to slow cooker. Add onions and garlic to drippings; cook and stir 1 minute. Stir in beer and mustard; pour over meat. Crumble bacon; add to slow cooker.
4. Cook, covered, on low 6-8 hours, or until meat and vegetables are tender. Remove roast; let stand 10 minutes before slicing.
5. Strain cooking juices. Reserve vegetables and juices; skim off fat. Return reserved vegetables and cooking juices to slow cooker. Stir in sour cream; heat through. Serve with roast; sprinkle with parsley.
1 serving 552 cal., 31g fat (12g sat. fat), 127mg chol., 926mg sod., 28g carb. (9g sugars, 6g fiber), 39g pro.

Bacon Cheeseburger Pasta

I make foods that are kid friendly and easy to reheat because my husband works long hours and often eats later than our children. If you like, use reduced-fat cheese and ground turkey for a lighter version.
—Melissa Stevens, Elk River, MN

Takes: 30 min. • **Makes:** 6 servings

- 8   oz. uncooked penne pasta
- 1   lb. ground beef
- 6   bacon strips, diced
- 1   can (10¾ oz.) condensed tomato soup, undiluted
- ½   cup water
- 1   cup shredded cheddar cheese
     Optional: Barbecue sauce and prepared mustard

1. Cook pasta according to the package directions. Meanwhile, in a large skillet, cook beef over medium heat until no longer pink, breaking meat into crumbles; drain and set meat aside.

2. In the same skillet, cook bacon until crisp; remove with a slotted spoon to paper towels to drain. Discard drippings. Drain pasta; add to the skillet. Stir in soup, water, beef and bacon; heat through.

3. Remove from heat and sprinkle with cheese. Cover and let stand until cheese is melted, 2-3 minutes. Serve with barbecue sauce and mustard if desired.

1 serving 389 cal., 16g fat (8g sat. fat), 62mg chol., 565mg sod., 36g carb. (5g sugars, 2g fiber), 25g pro.

Southwest Fish Tacos

These fish tacos are an adaptation of a dish I was served in Bermuda. They're quick because there's so little prep work involved.
—Jennifer Reid, Farmington, ME

Takes: 20 min. • **Makes:** 4 servings

- 1½ lbs. sole or cod fillets, cut into 1-in. strips
- 1 Tbsp. taco seasoning
- 3 Tbsp. butter, cubed
- 1 pkg. (10 oz.) angel hair coleslaw mix
- ½ cup minced fresh cilantro
- ½ cup mayonnaise
- 1 Tbsp. lime juice
- 1 tsp. sugar
- ¼ tsp. salt
- ¼ tsp. pepper
- 8 corn tortillas or taco shells, warmed
  Lime wedges

1. Sprinkle fish with the taco seasoning. In a large skillet, heat butter over medium heat; add fish. Cook until fish just begins to flake easily with a fork, 3-4 minutes on each side.
2. Meanwhile, in a small bowl, combine coleslaw, cilantro, mayonnaise, lime juice, sugar, salt and pepper.
3. Place fish in tortillas. Top with the coleslaw mixture; serve with lime wedges.
2 tacos 510 cal., 37g fat (11g sat. fat), 109mg chol., 1170mg sod., 20g carb. (4g sugars, 3g fiber), 23g pro.

"I used cod and this could not have been easier! It's perfect for a fast weeknight dinner and was a huge hit with all three of my kids. This is also good with some sliced avocado if you have any on hand."
—curlylis85, tasteofhome.com

Garlic Bread,
Page 178

Savory
Side
Dishes

Creamy Cheese Potatoes

This easy potato dish is a comfort-food classic. It's popular at all kinds of gatherings.
—Greg Christiansen, Parker, KS

Prep: 10 min. • **Cook:** 3¼ hours
Makes: 10 servings

1 can (10¾ oz.) condensed cream of chicken soup, undiluted
1 can (10¾ oz.) condensed cream of mushroom soup, undiluted
3 Tbsp. butter, melted
1 pkg. (30 oz.) frozen shredded hash brown potatoes, thawed
2 cups shredded cheddar cheese
1 cup sour cream
Minced fresh parsley, optional

1. In a 3-qt. slow cooker coated with cooking spray, combine the soups and butter. Stir in potatoes.
2. Cover and cook on low until potatoes are tender, 3-4 hours. Stir in cheese and sour cream. Cover and cook 15-30 minutes longer or until heated through. If desired, top with additional shredded cheddar cheese and minced fresh parsley.
¾ cup 278 cal., 17g fat (10g sat. fat), 52mg chol., 614mg sod., 21g carb. (2g sugars, 2g fiber), 9g pro.

Super Italian Chopped Salad

Antipasto ingredients are sliced and diced to make this substantial salad. I like to buy sliced meat from the deli and chop it all so we can get a bit of everything in each bite.
—Kim Molina, Duarte, CA

Takes: 25 min. • **Makes:** 10 servings

3 cups torn romaine
1 can (15 oz.) garbanzo beans or chickpeas, rinsed and drained
1 jar (6½ oz.) marinated artichoke hearts, drained and chopped
1 medium green pepper, chopped
2 medium tomatoes, chopped
1 can (2¼ oz.) sliced ripe olives, drained
5 slices deli ham, chopped
5 thin slices hard salami, chopped
5 slices pepperoni, chopped
3 slices provolone cheese, chopped
2 green onions, chopped
¼ cup olive oil
2 Tbsp. red wine vinegar
¼ tsp. salt
⅛ tsp. pepper
2 Tbsp. grated Parmesan cheese
Pepperoncini, optional

In a large bowl, combine the first 11 ingredients. For dressing, in a small bowl, whisk oil, vinegar, salt and pepper. Pour over salad; toss to coat. Sprinkle with cheese. Top with pepperoncini if desired.
Note Look for pepperoncini (pickled peppers) in the pickle and olive section of your grocery store.
¾ cup 185 cal., 13g fat (3g sat. fat), 12mg chol., 444mg sod., 11g carb. (3g sugars, 3g fiber), 7g pro.

Garlic Bread

This wonderful accompaniment could not be tastier or simpler to make. Minced fresh garlic is key to these flavor-packed crusty slices, which often get snapped up before they even have a chance to cool.
—Grace Yaskovic, Lake Hiawatha, NJ

Takes: 20 min. • **Makes:** 8 servings

- ½ cup butter, melted
- 3 to 4 garlic cloves, minced
- 1 loaf (1 lb.) French bread, halved lengthwise
- 2 Tbsp. minced fresh parsley

1. In a small bowl, combine butter and garlic. Brush over cut sides of bread; sprinkle with parsley. Place, cut side up, on a baking sheet.
2. Bake at 350° for 8 minutes. Broil 4-6 in. from the heat for 2 minutes or until golden brown. Slice and serve warm.
1 serving 258 cal., 13g fat (8g sat. fat), 31mg chol., 433mg sod., 30g carb. (3g sugars, 1g fiber), 6g pro.

Table for One

Garlic bread is very versatile, as this recipe proves. Best of all, it's a snap to make a single slice, using this recipe as a template. Simply mix garlic with melted butter and spread over a slice of bread (or as many slices as you like). If preparing a small batch, a toaster oven makes for a quick and easy bake.

Quick Green Beans with Bacon

Bits of bacon and onion dress up the green beans in this easy-to-prepare side dish. These beans lend a crisp, fresh flavor to any meal, from steaks to chicken.

—Mari Anne Warren, Milton, WI

Takes: 25 min. • **Makes:** 8 servings

- 8   cups fresh green beans, trimmed
- 4   bacon strips, chopped
- ½   cup chopped onion
- ¼   tsp. salt
- ⅛   tsp. pepper

1. Place beans in a large saucepan and cover with water. Bring to a boil. Cook, uncovered, until beans are crisp-tender, 8-10 minutes; drain. In a large skillet, cook bacon and onion over medium heat until bacon is crisp and onion is tender, stirring occasionally, 3-5 minutes.
2. Add beans to bacon mixture. Sprinkle with salt and pepper; toss to coat.

1 cup 62 cal., 2g fat (1g sat. fat), 6mg chol., 177mg sod., 8g carb. (4g sugars, 3g fiber), 4g pro.
Diabetic exchanges 1 vegetable, ½ fat.

Pickled Beets

I grew up with my mother's pickled beets. The beets she used came from our garden and were canned for the winter months. Even as a child I loved beets because they brought so much color to our table. Their tangy flavor is a great complement to the rest of the foods in a meal.

—Sara Lindler, Irmo, SC

Prep: 35 min. + chilling,
Cook: 5 min. • **Makes:** 8 servings

    8   medium fresh beets
    1   cup vinegar
    ½   cup sugar
    1½ tsp. whole cloves
    1½ tsp. whole allspice
    ½   tsp. salt

1. Scrub beets and trim tops to 1 in. Place in a Dutch oven; add water to cover. Bring to a boil. Reduce heat; simmer, covered, 25-30 minutes or until tender. Remove from water; cool. Peel beets and slice; place in a bowl and set aside.
2. In a small saucepan, combine vinegar, sugar, cloves, allspice and salt. Bring to a boil; boil 5 minutes. Pour over beets. Refrigerate at least 1 hour. Drain before serving.
1 cup 71 cal., 0 fat (0 sat. fat), 0 chol., 186mg sod., 18g carb. (16g sugars, 1g fiber), 1g pro.
Sweet-Sour Beets Cook beets as directed. In large saucepan, combine ½ cup sugar, 1 Tbsp. cornstarch and ¼ tsp. salt; stir in ½ cup cider vinegar. Bring to a boil over medium heat; cook and stir 1 minute or until thickened. Stir in 2 Tbsp. orange marmalade and 1 Tbsp. butter until melted. Reduce heat to low. Add beets; heat through.

Spanakopita Mashed Potatoes

Most of the recipes I make use only a handful of ingredients and have a healthier bent. I created this recipe after tasting a special baked potato. I wanted to capture the flavor but cut the prep time. By not peeling the potatoes, you not only keep some nutrients but also easily beat the clock. I love how the flecks of red and green make this versatile side dish look festive and special.

—Ashley Laymon, Lititz, PA

Prep: 10 min. • **Cook:** 25 min.
Makes: 6 servings

    6   medium red potatoes,
        quartered
    1   pkg. (6 oz.) fresh baby spinach
    ¼   cup 2% milk
    1   Tbsp. butter
    ½   tsp. salt
    ½   tsp. pepper
    ¾   cup crumbled feta cheese

1. Place potatoes in a large saucepan and cover with water. Bring to a boil. Reduce heat; cover and cook 15-20 minutes or until tender.
2. Meanwhile, in another large saucepan, bring ½ in. water to a boil. Add spinach; cover and boil 3-5 minutes or until wilted. Drain and coarsely chop; keep warm.
3. Drain potatoes and return to the saucepan. Add milk, butter, salt and pepper; mash until smooth. Fold in cheese and spinach.
¾ cup 145 cal., 5g fat (3g sat. fat), 13mg chol., 379mg sod., 20g carb. (2g sugars, 3g fiber), 6g pro.
Diabetic exchanges 1 starch, 1 fat.

Layered Veggie Tortellini Salad

Tortellini and a Parmesan dressing give this layered salad an unexpected twist. It's great for a potluck.
—Dennis Vitale, New Preston, CT

Takes: 30 min. • **Makes:** 10 servings

- 1 pkg. (16 oz.) frozen cheese tortellini
- 2 cups fresh broccoli florets
- 2 cups cherry tomatoes, quartered
- 2 celery ribs, finely chopped
- 1 can (2¼ oz.) sliced ripe olives, drained
- 1 cup shredded cheddar cheese

Parmesan Dressing
- ¾ cup mayonnaise
- 3 Tbsp. grated Parmesan cheese
- 2 Tbsp. lemon juice
- 2 Tbsp. heavy whipping cream
- 1 tsp. dried thyme

1. Cook tortellini according to the package directions; drain and rinse in cold water. In a 2½-qt. glass bowl, layer the tortellini, broccoli, tomatoes, celery, olives and cheddar cheese.

2. In a small bowl, whisk the dressing ingredients; spoon over salad or serve alongside. Cover and refrigerate until serving.

1 cup 286 cal., 20g fat (6g sat. fat), 32mg chol., 374mg sod., 18g carb. (2g sugars, 2g fiber), 8g pro.

"I made this for my son's birthday. It was so easy and so yummy. I will be making it again this weekend when a friend comes into town."

—onehoobgirl, tasteofhome.com

Lattice Corn Pie

This unique side dish is full of old-fashioned goodness, with tender diced potatoes and a fresh, sweet corn flavor. Once you've tasted this delicious pie, you'll never want to serve corn any other way!
—Kathy Spang, Manheim, PA

Prep: 25 min. • **Bake:** 35 min.
Makes: 8 servings

- 1   cup diced peeled potatoes
- ⅓   cup 2% milk
- 2   large eggs, room temperature
- 2   cups fresh or frozen corn, thawed
- 1   tsp. sugar
- ½   tsp. salt
- 2   sheets refrigerated pie crust

1. Preheat oven to 375°. Place potatoes in a small saucepan and cover with water. Bring to a boil. Reduce heat; cover and cook until tender, 6-8 minutes. Drain.
2. In a blender, combine the milk, eggs, corn, sugar and salt; cover and process until blended.
3. Unroll 1 sheet crust into a 9-in. pie plate. Trim crust to ½ in. beyond rim of plate; flute edge. Spoon potatoes into crust; top with corn mixture (crust will be full). Roll out remaining crust; make a lattice top with crust. Seal and flute edge.
4. Bake until crust is golden brown and filling is bubbly, 35-40 minutes.
1 piece 308 cal., 16g fat (7g sat. fat), 57mg chol., 373mg sod., 37g carb. (5g sugars, 1g fiber), 5g pro.

Green Bean Casserole

This green bean casserole has always been one of my favorite dishes—it's so easy to put together! You can make it before any guests arrive and keep it refrigerated until baking time.
—Anna Baker, Blaine, WA

Prep: 15 min. • **Bake:** 30 min.
Makes: 10 servings

- 2 lbs. fresh green beans, trimmed
- 2 cans (10¾ oz. each) condensed cream of mushroom soup, undiluted
- 1 cup 2% milk
- 2 tsp. soy sauce
- ⅛ tsp. pepper
- 1 can (6 oz.) french-fried onions, divided

1. In a large saucepan, bring 8 cups water to a boil. Add green beans; cook, uncovered, just until crisp-tender, 3-4 minutes. Drain.
2. In a bowl, combine soup, milk, soy sauce and pepper. Gently stir in beans. Spoon half the mixture into a 13x9-in. baking dish. Sprinkle with half the onions. Spoon the remaining bean mixture over the top. Sprinkle with remaining onions.
3. Bake at 350° until heated through and onions are brown and crispy, 30-35 minutes.

¾ cup 163 cal., 11g fat (3g sat. fat), 5mg chol., 485mg sod., 14g carb. (2g sugars, 1g fiber), 2g pro.

Ambrosia Salad

Because it's so easy to prepare, this tropical medley is great as a last-minute menu addition. Plus, it requires just 5 basic ingredients.
—Judi Bringegar, Liberty, NC

Prep: 10 min. + chilling
Makes: 4 servings

- 1 can (15 oz.) mandarin oranges, drained
- 1 can (8 oz.) pineapple tidbits, drained
- 1 cup miniature marshmallows
- 1 cup sweetened shredded coconut
- 1 cup sour cream

In a large bowl, combine the oranges, pineapple, marshmallows and coconut. Add sour cream and toss to mix. Cover and refrigerate for several hours.

1 cup 370 cal., 20g fat (14g sat. fat), 14mg chol., 101mg sod., 48g carb. (43g sugars, 2g fiber), 4g pro.

Lofty Origins

The name ambrosia derives from Greek mythology, where it imparted immortality and was known as food of the gods—the Greek gods ate ambrosia to maintain their strength. In present day, we know it as a deliciously fluffy fruit salad (or dessert) with tropical flavors.

Deluxe Mashed Potatoes

When it comes to mashed potatoes recipes, this is one of my favorites because they can be made ahead, refrigerated and then popped into the oven just prior to dinnertime. When my grandchildren come for dinner, I have to double this recipe. They love it!
—Vivian Bailey, Cedar Falls, IA

Prep: 30 min. • **Bake:** 35 min.
Makes: 6 servings

- 4 to 5 large potatoes (about 2½ lbs.)
- 3 oz. cream cheese, softened
- ½ cup sour cream
- 1 Tbsp. chopped chives
- ¾ tsp. onion salt
- ¼ tsp. pepper
- 1 Tbsp. butter
  Paprika, optional

Peel and cube the potatoes; place in a saucepan and cover with water. Cook over medium heat until tender; drain. Mash until smooth (do not add milk or butter). Stir in cream cheese, sour cream, chives, onion salt and pepper. Spoon into a greased 1½-qt. baking dish. Dot with butter; sprinkle with paprika if desired. Cover and bake at 350° for 35-40 minutes or until heated through.
¾ cup 301 cal., 10g fat (7g sat. fat), 34mg chol., 313mg sod., 45g carb. (5g sugars, 4g fiber), 7g pro.

Carrot Raisin Salad

This traditional salad is one of my mother-in-law's favorites. It's fun to eat because of the crunchy texture, and the raisins give it a slightly sweet flavor. Plus, I love how easy it is to toss together.
—Denise Baumert, Dalhart, TX

Takes: 10 min. • **Makes:** 8 servings

- 4 cups shredded carrots
- ¾ to 1½ cups raisins
- ¼ cup mayonnaise
- 2 Tbsp. sugar
- 2 to 3 Tbsp. 2% milk

Mix the first 4 ingredients. Stir in enough milk to reach desired consistency. Refrigerate until serving.
½ cup 122 cal., 5g fat (1g sat. fat), 1mg chol., 76mg sod., 19g carb. (14g sugars, 2g fiber), 1g pro.
Diabetic exchanges 1 vegetable, 1 fat, ½ starch, ½ fruit.

Roasted Sugar Snap Peas

This is a super fast and fresh way to dress up crisp sugar snap peas. It's a bright complement to so many spring dishes, and is pretty enough for company.
—*Taste of Home* Test Kitchen

Takes: 15 min. • **Makes:** 2 servings

- 1 pkg. (8 oz.) fresh sugar snap peas, trimmed
- 1 Tbsp. chopped shallot
- 2 tsp. olive oil
- ½ tsp. Italian seasoning
- ⅛ tsp. salt

Preheat oven to 400°. Toss together all ingredients; spread in a 15x10x1-in. pan. Roast until the peas are crisp-tender, 8-10 minutes, stirring once.
⅔ cup 91 cal., 5g fat (1g sat. fat), 0 chol., 153mg sod., 9g carb. (4g sugars, 3g fiber), 4g pro. **Diabetic exchanges** 2 vegetable, 1 fat.

Three-Bean Baked Beans

I got this recipe from my aunt and made a couple of changes to suit my taste. With ground beef and bacon mixed in, these satisfying beans are a big hit at backyard barbecues and church picnics. I'm always asked to bring my special beans.

—Julie Currington, Gahanna, OH

Prep: 20 min. • **Bake:** 1 hour
Makes: 12 servings

- ½ lb. ground beef
- 5 bacon strips, diced
- ½ cup chopped onion
- ⅓ cup packed brown sugar
- ¼ cup sugar
- ¼ cup ketchup
- ¼ cup barbecue sauce
- 2 Tbsp. molasses
- 2 Tbsp. prepared mustard
- ½ tsp. chili powder
- ½ tsp. salt
- 2 cans (15 oz. each) pork and beans, undrained
- 1 can (16 oz.) butter beans, rinsed and drained
- 1 can (16 oz.) kidney beans, rinsed and drained

1. Preheat oven to 350°. In a large skillet, cook and crumble beef with bacon and onion over medium heat until beef is no longer pink; drain.
2. Stir in sugars, ketchup, barbecue sauce, molasses, mustard, chili powder and salt until blended. Stir in beans. Transfer to a greased 2½-qt. baking dish. Bake, covered, 1 hour or until beans reach desired thickness.

Freeze option Freeze cooled bean mixture in freezer containers. To use, partially thaw in refrigerator overnight. Heat through in a saucepan, stirring occasionally; add water if necessary.

¾ cup 269 cal., 8g fat (2g sat. fat), 19mg chol., 708mg sod., 42g carb. (21g sugars, 7g fiber), 13g pro.

Caesar Salad

This crunchy, refreshing Caesar salad has a zippy, zesty dressing that provides a burst of flavor with each bite. It's a fantastic salad to perk up any spring or summer meal.

—Schelby Thompson, Camden Wyoming, DE

Takes: 10 min. • **Makes:** 6 servings

- 1 large bunch romaine, torn
- ¾ cup olive oil
- 3 Tbsp. red wine vinegar
- 1 tsp. Worcestershire sauce
- ½ tsp. salt
- ¼ tsp. ground mustard
- 1 large garlic clove, minced
- ½ fresh lemon
- Dash pepper
- ¼ to ½ cup shredded Parmesan cheese
- Caesar-flavored or garlic croutons

1. Place lettuce in a large salad bowl. Combine next 6 ingredients in a blender; process until smooth. Pour over lettuce and toss to coat.
2. Squeeze lemon juice over lettuce. Sprinkle with pepper, cheese and croutons.

1 cup 265 cal., 28g fat (4g sat. fat), 2mg chol., 268mg sod., 3g carb. (1g sugars, 1g fiber), 2g pro.

"Absolutely delicious! I've had many people request this recipe. It's so good!"

—leasamsar, tasteofhome.com

Corn & Broccoli in Cheese Sauce

Save room in the oven by making this savory side in your slow cooker. It is a standby in my house. My daughter likes to add leftover ham to create a hearty main course.
—Joyce Johnson, Uniontown, OH

Prep: 10 min. • **Cook:** 3 hours
Makes: 8 servings

- 1 pkg. (16 oz.) frozen corn, thawed
- 1 pkg. (16 oz.) frozen broccoli florets, thawed
- 4 oz. reduced-fat Velveeta, cubed
- ½ cup shredded cheddar cheese
- 1 can (10¼ oz.) reduced-fat reduced-sodium condensed cream of chicken soup, undiluted
- ¼ cup fat-free milk

1. In a 4-qt. slow cooker, combine the corn, broccoli and cheeses. In a small bowl, combine soup and milk; pour over vegetable mixture.
2. Cover and cook on low until heated through, 3-4 hours. Stir before serving.

¾ cup 148 cal., 5g fat (3g sat. fat), 16mg chol., 409mg sod., 21g carb. (4g sugars, 3g fiber), 8g pro.
Diabetic exchanges 1 starch, 1 medium-fat meat.

"Simple, satisfying comfort food. It's not fancy, but it is one of those recipes that you remember and look for again."
—cwbuff2, tasteofhome.com

Cauliflower Parmesan Casserole

Thick and creamy with a golden topping, this potluck dish tastes as comforting as it looks.
—Taste of Home Test Kitchen

Prep: 30 min. • **Bake:** 30 min.
Makes: 12 servings

- 3 pkg. (16 oz. each) frozen cauliflower, thawed
- 1 large onion, chopped
- ⅓ cup butter, cubed
- ⅓ cup all-purpose flour
- ½ tsp. salt
- ¼ tsp. ground mustard
- ¼ tsp. pepper
- 2 cups fat-free milk
- ½ cup grated Parmesan cheese

Topping
- ½ cup soft whole wheat bread crumbs
- 2 Tbsp. butter, melted
- ¼ tsp. paprika

1. Preheat oven to 350°. Place 1 in. water in a Dutch oven; add the cauliflower. Bring to a boil. Reduce heat; cover and cook until crisp-tender, 4-6 minutes. Drain and pat dry.
2. Meanwhile, in a large saucepan, saute onion in butter until tender. Stir in flour, salt, mustard and pepper until blended; gradually add milk. Bring to a boil; cook and stir until thickened, 1-2 minutes. Remove from the heat. Add cheese; stir until melted.
3. Place cauliflower in a greased 13x9-in. baking dish. Pour the sauce on top.
4. Combine the bread crumbs, butter and paprika. Sprinkle over sauce. Bake, uncovered, 30-35 minutes or until bubbly.

¾ cup 142 cal., 8g fat (5g sat. fat), 22mg chol., 257mg sod., 13g carb. (5g sugars, 3g fiber), 6g pro.

Hummingbird
Cake, Page 212

Mmm ... Dessert!

Apple Danish Bars

A friend shared this delightful recipe perfect for bountiful fall apples.
—Sandy Lynch, Decatur, IL

Prep: 20 min.
Bake: 40 min. + cooling
Makes: 24 servings

Pastry
3   cups all-purpose flour
½   tsp. salt
1   cup shortening
1   large egg yolk
½   cup 2% milk

Assembly
6   cups sliced peeled apples
1½ cups sugar
¼   cup butter, melted
2   Tbsp. all-purpose flour
1   tsp. ground cinnamon
1   large egg white, lightly beaten

Glaze
½   cup confectioners' sugar
2   to 3 tsp. water

1. In a bowl, combine flour and salt; cut in shortening until the mixture resembles coarse crumbs. Combine egg yolk and milk; add to flour mixture. Stir just until dough clings together. Divide dough in half.
2. On a lightly floured surface, roll half of dough into a 15x10-in. rectangle; transfer to a greased 15x10x1-in. baking pan. Set aside.
3. In a bowl, toss together the next 5 ingredients; spoon over pastry in pan. Roll out remaining dough into another 15x10-in. rectangle. Place over filling. Brush with egg white. Bake at 375° for 40 minutes or until golden brown. Cool on a wire rack.
4. For glaze, combine the confectioners' sugar and enough water to achieve a drizzling consistency. Drizzle over pastry. Cut into squares.
1 piece 230 cal., 11g fat (3g sat. fat), 15mg chol., 74mg sod., 32g carb. (18g sugars, 1g fiber), 2g pro.

Double Chocolate Truffles

Chocolate lovers of all kinds will appreciate these yummy truffles. Another nice flavor combination is to use orange extract instead of vanilla.
—Ruth Gordon, Lakewood, NY

Prep: 20 min. + chilling
Makes: 2½ dozen

1⅓ cups semisweet chocolate chips
3   Tbsp. butter
⅓   cup heavy whipping cream
1   tsp. vanilla extract
1   cup white baking chips
2   Tbsp. shortening, divided
1   cup milk chocolate chips

1. In a microwave-safe bowl, melt the semisweet chocolate chips and butter with cream; stir until smooth. Add vanilla; cool. Refrigerate until almost solid but still workable, about 1 hour.
2. Shape into ½-in. balls. In a microwave, melt white chips and 1 Tbsp. shortening; stir until smooth. Dip half of the balls in white chocolate mixture; allow excess to drip off. Place on waxed paper; let stand until set.
3. Microwave milk chocolate chips and remaining shortening; stir until smooth. Dip remaining balls in milk chocolate mixture; allow excess to drip off. Place on waxed paper; let stand until set.
4. If desired, drizzle truffles with melted chocolate of opposite color. Store in an airtight container.
1 truffle 122 cal., 9g fat (5g sat. fat), 9mg chol., 23mg sod., 11g carb. (7g sugars, 1g fiber), 1g pro.

Peanut Butter Icebox Dessert

Leftover crushed cookies create the yummy crust for this crowd-pleasing dessert. It's covered with a smooth cream cheese mixture, chocolate pudding and whipped topping for a lovely layered look.

—Nancy Mueller, Highlands Ranch, CO

Prep: 20 min. + chilling
Makes: 15 servings

- 16 Nutter Butter cookies, crushed, divided
- ¼ cup sugar
- ¼ cup butter, melted
- 1 pkg. (8 oz.) cream cheese, softened
- 1⅓ cups confectioners' sugar
- 1 carton (8 oz.) frozen whipped topping, thawed, divided
- 2½ cups cold 2% milk
- 2 pkg. (3.9 oz. each) instant chocolate pudding mix

1. In a large bowl, combine 1¾ cups crushed cookies, sugar and butter; press into an ungreased 13x9-in. baking dish. Bake at 350° until golden brown, 6-8 minutes; cool on a wire rack.
2. In a large bowl, beat cream cheese and confectioners' sugar until smooth; fold in 1½ cups whipped topping. Spread over cooled crust.
3. In another large bowl, beat milk and pudding mix on low speed until thickened, about 2 minutes. Spread over cream cheese layer. Top with the remaining whipped topping; sprinkle with the remaining ¼ cup crushed cookies. Cover and refrigerate for at least 1 hour before serving.
1 piece 323 cal., 15g fat (9g sat. fat), 27mg chol., 217mg sod., 43g carb. (31g sugars, 1g fiber), 4g pro.

Milky Way Pudgy Pie

My favorite pudgy pies have Milky Way candy bars, graham cracker crumbs and marshmallows. So irresistible. And buttered bread is a must.

—Susan Hein, Burlington, WI

Takes: 10 min. • **Makes:** 1 serving

- 1 Tbsp. butter, softened
- 2 slices white bread
- 1 Tbsp. graham cracker crumbs
- 1 fun-size Milky Way candy bar, chopped
- 2 Tbsp. miniature marshmallows

1. Spread butter over bread slices. Place 1 slice in a sandwich iron, buttered side down. Top with cracker crumbs, chopped candy, marshmallows and remaining bread slice, buttered side up. Close iron.
2. Cook over a hot campfire until golden brown and marshmallows are melted, 3-6 minutes, turning occasionally.
1 sandwich 380 cal., 17g fat (10g sat. fat), 32mg chol., 438mg sod., 51g carb. (19g sugars, 2g fiber), 6g pro.

"These are great sweet grilled sandwiches. You can use all sorts of candy bars in these. You can also use marshmallow creme instead of miniature marshmallows. These are perfect to make on campouts."

—randcbruns, tasteofhome.com

Pumpkin Creme Brulee

I've never met a creme brulee that I didn't love! I'm not a big pumpkin fan, but this is fantastic.

—Tamara Leonard Merritt, Raleigh, NC

Prep: 20 min.
Bake: 25 min. + chilling
Makes: 8 servings

8   large egg yolks
⅓   cup plus ½ cup sugar, divided
3   cups heavy whipping cream
¾   cup canned pumpkin
1½ tsp. vanilla extract
½   tsp. ground cinnamon
¼   tsp. each ground ginger, nutmeg and cloves

1. In a small bowl, whisk egg yolks and ⅓ cup sugar. In a small saucepan, heat cream over medium heat until bubbles form around sides of pan. Remove from the heat; stir a small amount of hot cream into egg yolk mixture. Return all to the pan, stirring constantly. Stir in the pumpkin, vanilla and spices.

2. Transfer to eight 6-oz. ramekins or custard cups. Place ramekins in a baking pan; add 1 in. of boiling water to pan. Bake, uncovered, at 325° for 25-30 minutes or until centers are just set (mixture will jiggle). Remove ramekins from water bath; cool for 10 minutes. Cover and refrigerate for at least 4 hours.

3. If using a creme brulee torch, sprinkle with remaining ½ cup sugar. Heat sugar with the torch until caramelized. Serve immediately.

4. If broiling the custards, place ramekins on a baking sheet; let stand at room temperature for 15 minutes. Sprinkle with remaining ½ cup sugar. Broil 8 in. from the heat for 4-7 minutes or until sugar is caramelized. Refrigerate for 1-2 hours or until firm.

1 serving 452 cal., 38g fat (22g sat. fat), 327mg chol., 43mg sod., 26g carb. (22g sugars, 1g fiber), 5g pro.

White Chocolate Macadamia Cookies

White baking chips and macadamia nuts are a fantastic change of pace from chocolate chip cookies.

—Cathy Lennon, Newport, TN

Prep: 15 min.
Bake: 10 min./batch
Makes: 2½ dozen

½   cup butter, softened
⅔   cup sugar
1   large egg, room temperature
1   tsp. vanilla extract
1   cup plus 2 Tbsp. all-purpose flour
½   tsp. baking soda
1   cup macadamia nuts, chopped
1   cup white baking chips

1. Preheat oven to 350°. In a large bowl, cream butter and sugar until light and fluffy, 5-7 minutes. Beat in egg and vanilla. Combine flour and baking soda; gradually beat into creamed mixture. Stir in nuts and baking chips.

2. Drop by tablespoonfuls 2 in. apart onto ungreased baking sheets. Bake 10-13 minutes or until golden brown. Cool on pans 1 minute. Remove to wire racks.

1 cookie 127 cal., 8g fat (4g sat. fat), 16mg chol., 69mg sod., 12g carb. (8g sugars, 1g fiber), 1g pro.

Did You Know?

Because it contains no cocoa solids, white chocolate technically isn't a chocolate at all. It does contain cocoa butter, which gives white chocolate its rich, buttery texture. Top-quality white chocolate contains a high percentage of cocoa butter.

Fudgy Brownies with Peanut Butter Pudding Frosting

Rich brownies are topped with a peanut butter pudding frosting to make this a recipe the whole family will love. These are perfect for a potluck, bake sale or yummy after-dinner treat.
—Amy Crook, Syracuse, UT

Prep: 20 min. + chilling
Bake: 25 min.
Makes: 2½ dozen

1   pkg. fudge brownie mix (13x9-in. pan size)
1½ cups confectioners' sugar
½   cup butter, softened
2   to 3 Tbsp. peanut butter
2   Tbsp. cold 2% milk
4½ tsp. instant vanilla pudding mix
1   can (16 oz.) chocolate fudge frosting

1. Prepare and bake brownies according to package directions. Cool on a wire rack.
2. Meanwhile, in a small bowl, beat confectioners' sugar, butter, peanut butter, milk and pudding mix until smooth. Spread over brownies. Refrigerate for 30 minutes or until firm. Frost with chocolate frosting just before cutting.
1 brownie 236 cal., 12g fat (4g sat. fat), 23mg chol., 145mg sod., 31g carb. (23g sugars, 1g fiber), 2g pro.

"I made these for a family gathering because I knew the kids wanted brownies. Now they're requested and often hidden from the kids. Easy, rich and yummy!"

—wfqq135z, tasteofhome.com

Orange Jelly Candies

After taking a couple of classes, candy making became one of my favorite pastimes—and this is one of my top go-to recipes.
—Leah Jackson, Washington, UT

Prep: 15 min.
Cook: 10 min. + standing
Makes: 81 pieces

- 2 tsp. butter
- 1 pkg. (1¾ oz.) powdered fruit pectin
- ½ tsp. baking soda
- ¾ cup water
- 1 cup sugar
- 1 cup light corn syrup
- ⅛ tsp. orange oil
- 5 drops each red and yellow food coloring
  Additional sugar

1. Butter a 9-in. square pan with 2 tsp. butter; set aside. In a large saucepan, combine the pectin, baking soda and water (mixture will be foamy). In another saucepan, combine sugar and corn syrup. Bring both mixtures to a boil. Cook until foam on pectin mixture thins slightly and sugar mixture comes to a full rolling boil, about 4 minutes. Gradually add pectin mixture to boiling sugar mixture, stirring constantly. Boil for 1 minute, stirring constantly.
2. Remove from the heat. Stir in orange oil and food coloring. Immediately pour into prepared pan. Let stand at room temperature for 3 hours or until set.
3. Sprinkle waxed paper with sugar; invert pan onto sugar. With a knife dipped in warm water, cut candy into 1-in. squares; roll in additional sugar. Place on a wire rack. Let stand, uncovered, at room temperature overnight. Store in an airtight container.

1 piece 22 cal., 0 fat (0 sat. fat), 0 chol., 11mg sod., 6g carb. (4g sugars, 0 fiber), 0 pro.

Carnival Caramel Apples

With four kids (one child whose birthday is November 1), we celebrate Halloween in style at our house. These caramel apples are a tried-and-true favorite year after year.
—Gail Prather, Bethel, MN

Prep: 20 min.
Cook: 25 min. + cooling
Makes: 12 apples

- ½ cup butter, cubed
- 2 cups packed brown sugar
- 1 cup light corn syrup
  Dash salt
- 1 can (14 oz.) sweetened condensed milk
- 1 tsp. vanilla extract
- 12 wooden pop sticks
- 12 medium tart apples, washed and dried
- 1 cup salted peanuts, chopped

1. In a large heavy saucepan, melt butter; add the brown sugar, corn syrup and salt. Cook and stir over medium heat until mixture comes to a boil, 10-12 minutes. Stir in milk. Cook and stir until a candy thermometer reads 248° (firm-ball stage). Remove from the heat; stir in vanilla.
2. Insert pop sticks into apples. Dip each apple into the hot caramel mixture; turn to coat. Dip bottom of apples into peanuts. Place on greased waxed paper until set.
Note We recommend that you test your candy thermometer before each use by bringing water to a boil; the thermometer should read 212°. Adjust your recipe temperature up or down based on your test.
1 apple 526 cal., 17g fat (7g sat. fat), 32mg chol., 231mg sod., 94g carb. (82g sugars, 4g fiber), 6g pro.

Grandma's Red Velvet Cake

It's just not Christmas at our house until this festive cake appears. This is different from other red velvets I've had; the icing is as light as snow. For quicker assembly, you can leave the layers untrimmed and simply frost the top and side of the cake with icing.
—Kathryn Davison, Charlotte, NC

Prep: 30 min.
Bake: 20 min. + cooling
Makes: 14 servings

- ½ cup butter, softened
- 1½ cups sugar
- 2 large eggs, room temperature
- 2 bottles (1 oz. each) red food coloring
- 1 Tbsp. white vinegar
- 1 tsp. vanilla extract
- 2¼ cups cake flour
- 2 Tbsp. baking cocoa
- 1 tsp. baking soda
- 1 tsp. salt
- 1 cup buttermilk

Frosting

- ½ cup cold water
- 1 Tbsp. cornstarch
- 2 cups butter, softened
- 2 tsp. vanilla extract
- 3½ cups confectioners' sugar

1. Preheat oven to 350°. Cream butter and sugar until light and fluffy, 5-7 minutes. Add eggs, 1 at a time, beating well after each addition. Beat in food coloring, vinegar and vanilla. In another bowl, whisk together flour, cocoa, baking soda and salt; add to creamed mixture alternately with buttermilk, beating well after each addition.

2. Pour into 2 greased and floured 9-in. round baking pans. Bake until a toothpick inserted in the center comes out clean, 20-25 minutes. Cool layers 10 minutes before removing from pans to wire racks to cool completely. Trim ¼ in. off the top of each cake layer; crumble trimmings onto a baking sheet. Let crumbs stand at room temperature while making frosting.

3. For frosting, combine water and cornstarch in a small saucepan over medium heat. Stir until thickened and opaque, 2-3 minutes. Cool to room temperature. Beat butter and vanilla until light and fluffy. Beat in cornstarch mixture. Gradually add confectioners' sugar; beat until light and fluffy. Spread between layers and over top and side of cake. Press reserved cake crumbs into side of cake.

Note For a snow effect, sprinkle confectioners' sugar over frosted cake top.

1 piece 595 cal., 34g fat (21g sat. fat), 115mg chol., 564mg sod., 71g carb. (52g sugars, 1g fiber), 4g pro.

"Delicious cake with a tender and moist crumb! I used gel food coloring so I didn't need quite as much to get a beautiful red color. This is perfect for Valentine's Day!"

—Adrienne189, tasteofhome.com

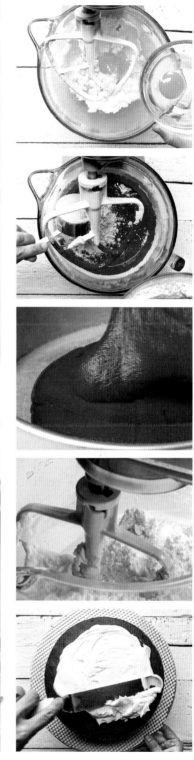

Mini Pineapple Upside-Down Cake

Now you can enjoy this traditional favorite without making a huge pan! This delectable recipe makes a mini cake that serves four people.
—Edna Hoffman, Hebron, IN

Prep: 15 min. • **Bake:** 30 min.
Makes: 4 servings

- 1 can (8 oz.) sliced pineapple
- ¼ cup packed brown sugar
- 3 Tbsp. butter, melted, divided
- 4 maraschino cherries
- 4 pecan halves
- ¾ cup all-purpose flour
- ⅓ cup sugar
- 1 tsp. baking powder
- ¼ tsp. salt
- ⅛ tsp. ground allspice
- 1 large egg, room temperature, lightly beaten
- ¼ cup 2% milk

1. Drain pineapple, reserving 1 Tbsp. juice. Set pineapple aside. In a small bowl, combine brown sugar and 2 Tbsp. butter; stir until sugar is dissolved.

2. Pour into an ungreased 6-in. round baking pan. Arrange pineapple slices in a single layer in pan; place cherries and pecans in center of pineapple slices.

3. In a small bowl, combine the flour, sugar, baking powder, salt and allspice. Beat in the egg, milk, the reserved pineapple juice and the remaining butter just until combined. Spoon over pineapple.

4. Bake at 350° for 30-35 minutes or until cake springs back when lightly touched. Cool for 5 minutes before inverting onto a serving plate. Serve warm.

1 piece 353 cal., 11g fat (6g sat. fat), 77mg chol., 369mg sod., 59g carb. (40g sugars, 1g fiber), 5g pro.

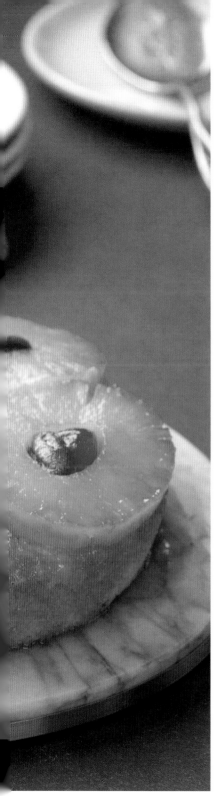

Grandma's Rice Pudding

You can whip up this classic dessert on short notice if you keep cooked rice on hand. Cooked rice can be frozen in an airtight container for up to three months. Just thaw it in the refrigerator or microwave when you're ready to use it.

—Margaret DeChant, Newberry, MI

Prep: 10 min. • **Bake:** 45 min.
Makes: 6 servings

- 1½ cups cooked rice
- ¼ cup raisins
- 2 large eggs
- 1½ cups whole milk
- ½ cup sugar
- ½ tsp. ground nutmeg
  Additional milk, optional

1. Place rice and raisins in a greased 1-qt. casserole. In a small bowl, whisk the eggs, milk, sugar and nutmeg; pour over rice.
2. Bake, uncovered, at 375° for 45-50 minutes or until a knife inserted in the center comes out clean. Cool. Pour milk over each serving if desired. Refrigerate leftovers.

1 cup 197 cal., 4g fat (2g sat. fat), 79mg chol., 52mg sod., 36g carb. (23g sugars, 0 fiber), 5g pro.

Perfect Leftovers

Rice puddings tend to thicken as they cool. To thin when reheating, stir in 1 or 2 Tbsp. of milk.

Coffee-Chocolate Cake

This dark, moist cake is perfect for birthdays. The basic buttery frosting has an unmatchable homemade taste. With a few simple variations, you can come up with different colors and flavors.

—*Taste of Home* Test Kitchen

Prep: 25 min.
Bake: 25 min. + cooling
Makes: 12 servings

 2 cups sugar
 1 cup canola oil
 1 cup whole milk
 1 cup brewed coffee, room temperature
 2 large eggs, room temperature
 1 tsp. vanilla extract
 2 cups all-purpose flour
 ¾ cup baking cocoa
 2 tsp. baking soda
 1 tsp. baking powder
 1 tsp. salt

Buttercream Frosting

 1 cup butter, softened
 8 cups confectioners' sugar
 2 tsp. vanilla extract
 ½ to ¾ cup whole milk

1. In a large bowl, beat the sugar, oil, milk, coffee, eggs and vanilla until well blended. Combine the flour, cocoa, baking soda, baking powder and salt; gradually beat into sugar mixture until blended.

2. Pour into 2 greased and floured 9-in. round baking pans. Bake at 325° for 25-30 minutes or until a toothpick inserted in the center comes out clean. Cool in pans for 10 minutes before removing to wire racks to cool completely.

3. For frosting, in a large bowl, beat butter until fluffy. Beat in confectioners' sugar and vanilla. Add milk until frosting reaches desired consistency. Spread frosting between layers and over top and side of cake.

1 piece 859 cal., 36g fat (13g sat. fat), 80mg chol., 621mg sod., 133g carb. (109g sugars, 2g fiber), 5g pro.

"This cake is so moist and delicious! My whole family loved it, even the ones who don't like cake. We will be making this again and again! My husband already requested it for his birthday in October."

—sjgapeterson, tasteofhome.com

Walnut Baklava

Here's my recipe for the traditional sweet and nutty Greek pastry. It's a tasty end to any meal.
—Josie Bochek, Sturgeon Bay, WI

Prep: 1¼ hours
Bake: 45 min.
Makes: 3 dozen

- 4 cups finely chopped walnuts
- ¼ cup sugar
- 1 Tbsp. ground cinnamon
- 1 cup butter, melted
- 1 pkg. (16 oz.) frozen phyllo dough, thawed

Syrup
- 1 cup sugar
- ½ cup water
- ¼ cup honey
- 1 tsp. lemon juice
- 1 tsp. vanilla extract

1. In a small bowl, combine the walnuts, sugar and cinnamon; set aside. Grease a 13x9-in. baking dish with some of the melted butter. Unroll phyllo dough sheets (keep dough covered with a damp towel while assembling).
2. Place 1 sheet of phyllo in baking dish; brush with butter. Top with a second sheet; brush with butter. Fold long ends under to fit the dish. Sprinkle with about ¼ cup nut mixture. Repeat 18 times, layering 2 sheets, brushing with butter and sprinkling with nut mixture. Top with remaining dough; brush with butter. Cut into 2-in. diamonds with a sharp knife.
3. Bake at 350° for 45-55 minutes or until golden brown. Meanwhile, in a saucepan, combine the syrup ingredients; bring to a boil. Reduce heat; simmer, uncovered, for 10 minutes. Pour over warm baklava. Cool on a wire rack.
1 piece 197 cal., 13g fat (4g sat. fat), 14mg chol., 102mg sod., 18g carb. (9g sugars, 1g fiber), 5g pro.

Lara's Tender Gingersnaps

Soft gingersnaps herald the tastes and smells of the Christmas season, but they are perfect for any fall or winter gathering. I enjoy the flavors of cloves, cinnamon and ginger blended into one delicious cookie.
—Lara Pennell, Mauldin, SC

Prep: 15 min. + chilling
Bake: 10 min./batch + cooling
Makes: 3 dozen

- 1 cup packed brown sugar
- ¾ cup butter, melted
- 1 large egg, room temperature
- ¼ cup molasses
- 2¼ cups all-purpose flour
- 1½ tsp. ground ginger
- 1 tsp. baking soda
- 1 tsp. ground cinnamon
- ½ tsp. ground cloves
- ¼ cup sugar or coarse sugar

1. In a large bowl, beat brown sugar and butter until blended. Beat in egg and molasses. Combine the flour, ginger, baking soda, cinnamon and cloves; gradually add to brown sugar mixture and mix well (dough will be stiff). Cover and refrigerate for at least 2 hours.
2. Preheat oven to 350°. Shape dough into 1-in. balls. Roll in sugar. Place 2 in. apart on greased baking sheets.
3. Bake until set, 9-11 minutes. Cool for about 1 minute; remove from pans to wire racks to cool completely.
1 cookie 100 cal., 4g fat (2g sat. fat), 15mg chol., 70mg sod., 15g carb. (9g sugars, 0 fiber), 1g pro.

Strawberry Pretzel Dessert

A salty pretzel crust nicely contrasts with the cream cheese and gelatin layers in this all-time favorite dessert.
—Aldene Belch, Flint, MI

Prep: 30 min. + chilling
Makes: 16 servings

2 cups crushed pretzels (about 8 oz.)
¾ cup butter, melted
3 Tbsp. sugar
Filling
2 cups whipped topping
1 pkg. (8 oz.) cream cheese, softened
1 cup sugar
Topping
2 pkg. (3 oz. each) strawberry gelatin
2 cups boiling water
2 pkg. (16 oz. each) frozen sweetened sliced strawberries, thawed
Optional: Additional whipped topping and pretzels

1. Preheat oven to 350°. In a bowl, combine the pretzels, butter and sugar. Press into an ungreased 13x9-in. baking dish. Bake for 10 minutes. Cool on a wire rack.
2. For filling, in a small bowl, beat whipped topping, cream cheese and sugar until smooth. Spread over pretzel crust. Refrigerate until chilled.
3. For topping, dissolve gelatin in boiling water in a large bowl. Stir in sweetened strawberries; chill until partially set. Carefully spoon over filling. Chill until firm, 4-6 hours. Cut into squares. Serve with additional whipped topping and additional pretzels if desired.
1 piece 295 cal., 15g fat (10g sat. fat), 39mg chol., 305mg sod., 38g carb. (27g sugars, 1g fiber), 3g pro.

Chocolate Double Chip Cookies

My young grandsons love these cookies, and I love to make them. I bake bread and rolls about once a week and also make all of our family's Christmas cookies and candy.
—Jim Roth, East Peoria, IL

Prep: 25 min.
Bake: 10 min./batch
Makes: about 6 dozen

2 cups semisweet chocolate chips
½ cup butter
3 large eggs, room temperature
½ cup sugar
2 tsp. vanilla extract
2¼ cups all-purpose flour
1 tsp. baking soda
½ tsp. salt
1 pkg. (10 oz.) vanilla or white chips

1. In a microwave or heavy saucepan, melt chocolate chips and butter; stir until smooth. Remove from the heat; cool for 10 minutes. In a bowl, beat the eggs, sugar and vanilla until light and fluffy. Add chocolate mixture and mix well. Combine flour, baking soda and salt; gradually add to the creamed mixture. Stir in vanilla chips (batter will be sticky). Drop by rounded tablespoonfuls 2 in. apart onto ungreased baking sheets.
2. Bake at 350° for 10-12 minutes or until set. Cool for 2 minutes before removing from pans to wire racks.
1 cookie 100 cal., 6g fat (3g sat. fat), 13mg chol., 50mg sod., 13g carb. (9g sugars, 1g fiber), 1g pro.

Peanut Butter Kiss Cookies

Everyone who tries these beloved gems is amazed that they use only five ingredients. Baking cookies doesn't get much easier than this.
—Dee Davis, Sun City, AZ

Prep: 20 min.
Bake: 10 min./batch
Makes: 2½ dozen

- 1   cup peanut butter
- 1   cup sugar
- 1   large egg, room temperature
- 1   tsp. vanilla extract
- 30 milk chocolate kisses

1. Preheat oven to 350°. Cream peanut butter and sugar until light and fluffy, 5-7 minutes. Beat in egg and vanilla.
2. Roll into 1¼-in. balls. Place 2 in. apart on ungreased baking sheets. Bake until tops are slightly cracked, 10-12 minutes. Immediately press 1 chocolate kiss into center of each cookie. Cool for 5 minutes before removing from pans to wire racks.
Note This recipe does not contain flour. Reduced-fat or generic brands of peanut butter are not recommended for this recipe.
1 cookie 102 cal., 6g fat (2g sat. fat), 7mg chol., 43mg sod., 11g carb. (10g sugars, 1g fiber), 2g pro.

"This was absolutely great. I'm only 12 years old, and I did it all by myself."
—jsaldierna, tasteofhome.com

Pumpkin Spice Cupcakes

I make these flavorful pumpkin cupcakes each Halloween, but they're wonderful year-round.
—Amber Butzer, Gladstone, OR

Prep: 30 min.
Bake: 30 min. + cooling
Makes: 2 dozen

- 2   cups sugar
- 1   can (15 oz.) pumpkin
- 4   large eggs, room temperature
- 1   cup canola oil
- 2   cups all-purpose flour
- 2   tsp. baking powder
- 2   tsp. ground cinnamon
- 1   tsp. baking soda
- ½   tsp. salt
- ½   tsp. ground ginger
- ¼   tsp. ground cloves
- 1   cup raisins

Cream Cheese Frosting

- ⅓   cup butter, softened
- 3   oz. cream cheese, softened
- 1   tsp. vanilla extract
- 2   cups confectioners' sugar
- ½   cup chopped walnuts, toasted

1. Preheat oven to 350°. Beat sugar, pumpkin, eggs and oil until well blended. In another bowl, whisk next 7 ingredients; gradually beat into pumpkin mixture. Stir in raisins.
2. Fill each of 24 paper-lined muffin cups ⅔ full with batter. Bake until a toothpick inserted in center comes out clean, 28-32 minutes. Cool 10 minutes before removing from pans to wire racks to cool completely.
3. For frosting, beat butter and cream cheese until smooth. Beatin vanilla. Gradually add the confectioners' sugar. Frost cupcakes; sprinkle with walnuts. Refrigerate leftovers.
Note To toast nuts, bake in a shallow pan in a 350° oven for 5-10 minutes or cook in a skillet over low heat until lightly browned, stirring occasionally.
1 cupcake 313 cal., 16g fat (3g sat. fat), 41mg chol., 187mg sod., 42g carb. (31g sugars, 1g fiber), 3g pro.

Turtle Praline Tart

This rich dessert is my own creation, and I'm very proud of it. It's easy enough to make for everyday meals but special enough to serve guests or take to a potluck.

—Kathy Specht, Clinton, MT

Prep: 35 min. + chilling
Makes: 16 servings

1	sheet refrigerated pie crust
36	caramels
1	cup heavy whipping cream, divided
3½	cups pecan halves
½	cup semisweet chocolate chips, melted

1. Preheat oven to 450°. Unroll pie crust on a lightly floured surface. Transfer to an 11-in. fluted tart pan with removable bottom; trim edges.
2. Line unpricked pie crust with a double thickness of heavy-duty foil. Bake 8 minutes. Remove foil; bake until light golden brown, 5-6 minutes longer. Cool on a wire rack.
3. In a large saucepan, combine caramels and ½ cup cream. Cook and stir over medium-low heat until caramels are melted. Stir in pecans. Spread filling evenly into crust. Drizzle with melted chocolate.
4. Refrigerate until set, about 30 minutes. Whip remaining cream; serve with tart.

1 piece 335 cal., 24g fat (4g sat. fat), 4mg chol., 106mg sod., 31g carb. (19g sugars, 3g fiber), 4g pro.

Lemonade Icebox Pie

High and fluffy, this pie has a creamy consistency that we really appreciate. It's comes to mind immediately when I plan summer meals.
—Cheryl Wilt, Eglon, WV

Prep: 15 min. + chilling
Makes: 8 servings

- 1   pkg. (8 oz.) cream cheese, softened
- 1   can (14 oz.) sweetened condensed milk
- ¾   cup thawed lemonade concentrate
- 1   carton (8 oz.) frozen whipped topping, thawed
      Yellow food coloring, optional
- 1   graham cracker crust (9 in.)

In a large bowl, beat cream cheese and milk until smooth. Beat in lemonade concentrate. Fold in whipped topping and, if desired, food coloring. Pour into crust. Cover and refrigerate until set.

Note Sweetened condensed milk is made with cow's milk from which water has been removed and to which sugar has been added, yielding a very thick, sweet canned product. It is used most often in candy and dessert recipes.

1 piece 491 cal., 24g fat (15g sat. fat), 48mg chol., 269mg sod., 61g carb. (52g sugars, 0 fiber), 7g pro.

Orange Icebox Pie Substitute ¾ cup thawed orange juice concentrate for lemonade, add ½ tsp. grated orange peel and omit food coloring.

Creamy Pineapple Pie Substitute 1 can (8 oz.) crushed, undrained pineapple and ¼ cup lemon juice for lemonade. Omit cream cheese and food coloring.

Cool Lime Pie Substitute ¾ cup thawed limeade concentrate for lemonade and use green food coloring instead of yellow.

Hummingbird Cake

This impressive cake is my dad's favorite, so I always make it for his birthday. The beautiful, old-fashioned layered delight makes a memorable celebration dessert any time of year.
—Nancy Zimmerman,
Cape May Court House, NJ

Prep: 40 min.
Bake: 25 min. + cooling
Makes: 14 servings

2   cups mashed ripe bananas
1½ cups canola oil
3   large eggs, room temperature
1   can (8 oz.) unsweetened
     crushed pineapple, undrained
1½ tsp. vanilla extract
3   cups all-purpose flour
2   cups sugar
1   tsp. salt
1   tsp. baking soda
1   tsp. ground cinnamon
1   cup chopped walnuts

Pineapple Frosting
¼   cup shortening
2   Tbsp. butter, softened
1   tsp. grated lemon zest
¼   tsp. salt
6   cups confectioners' sugar
½   cup unsweetened pineapple
     juice
2   tsp. half-and-half cream
     Chopped walnuts, optional

1. In a large bowl, beat the bananas, oil, eggs, pineapple and vanilla until well blended. In another bowl, combine the flour, sugar, salt, baking soda and cinnamon; gradually beat into banana mixture until blended. Stir in walnuts.

2. Pour into 3 greased and floured 9-in. round baking pans. Bake at 350° until a toothpick inserted in the center comes out clean, 25-30 minutes. Cool for 10 minutes before removing from pans to wire racks to cool completely.

3. For frosting, in a large bowl, beat the shortening, butter, lemon zest and salt until fluffy. Add confectioners' sugar alternately with pineapple juice. Beat in cream. Spread between layers and over top and side of cake. If desired, sprinkle with walnuts.

1 piece 777 cal., 35g fat (6g sat. fat), 50mg chol., 333mg sod., 113g carb. (85g sugars, 2g fiber), 7g pro.

To Make Ahead

To make hummingbird cake ahead of time, simply prepare and bake the cake layers. Once cool, the layers can be wrapped and kept in the fridge for 1-2 days or frozen for up to 1 month. Similarly, you can make the frosting ahead of time and keep it in the fridge for 1-2 days before it's time to frost the cake. Let cake layers and frosting come to room temperature before assembling.

Peach Pie

I acquired this delicious peach pie filling recipe some 40 years ago, when my husband and I first moved to southern Iowa and had peach trees growing in our backyard. It's been a family favorite since then and always brings back memories of both summer and those happy early years.
—June Mueller, Sioux City, IA

Prep: 35 min. + standing
Bake: 50 min. + cooling
Makes: 8 servings

- ½ cup sugar
- ¼ cup packed brown sugar
- 4½ cups sliced peeled peaches
  Dough for double-crust pie
- 3 Tbsp. cornstarch
- ¼ tsp. ground nutmeg
- ¼ tsp. ground cinnamon
- ⅛ tsp. salt
- 2 tsp. lemon juice
- 1 Tbsp. butter
  Vanilla ice cream, optional

1. In a large bowl, combine sugars; add peaches and toss gently. Cover and let stand for 1 hour. On a lightly floured surface, roll 1 half of dough to a ⅛-in.-thick circle; transfer to a 9-in. pie plate or iron skillet. Trim even with rim. Refrigerate while preparing filling.
2. Preheat oven to 400°. Drain peaches, reserving juice. In a small saucepan, combine cornstarch, nutmeg, cinnamon and salt; gradually stir in reserved juice. Bring to a boil; cook and stir until thickened, about 2 minutes. Remove from the heat; stir in lemon juice and butter. Gently fold in peaches. Pour into crust.
3. Roll remaining dough to a ⅛-in.-thick circle; cut into 1½-in.-wide strips. Arrange over filling in a lattice pattern. Trim and seal strips to edge of bottom crust; flute edge. Cover edge loosely with foil. Bake 40 minutes; remove foil. Bake until crust is golden brown and filling is bubbly, 10-20 minutes longer. Cool on a wire rack. If desired, serve with vanilla ice cream.

Dough for double-crust pie
Combine 2½ cups all-purpose flour and ½ tsp. salt; cut in 1 cup cold butter until crumbly. Gradually add ⅓ -⅔ cup ice water, tossing with a fork until dough holds together when pressed. Divide dough in half. Shape each into a disk; wrap and refrigerate 1 hour.

1 piece 477 cal., 25g fat (15g sat. fat), 64mg chol., 360mg sod., 60g carb. (27g sugars, 2g fiber), 5g pro.

Pot of S'mores

This easy Dutch-oven version of the popular campout treat is so good and gooey. The hardest part is waiting for it to cool a bit so you can dig in. Yum!
—June Dress, Meridian, ID

Takes: 25 min. • **Makes:** 12 servings

- 1 pkg. (14½ oz.) graham crackers, crushed
- ½ cup butter, melted
- 1 can (14 oz.) sweetened condensed milk
- 2 cups semisweet chocolate chips
- 1 cup butterscotch chips
- 2 cups miniature marshmallows

1. Prepare grill or campfire for low heat, using 16-18 charcoal briquettes or large wood chips.
2. Line a cast-iron Dutch oven with heavy-duty aluminum foil. Combine cracker crumbs and butter; press into bottom of pan. Pour milk over crust and sprinkle with chocolate and butterscotch chips. Top with marshmallows.
3. Cover Dutch oven. When briquettes or wood chips are covered with white ash, place Dutch oven directly on top of 6 of them. Using long-handled tongs, place remaining briquettes on pan cover.
4. Cook until marshmallows begin to melt, about 15 minutes. To check for doneness, use the tongs to carefully lift the cover.
1 serving 584 cal., 28g fat (17g sat. fat), 31mg chol., 326mg sod., 83g carb. (47g sugars, 3g fiber), 8g pro.

"Wow, are these ever good! We made them in our backyard fire pit and love them!"

—AngelRyan75, tasteofhome.com

Apple Pie Cupcakes with Cinnamon Buttercream

These apple pie cupcakes are always a hit! They are so easy to make and the flavor just screams fall. Of course, they're just as delicious any other time of year.

—Jennifer Stowell, Deep River, IA

Prep: 20 min.
Bake: 20 min. + cooling
Makes: 2 dozen

- 1   pkg. yellow cake mix (regular size)
- 2   Tbsp. butter
- 4   medium tart apples, peeled and finely chopped (about 4 cups)
- ¾   cup packed brown sugar
- 1   Tbsp. cornstarch
- 1   Tbsp. water

Frosting
- 1   cup butter, softened
- 3   cups confectioners' sugar
- 2   Tbsp. heavy whipping cream
- 1   tsp. vanilla extract
- 1½ tsp. ground cinnamon
      Thinly sliced apples, optional

1. Prepare and bake cake mix according to package directions for 24 cupcakes; cool cupcakes completely.

2. In a large skillet, heat butter over medium heat. Add apples and brown sugar; cook and stir until apples are tender, 10-12 minutes. In a small bowl, mix cornstarch and water until smooth; stir into pan. Bring to a boil; cook and stir until thickened, 1-2 minutes. Remove from heat; cool completely.

3. Using a paring knife, cut a 1-in.-wide cone-shaped piece from the top of each cupcake; discard removed portion. Fill cavity with apple mixture.

4. In a large bowl, combine the 5 frosting ingredients; beat until smooth. Frost the cupcakes. If desired, garnish with apple slices just before serving.

1 cupcake 300 cal., 15g fat (7g sat. fat), 48mg chol., 221mg sod., 41g carb. (32g sugars, 1g fiber), 1g pro.

Chocolate-Covered Cheesecake Squares

Satisfy your cheesecake craving with these bite-sized delights! The party favorites are perfect for the holidays when there are so many sweets to choose from.

—Esther Neustaeter, La Crete, AB

Prep: 1½ hours + standing
Bake: 35 min. + freezing
Makes: 49 squares

- 1 cup graham cracker crumbs
- ¼ cup finely chopped pecans
- ¼ cup butter, melted

Filling
- 2 pkg. (8 oz. each) cream cheese, softened
- ½ cup sugar
- ¼ cup sour cream
- 2 large eggs, room temperature, lightly beaten
- ½ tsp. vanilla extract

Coating
- 24 oz. semisweet chocolate, chopped
- 3 Tbsp. shortening

1. Preheat oven to 325°. Line a 9-in. square baking pan with foil and grease the foil. In a small bowl, combine graham cracker crumbs, pecans and butter. Press onto bottom of prepared pan.

2. In a large bowl, beat cream cheese, sugar and sour cream until smooth. Add eggs and vanilla; beat on low speed just until combined. Pour over crust. Bake until center is almost set, 35-40 minutes. Cool on a wire rack. Freeze overnight.

3. In a microwave, melt chocolate and shortening; stir until smooth. Cool slightly.

4. Using foil, lift cheesecake out of pan. Gently peel off foil. Cut cheesecake into 1¼-in. squares; refrigerate. Remove a few squares at a time for dipping, keeping remaining squares refrigerated until ready to dip.

5. Using a toothpick, completely dip squares, 1 at a time, into melted chocolate mixture; allow excess to drip off. Place on waxed paper-lined baking sheets. Spoon additional chocolate over the tops if necessary to coat. (Reheat chocolate if needed to finish dipping.) Let stand for 20 minutes or until set. Store in an airtight container in the refrigerator or freezer.

1 piece 141 cal., 10g fat (6g sat. fat), 22mg chol., 48mg sod., 12g carb. (10g sugars, 1g fiber), 2g pro.

Mint Oreo Milkshakes

These kid-pleasing shakes are sure to be a hit at Christmas. Top them off with whipped cream and crushed cookies.
—*Taste of Home* Test Kitchen

Takes: 10 min. • **Makes:** 5 servings

- 1½ cups 2% milk
- 4½ cups vanilla ice cream
- 15 mint creme Oreo cookies, crushed
- ½ tsp. peppermint extract
  Whipped cream and additional crushed mint creme Oreo cookies

In a blender, combine the milk, ice cream, cookies and extract; cover and process until smooth. Pour into chilled glasses. Garnish with whipped cream and additional cookies. Serve immediately.
1 cup 487 cal., 25g fat (11g sat. fat), 58mg chol., 312mg sod., 62g carb. (44g sugars, 2g fiber), 8g pro.

Dream Up Your Own Milkshake Flavors

- Instead of mint-flavored Oreos and peppermint extract, use regular Oreo cookies and vanilla extract.

- Reach for chocolate ice cream and Chocolate Creme Oreos; omit extract.

- Make their day with Birthday Cake Oreos, rainbow sprinkles and a few drops of butter extract instead of the peppermint extract.

Apricot Almond Torte

This pretty cake takes a bit of time, so I like to make the layers in advance and assemble it the day of serving, which make it an easier option for entertaining.
—Trisha Kruse, Eagle, ID

Prep: 45 min.
Bake: 25 min. + cooling
Makes: 12 servings

- 3 large eggs
- 1½ cups sugar
- 1 tsp. vanilla extract
- 1¾ cups all-purpose flour
- 1 cup ground almonds, toasted
- 2 tsp. baking powder
- ½ tsp. salt
- 1½ cups heavy whipping cream, whipped

Frosting
- 1 pkg. (8 oz.) cream cheese, softened
- 1 cup sugar
- ⅛ tsp. salt
- 1 tsp. almond extract
- 1½ cups heavy whipping cream, whipped
- 1 jar (10 to 12 oz.) apricot preserves
- ½ cup slivered almonds, toasted

1. Preheat oven to 350°. In a large bowl, beat eggs, sugar and vanilla on high speed until thick and lemon-colored. Combine flour, almonds, baking powder and salt; gradually fold into egg mixture alternately with the whipped cream.
2. Transfer to 2 greased and floured 9-in. round baking pans. Bake until a toothpick inserted in the center comes out clean, 22-28 minutes. Cool 10 minutes before removing from pans to wire racks to cool completely.
3. For frosting, in a large bowl, beat cream cheese, sugar and salt until smooth. Beat in extract. Fold in whipped cream.
4. Cut each cake horizontally into 2 layers. Place 1 layer on a serving plate; spread with 1 cup frosting. Top with another cake layer; spread with half the preserves. Repeat layers. Frost side of cake; decorate the top edge with remaining frosting. Sprinkle with almonds.
1 piece 546 cal., 25g fat (12g sat. fat), 115mg chol., 284mg sod., 75g carb. (51g sugars, 2g fiber), 8g pro.

Chocolate Chip Blondies

Folks who love chocolate chip cookies can enjoy that same flavor in these golden bars. They can be mixed up in a jiffy and taste wonderful—perfect for occasions when company drops by unexpectedly or you need a treat in a hurry.

—Rhonda Knight, Hecker, IL

Takes: 30 min. • **Makes:** 3 dozen

- 1½ cups packed brown sugar
- ½ cup butter, melted
- 2 large eggs, lightly beaten, room temperature
- 1 tsp. vanilla extract
- 1½ cups all-purpose flour
- ½ tsp. baking powder
- ½ tsp. salt
- 1 cup semisweet chocolate chips

1. In a large bowl, combine the brown sugar, butter, eggs and vanilla just until blended. Combine the flour, baking powder and salt; add to brown sugar mixture. Stir in chocolate chips.

2. Spread mixture into a greased 13x9-in. baking pan. Bake at 350° until a toothpick inserted in the center comes out clean, 18-20 minutes. Cool on a wire rack. Cut into bars.

1 blondie 102 cal., 4g fat (2g sat. fat), 19mg chol., 72mg sod., 16g carb. (12g sugars, 0 fiber), 1g pro.

Go Over the Top

To make extravagant sundaes, serve these bars with chocolate or mint chip ice cream, warm fudge sauce, dollops of whipped cream, and chopped nuts or chocolate candies.

Old-Fashioned Chocolate Pudding

One of the nice things about this easy pudding is you don't have to stand and stir it. It's a must for my family year-round! I also make it into a pie with a graham cracker crust that our grandchildren love.

—Amber Sampson, Somonauk, IL

Prep: 10 min. + chilling
Cook: 30 min. cooling
Makes: 4 servings

- 2 cups whole milk
- 2 Tbsp. butter
- 2 oz. unsweetened chocolate, chopped
- ⅔ cup sugar
- ⅓ cup all-purpose flour
- ¼ tsp. salt
- 2 large egg yolks, beaten
- ½ tsp. vanilla extract
  Whipped cream, optional

1. In a double boiler or metal bowl over simmering water, heat the milk, butter and chocolate until chocolate is melted (chocolate may appear curdled).

2. Combine sugar, flour and salt. Sprinkle over chocolate mixture (do not stir). Cover and continue to cook in a double boiler over medium-low heat for 20 minutes. With a wooden spoon, stir until smooth. Remove from the heat.

3. Stir a small amount of the hot mixture into egg yolks; return all to the pan, stirring constantly. Cook and stir until mixture is thickened and a thermometer reads 160°. Remove from heat; stir in vanilla. Cool for 15 minutes, stirring occasionally. Transfer to dessert dishes.

4. Cover and refrigerate for 1 hour. If desired, top with whipped cream.
⅔ cup 413 cal., 20g fat (11g sat. fat), 120mg chol., 254mg sod., 52g carb. (40g sugars, 3g fiber), 8g pro.

Lemon Anise Biscotti

With the growing popularity of gourmet coffees, cappuccino and espresso, I'm finding lots of people enjoy these classic Sicilian dipping cookies.

—Carrie Sherrill, Forestville, WI

Prep: 25 min.
Bake: 40 min. + cooling
Makes: 3 dozen

2 large eggs, room temperature
1 cup sugar
¼ cup canola oil
½ tsp. lemon extract
¼ tsp. vanilla extract
2 cups all-purpose flour
1 tsp. baking powder
½ tsp. salt
4 tsp. grated lemon zest
2 tsp. aniseed, crushed

Optional Glaze
2 cups confectioners' sugar
3 to 4 Tbsp. lemon juice
Grated lemon zest

1. Preheat oven to 350°. In a small bowl, beat eggs and sugar for 2 minutes or until thickened. Add oil and extracts; mix well. Combine flour, baking powder and salt; beat into egg mixture. Beat in lemon zest and aniseed.

2. Divide dough in half. On a lightly floured surface, shape each portion into a 12x2-in. rectangle. Transfer to a baking sheet lined with parchment. Flatten to ½-in. thickness.

3. Bake until golden and tops begin to crack, 30-35 minutes. Carefully remove to wire racks; cool for 5 minutes.

4. Transfer to a cutting board; cut with a serrated knife into scant ¾-in. slices. Place cut side down on ungreased baking sheets. Bake 5 minutes. Turn and bake until firm and golden brown, 5-7 minutes. Remove to wire racks to cool completely. If using glaze, whisk confectioners' sugar and lemon juice in a small bowl. Drizzle over biscotti; sprinkle with lemon zest. Store in an airtight container.

1 cookie 65 cal., 2g fat (0 sat. fat), 10mg chol., 50mg sod., 11g carb. (6g sugars, 0 fiber), 1g pro.

Thick Strawberry Shakes

Cool off with a thick and rich treat that will remind you of a malt shoppe!
—Kathryn Conrad, Milwaukee, WI

Takes: 5 min. • **Makes:** 2 servings

- ⅓ cup 2% milk
- 1½ cups vanilla ice cream
- ½ cup frozen unsweetened strawberries
- 1 Tbsp. strawberry preserves

In a blender, combine all ingredients; cover and process until smooth. Pour into chilled glasses; serve immediately.

1 cup 257 cal., 12g fat (7g sat. fat), 47mg chol., 100mg sod., 35g carb. (28g sugars, 1g fiber), 5g pro.

"This was absolutely delicious. I made this shake with fresh strawberries and unsweetened soy milk. I left out the preserves as I do not like overly sweet shakes. It was creamy and delicious. Perfect for any age."
—Penny409, tasteofhome.com

Pecan Pumpkin Pie

A rich, crispy pecan topping and maple syrup give this creamy pumpkin pie a crunchy, mouthwatering twist. It's like getting two pies in one. Yum!
—Deborah Whitley, Nashville, TN

Prep: 10 min.
Bake: 55 min. + chilling
Makes: 8 servings

	Dough for single-crust pie
2	large eggs
1	can (15 oz.) pumpkin
½	cup maple syrup
¼	cup sugar
¼	cup heavy whipping cream
1	tsp. ground cinnamon
½	tsp. ground nutmeg

Topping

2	large eggs, lightly beaten
1	cup chopped pecans
½	cup sugar
½	cup maple syrup
	Whipped topping, optional

1. Preheat oven to 425°. On a lightly floured surface, roll dough to a ⅛-in.-thick circle; transfer to a 9-in. pie plate. Trim crust to ½ in. beyond rim of plate; flute edge. In a large bowl, beat eggs, pumpkin, syrup, sugar, cream, cinnamon and nutmeg until smooth; pour into crust.
2. For topping, in a large bowl, combine eggs, pecans, sugar and syrup; spoon over top.
3. Bake for 15 minutes. Reduce oven temperature to 350°. Bake until crust is golden brown and top of pie is set, 40-45 minutes longer. Cool on a wire rack for 1 hour. Refrigerate overnight. If desired, serve with whipped topping.

Dough for single-crust pie
Combine 1¼ cups all-purpose flour and ¼ tsp. salt; cut in ½ cup cold butter until crumbly. Gradually add 3-5 Tbsp. ice water, tossing with a fork until dough holds together when pressed. Shape into a disk; wrap and refrigerate 1 hour.
1 piece 524 cal., 27g fat (11g sat. fat), 132mg chol., 200mg sod., 68g carb. (46g sugars, 4g fiber), 7g pro.

Pie Tips

Should I blind bake the crust? You don't need to blind bake the crust for this pie. It bakes in the oven long enough that the crust will cook as the filling cooks.

How do I prevent a soggy bottom crust on this pie? Bake the pie in the lower third of the oven.

How do I stop my crust from burning? Use a pie shield to protect the crust. If you don't have one, you can improvise one by shaping aluminum foil around the top edge of the pie.

Easy Fudgy Brownies

I can stir up these moist and chocolaty brownies in a snap. They're oh-so-easy to make and oh-so-scrumptious to eat!

Evie Gloistein, Susanville, CA

Prep: 15 min. • **Bake:** 35 min.
Makes: 32 brownies

- ½ cup butter, cubed
- 4 oz. unsweetened chocolate, chopped
- 2 cups sugar
- 4 large eggs, lightly beaten
- 1 tsp. vanilla extract
- ½ cup all-purpose flour
- ½ tsp. salt
- 2 cups chopped pecans, optional
  Confectioners' sugar, optional

1. In a microwave, melt butter and chocolate; stir until smooth. Cool slightly. In a large bowl, beat sugar and eggs. Stir in vanilla and chocolate mixture. Combine flour and salt; gradually add to chocolate mixture. Stir in pecans if desired.
2. Spread into 2 greased 8-in. square baking pans. Bake at 325° for 35-40 minutes or until a toothpick inserted in the center comes out clean. Cool on a wire rack. Dust with confectioners' sugar if desired. Cut into bars.
1 brownie 113 cal., 5g fat (3g sat. fat), 31mg chol., 70mg sod., 15g carb. (13g sugars, 1g fiber), 2g pro.

Banana Chocolate Chip Cookies

These soft cookies have a cakelike texture and lots of banana flavor that everyone seem to love. It's one of the best banana cookie recipes I've found.
—Vicki Raatz, Waterloo, WI

Prep: 20 min. • **Bake:** 15 min./batch
Makes: 3 dozen

- ⅓ cup butter, softened
- ½ cup sugar
- 1 large egg, room temperature
- ½ cup mashed ripe banana
- ½ tsp. vanilla extract
- 1¼ cups all-purpose flour
- 1 tsp. baking powder
- ¼ tsp. salt
- ⅛ tsp. baking soda
- 1 cup semisweet chocolate chips

1. In a small bowl, cream butter and sugar until light and fluffy, 5-7 minutes. Beat in the egg, banana and vanilla. Combine the flour, baking powder, salt and baking soda; gradually add to creamed mixture and mix well. Stir in chocolate chips.
2. Drop by tablespoonfuls 2 in. apart onto baking sheets coated with cooking spray. Bake at 350° for 13-16 minutes or until edges are lightly browned. Remove to wire racks to cool.
1 cookie 69 cal., 3g fat (2g sat. fat), 10mg chol., 50mg sod., 10g carb. (6g sugars, 0 fiber), 1g pro. **Diabetic exchanges** ½ starch, ½ fat.

Bread Pudding with White Chocolate Sauce

A delectable white chocolate sauce is the crowning touch on servings of this comforting cinnamon bread pudding.

—Kathy Rundle, Fond du Lac, WI

Prep: 30 min. + standing
Bake: 55 min.
Makes: 12 servings (1½ cups sauce)

- 16 slices cinnamon bread, crusts removed, cubed
- 1 cup dried cranberries
- ¾ cup white baking chips
- ¾ cup chopped pecans
- ¼ cup butter, melted
- 6 large eggs, lightly beaten
- 4 cups 2% milk
- ¾ cup plus 1 Tbsp. sugar, divided
- 1 tsp. vanilla extract
- ¼ tsp. ground cinnamon
- ¼ tsp. ground allspice

Sauce

- ⅔ cup heavy whipping cream
- 2 Tbsp. butter
- 8 oz. white baking chocolate, chopped

1. Preheat oven to 375°. In a greased 13x9-in. baking dish, layer half of the bread cubes, cranberries, baking chips and pecans. Repeat layers. Drizzle with butter.

2. In a large bowl, whisk eggs, milk, ¾ cup sugar, vanilla, cinnamon and allspice until blended; pour over bread mixture. Let stand for 15-30 minutes.

3. Sprinkle with remaining sugar. Bake, uncovered, until a knife inserted in the center comes out clean, 55-65 minutes. Cover loosely with foil during the last 15 minutes if top browns too quickly.

4. In a small saucepan, bring cream and butter to a boil. Add chocolate and remove from the heat (do not stir). Let stand for 5 minutes; whisk until smooth. Serve with warm bread pudding.

1 piece with 2 Tbsp. sauce 495 cal., 29g fat (13g sat. fat), 153mg chol., 300mg sod., 54g carb. (31g sugars, 4g fiber), 12g pro.

Bread Pudding Tips

Can I use other types of bread to make this bread pudding? Absolutely! Other day-old bread or leftover bread you have on hand, such as brioche, French bread or challah, will work too. You might, however, need to adjust the spices and add more cinnamon.

Can I make this ahead of time? Yes, bread pudding recipes are good time-savers because they can be prepped or baked ahead of time. They warm up well in the microwave or oven.

One-Bowl Chocolate Cake

This cake mixes up quickly and bakes while we enjoy our dinner. My son, David, loves to help decorate it.
—Coleen Martin, Brookfield, WI

Prep: 15 min.
Bake: 35 min. + cooling
Makes: 15 servings

- 2 cups all-purpose flour
- 2 cups sugar
- ½ cup baking cocoa
- 2 tsp. baking soda
- 1 tsp. baking powder
- ½ tsp. salt
- 2 large eggs, room temperature, lightly beaten
- 1 cup canola oil
- 1 cup buttermilk
- 1 cup hot water
- Frosting of your choice
- Colored sprinkles, optional

1. Preheat oven to 350°. Grease a 13x9-in. baking pan. In a large bowl, whisk the first 6 ingredients. Stir in eggs, oil and buttermilk. Add water; stir until combined.
2. Transfer batter to prepared pan. Bake 35-40 minutes or until a toothpick inserted in center comes out clean. Cool completely in pan on a wire rack. Frost cake. If desired, decorate with sprinkles.
1 piece 297 cal., 15g fat (2g sat. fat), 27mg chol., 281mg sod., 39g carb. (25g sugars, 1g fiber), 3g pro.

"Definitely a five-star chocolate cake recipe in my family! Stayed moist for days, even though my husband and I could have devoured it the same day. Easy and simple to put together when you're short on time."

—Vicki385, tasteofhome.com

Fudge Sundae Pie

My son always asks for this guilt-free frozen yogurt pie for his birthday. Complete with peanut butter, fudge topping and nuts, it tastes ice cream parlor good ... but it's healthier.
—Margaret Riley, Tallahassee, FL

Prep: 20 min. + freezing
Makes: 8 servings

- ¼ cup plus 3 Tbsp. light corn syrup, divided
- 3 Tbsp. butter
- 2 Tbsp. brown sugar
- 2½ cups crisp rice cereal
- ¼ cup reduced-fat creamy peanut butter
- ¼ cup fat-free hot fudge ice cream topping, warmed
- ¼ cup chopped unsalted peanuts
- 4 cups fat-free vanilla frozen yogurt, softened

1. In a large saucepan, combine ¼ cup corn syrup, butter and brown sugar. Bring to a boil; cook and stir for 1 minute.
2. Remove from the heat; stir in cereal until blended. Press into a greased 9-in. pie plate.
3. In a small bowl, combine the peanut butter, hot fudge topping and remaining corn syrup. Set aside ⅓ cup for topping. Spread remaining mixture over crust; sprinkle with half the peanuts. Top with frozen yogurt. Freeze, covered, for 6 hours or until firm.
4. Warm reserved peanut butter mixture; drizzle over pie. Sprinkle with remaining peanuts. Let stand at room temperature for 5 minutes before cutting.
1 piece 300 cal., 7g fat (2g sat. fat), 7mg chol., 253mg sod., 53g carb. (33g sugars, 1g fiber), 9g pro.

Apple & Herb Roasted
Turkey, Page 247

Celebrate

Valentine Heart Brownies

Steal hearts this Valentine's Day with brownies that have yummy frosting centers. They're simply irresistible.
—Taste of Home Test Kitchen

Prep: 30 min.
Bake: 20 min. + cooling
Makes: 15 servings

- 1 pkg. fudge brownie mix (13x9-in. pan size)
- ¼ tsp. mint extract
- ½ cup butter, softened
- 1½ cups confectioners' sugar
- ¼ tsp. vanilla extract
  Red paste food coloring, optional
- ¼ cup baking cocoa
  Heart-shaped sprinkles, optional

1. Prepare brownie mix according to package directions, adding mint extract to batter. Transfer to a greased 13x9-in. baking pan. Bake at 350° for 20-25 minutes or until a toothpick inserted in the center comes out clean. Cool completely on a wire rack.
2. Meanwhile, cream the butter, confectioners' sugar, vanilla and, if desired, food coloring until light and fluffy, 3-4 minutes. Transfer to a pastry bag. Set aside.
3. Line a baking sheet with parchment. Dust with cocoa; set aside. Cut brownies into 15 rectangles. Using a 1½-in. heart-shaped cookie cutter, cut out a heart from the center of each brownie. Reserve cutout centers for another use. Place brownies on prepared baking sheet. Pipe frosting into centers of brownies. If desired, top with sprinkles.
1 brownie 334 cal., 18g fat (6g sat. fat), 42mg chol., 201mg sod., 41g carb. (30g sugars, 1g fiber), 3g pro.

Be-Mine Sandwich Cookies

These simple cookies are the first thing to disappear from dessert tables. They're cute, colorful and extremely fast to make.
—Darcie Cross, Novi, MI

Takes: 20 min. • **Makes:** 50 cookies

- 6 oz. white or milk chocolate candy coating, coarsely chopped
- 50 Oreo cookies
  Assorted candy sprinkles or decorations

In a microwave, melt 2 oz. of candy coating at a time, stirring until smooth. Spread over cookie tops; decorate immediately. Place on waxed paper until set.
1 cookie 65 cal., 3g fat (1g sat. fat), 0 chol., 67mg sod., 9g carb. (6g sugars, 0 fiber), 1g pro.

"Even kids can put these together easily. Depending on the color of the sprinkles, these are perfect for any occasion. Something kids can make and give to teachers and friends."
—frombraziltoyou, tasteofhome.com

St. Paddy's Irish Beef Dinner

A variation on shepherd's pie, this hearty dish brings together saucy beef with mashed potatoes, parsnips and other vegetables. It's always the star of our March 17 meal.

—Lorraine Caland, Shuniah, ON

Prep: 25 min. • **Cook:** 35 min.
Makes: 4 servings

- 2 medium Yukon Gold potatoes
- 2 small parsnips
- ¾ lb. lean ground beef (90% lean)
- 1 medium onion, chopped
- 2 cups finely shredded cabbage
- 2 medium carrots, halved and sliced
- 1 tsp. dried thyme
- 1 tsp. Worcestershire sauce
- 1 Tbsp. all-purpose flour
- ¼ cup tomato paste
- 1 can (14½ oz.) reduced-sodium chicken or beef broth
- ½ cup frozen peas
- ¾ tsp. salt, divided
- ½ tsp. pepper, divided
- ¼ cup 2% milk
- 1 Tbsp. butter

1. Peel potatoes and parsnips and cut into large pieces; place in a large saucepan and cover with water. Bring to a boil. Reduce heat; cover and cook for 10-15 minutes or until tender. Drain.
2. Meanwhile, in a large skillet, cook beef and onion over medium heat until meat is no longer pink; drain. Stir in the cabbage, carrots, thyme and Worcestershire sauce.
3. In a small bowl, combine the flour, tomato paste and broth until smooth. Gradually stir into the meat mixture. Bring to a boil. Reduce heat; cover and simmer for 15-20 minutes or until the vegetables are tender. Stir in peas, ¼ tsp. salt and ¼ tsp. pepper.
4. Drain the potatoes and parsnips; mash with milk, butter and the remaining ½ tsp. salt and ¼ tsp. pepper. Serve with the meat mixture.
1 serving 369 cal., 11g fat (5g sat. fat), 62mg chol., 849mg sod., 46g carb. (13g sugars, 8g fiber), 24g pro.
Diabetic exchanges 3 lean meat, 2 starch, 2 vegetable.

St. Paddy's Irish Beef Dinner Tips

How do I store this recipe?
Store the mashed potatoes and parsnips and the beef mixture in separate airtight containers in the fridge. Both components should last 3 to 4 days.

What are some variations of this recipe? The easiest way to switch up this dinner is by adding another vegetable, such as corn, into the mix.

Colcannon Potatoes

Every Irish family has its own version of this classic dish. My recipe comes from my father's family in Ireland. It's always part of my St. Patrick's Day menu, along with lamb chops, carrots and soda bread.

—Marilou Robinson, Portland, OR

Prep: 25 min. • **Cook:** 35 min.
Makes: 12 servings

- 1   medium head cabbage (about 2 lbs.), shredded
- 4   lbs. medium potatoes (about 8), peeled and quartered
- 2   cups whole milk
- 1   cup chopped green onions
- 1½ tsp. salt
- ½   tsp. pepper
- ¼   cup butter, melted
      Minced fresh parsley
      Crumbled cooked bacon

1. Place cabbage and 2 cups water in a large saucepan; bring to a boil. Reduce heat; simmer, covered, until cabbage is tender, about 10 minutes. Drain, reserving the cooking liquid; keep the cabbage warm in a separate dish.
2. In same pan, combine potatoes and reserved cooking liquid. Add additional water to cover potatoes; bring to a boil. Reduce heat; cook, uncovered, until potatoes are tender, 15-20 minutes. Meanwhile, place milk, green onions, salt and pepper in a small saucepan; bring just to a boil and remove from heat.
3. Drain potatoes; place in a large bowl and mash. Add milk mixture; beat just until blended. Stir in cabbage. To serve, drizzle with butter; top with parsley and bacon.
1 cup 168 cal., 5g fat (3g sat. fat), 14mg chol., 361mg sod., 27g carb. (6g sugars, 4g fiber), 4g pro.
Diabetic exchanges 2 starch, 1 fat.

Homemade Irish Soda Bread

Some people consider bread to be the most important part of a meal—and this Irish bread satisfies such folks! This recipe is by far the best soda bread I've ever tried. With the addition of raisins, it is moist and delicious!

—Evelyn Kenney, Trenton, NJ

Prep: 20 min. • **Bake:** 1 hour
Makes: 1 loaf

- 4   cups all-purpose flour
- ¼   cup sugar
- 1   tsp. salt
- 1   tsp. baking powder
- 1   tsp. baking soda
- ¼   cup cold butter, cubed
- 1⅓ cups buttermilk
- 1   large egg
- 2   cups raisins
- 3   to 4 Tbsp. caraway seeds
- 2   Tbsp. 2% milk

1. Preheat oven to 375°. In a large bowl, combine flour, sugar, salt, baking powder and baking soda. Cut in butter until the mixture resembles coarse crumbs. In a separate bowl, whisk buttermilk and egg; stir into the dry ingredients just until moistened. Stir in raisins and caraway seeds.
2. Turn out dough onto a floured surface. Knead gently 8-10 times. Shape into a ball and place on a greased baking pan. Pat into a 7-in. round loaf. Cut a 4-in. cross about ¼ in. deep on top to allow for expansion. Brush top with milk.
3. Bake until golden brown, about 1 hour. Remove from pan to wire rack to cool.
1 piece 223 cal., 4g fat (2g sat. fat), 20mg chol., 326mg sod., 43g carb. (15g sugars, 2g fiber), 5g pro.

Cider-Glazed Ham

Here is a heartwarming and classic way to serve ham. Apple cider and mustard perfectly accent the ham's rich, smoky flavor.
—Jennifer Foos-Furer, Marysville, OH

Prep: 15 min. • **Cook:** 4 hours
Makes: 8 servings

1	boneless fully cooked ham (3 lbs.)
1¾	cups apple cider or juice
¼	cup packed brown sugar
¼	cup Dijon mustard
¼	cup honey
2	Tbsp. cornstarch
2	Tbsp. cold water

1. Place ham in a 5-qt. slow cooker. In a small bowl, combine cider, brown sugar, mustard and honey; pour over the ham. Cover and cook on low for 4-5 hours or until heated through. Remove ham; keep warm.
2. Pour cooking juices into a small saucepan. Combine cornstarch and water until smooth; stir into the cooking juices. Bring to a boil; cook and stir for 2 minutes or until thickened. Serve with ham.

4 oz. cooked ham with about ¼ cup glaze 280 cal., 6g fat (2g sat. fat), 86mg chol., 1954mg sod., 26g carb. (21g sugars, 0 fiber), 31g pro.

Baked Cider-Glazed Ham Place ham on a rack in a shallow roasting pan. Score the surface of the ham, making diamond shapes ½ in. deep. Pour cider over ham. Combine the brown sugar, mustard and honey; spread over ham. Cover and bake at 325° for 45 minutes. Uncover; bake 15-30 minutes longer or until a meat thermometer reads 140°, basting occasionally. Serve as directed.

Orange-Glazed Ham Substitute orange juice for the apple cider.

Peeps Sunflower Cake

With yellow Peeps as the petals of a sunflower, and chocolate chips as the seeds, this pretty cake is a fun finish to any springtime meal.
—Bethany Eledge, Cleveland, TN

Prep: 15 min.
Bake: 30 min. + cooling
Makes: 12 servings

1	yellow cake mix (regular size)
2	cans (16 oz. each) chocolate frosting
19	to 20 yellow chick Peeps candies
1½	cups semisweet chocolate chips (assorted sizes)

1. Prepare and bake cake mix according to package directions, using 2 parchment-lined and greased 9-in. round baking pans. Cool in pans 10 minutes before removing to wire racks; remove paper. Cool completely.
2. If cake layers have rounded tops, trim with a long serrated knife to make level. Spread frosting between layers and over top and side of cake.
3. For petals, arrange Peeps around edge of cake, curving slightly and being careful not to separate chicks. For sunflower seeds, arrange chocolate chips in center of cake.

1 piece 679 cal., 30g fat (10g sat. fat), 47mg chol., 417mg sod., 105g carb. (83g sugars, 2g fiber), 5g pro.

Decorating Pointers

- Thick frosting tends to tear cake. For easier spreading, thin it with 1-2 tsp. water.
- Tweezers come in handy when arranging the chocolate chips.

Lemon Meringue Angel Cake

I've been told that this dessert tastes exactly like a lemon meringue pie and that it's the best angel food cake anyone could ask for. I'm not sure about all of that, but it is delightful to serve, and each slice is virtually fat free.

—Sharon Kurtz, Emmaus, PA

Prep: 40 min.
Bake: 50 min. + cooling
Makes: 14 servings

- 12 large egg whites, room temperature
- 1½ cups sugar, divided
- 1 cup cake flour
- 2 tsp. cream of tartar
- 1½ tsp. vanilla extract
- ¼ tsp. salt
- 1 jar (10 oz.) lemon curd

Meringue
- 4 large egg whites, room temperature
- ¾ tsp. cream of tartar
- ½ cup sugar

1. Place egg whites in a large bowl. Sift ½ cup sugar and the flour together twice; set aside.
2. Add cream of tartar, vanilla and salt to egg whites; beat on medium speed until foamy. Gradually beat in the remaining 1 cup sugar, 2 Tbsp. at a time, on high until stiff glossy peaks form and the sugar is dissolved. Gradually fold in the flour mixture, about ½ cup at a time.
3. Gently spoon batter into an ungreased 10-in. tube pan. Cut through batter with a knife to remove any air pockets. Bake on lowest oven rack at 350° until golden brown and entire top appears dry, 35-40 minutes. Immediately invert pan; cool completely, about 1 hour.

4. Run a knife around side and center tube of pan. Remove cake; split into 2 horizontal layers. Place cake bottom on a parchment-lined baking sheet. Spread with lemon curd; replace cake top.
5. For meringue, in a small bowl, beat egg whites and cream of tartar on medium until soft peaks form. Gradually beat in sugar, 1 Tbsp. at a time, on high until stiff glossy peaks form and the sugar is dissolved. Spread over top and side of cake.

6. Bake at 350° until golden brown, 15-18 minutes. Transfer to a serving plate. Refrigerate leftovers.
1 piece 238 cal., 1g fat (1g sat. fat), 15mg chol., 121mg sod., 51g carb. (41g sugars, 0 fiber), 5g pro.

"I made this for Easter. It was a huge hit! I followed the recipe and it turned out perfect! The flavors, tart and sweet, made for a delicious cake. It even traveled well! I will definitely make this again!"

—Barefoot8251, tasteofhome.com

Orange-Glazed Bunny Rolls

Orange marmalade gives the icing on these tender yeast rolls a pleasant citrus flavor. These are shaped like a bunny, complete with tail, but shape the rolls any way you like for any special occasion.

—Gerri Brown, Canfield, OH

Prep: 45 min. + rising
Bake: 15 min. + cooling
Makes: 1 dozen

- 2 pkg. (¼ oz. each) active dry yeast
- ¼ cup warm water (110° to 115°)
- 1 cup warm 2% milk (110° to 115°)
- ½ cup shortening
- 2 large eggs, room temperature
- ⅓ cup sugar
- ¼ cup orange juice
- 2 Tbsp. grated orange zest
- 1 tsp. salt
- 5 to 5½ cups all-purpose flour

Glaze
- 2 cups confectioners' sugar
- ¼ cup water
- 1 Tbsp. orange marmalade
- ½ tsp. butter, softened

1. In a large bowl, dissolve yeast in warm water. Add milk, shortening, eggs, sugar, orange juice, orange zest, salt and 3 cups flour; beat until smooth. Stir in enough remaining flour to form a soft dough.
2. Turn onto a floured surface; knead until smooth and elastic, 6-8 minutes. Place in a greased bowl, turning once to grease top. Cover and let rise in a warm place until doubled, about 1 hour.
3. Punch dough down; turn on a lightly floured surface. Divide into 13 pieces. Shape 12 pieces into 12-in. ropes. Fold each in half; twist top half of the open end twice to form ears. Place 2 in. apart on greased baking sheets. Shape remaining dough into 12 balls. Place 1 ball on the loop end of each roll; press into dough. Cover and let rise until doubled, about 30 minutes.
4. Bake at 375° until golden brown, 12-15 minutes. Cool on wire racks. Combine glaze ingredients. Spread over rolls.
1 roll 399 cal., 10g fat (3g sat. fat), 39mg chol., 222mg sod., 69g carb. (27g sugars, 2g fiber), 8g pro.

Herbed Asparagus Salad

This salad is a wonderful way to serve fresh-cut asparagus. The tarragon and oregano are a nice surprise in the lemony vinaigrette, and sliced cooked eggs make a pretty garnish.

—Dawn Szalai, Edwardsburg, MI

Prep: 20 min. + chilling
Makes: 8 servings

- 2 lbs. fresh asparagus, cut into 1-in. pieces
- ¾ cup canola oil
- ½ cup lemon juice
- 1½ tsp. sugar
- 1 tsp. salt
- ½ tsp. dried oregano
- ½ tsp. dried tarragon
- ½ tsp. coarsely ground pepper
- 1 garlic clove, minced
- 8 cups torn mixed salad greens
- 3 hard-boiled large eggs, sliced

1. In a large saucepan, bring ½ in. of water to a boil. Add asparagus; boil, covered, for 3 minutes. Drain and immediately place asparagus in ice water. Drain and pat dry. Place in a large bowl.
2. In a small bowl, whisk oil, lemon juice, sugar, salt, oregano, tarragon, pepper and garlic. Pour over the asparagus; cover and refrigerate for at least 2 hours.
3. Place salad greens on a serving platter. With a slotted spoon, arrange asparagus over greens. Garnish with egg slices.
1 serving 240 cal., 23g fat (3g sat. fat), 80mg chol., 339mg sod., 7g carb. (3g sugars, 2g fiber), 5g pro.

Patriotic Ice Cream Cupcakes

These frosty cupcakes are practically a fireworks display on their own. The little treats feature red velvet cake, blue moon ice cream, a creamy white topping and star-spangled sprinkles.
—*Taste of Home* Test Kitchen

Prep: 30 min. + freezing
Bake: 15 min. + cooling
Makes: 3 dozen

- 1 pkg. red velvet cake mix (regular size)
- 1½ qt. blue moon ice cream, softened if necessary
- 1 jar (7 oz.) marshmallow creme
- 3 cups heavy whipping cream
  Red, white and blue sprinkles

1. Preheat oven to 350°. Line 36 muffin cups with paper liners; set aside.

2. Prepare cake batter according to package directions. Fill the prepared cups about one-third full. Bake until a toothpick inserted in the center comes out clean, 11-14 minutes. Cool 10 minutes before removing from pans to wire racks; cool completely.

3. Working quickly, spread ice cream onto cupcakes. Freeze until firm, at least 1 hour.

4. Place marshmallow creme in a large bowl. Add whipping cream; beat until blended and stiff peaks form. Pipe or spread over cupcakes. Decorate with sprinkles. Serve immediately or freeze until firm.

Note Vanilla ice cream tinted with blue food coloring may be substituted for the blue moon ice cream.

1 cupcake 220 cal., 13g fat (6g sat. fat), 46mg chol., 139mg sod., 21g carb. (16g sugars, 0 fiber), 4g pro.

Red, White & Blue Berry Pie

To me, this colorful pie is the epitome of summer. Bright blueberries and raspberries sandwich a white cream cheese layer. I can't imagine a holiday party without this tasty and festive treat!

—Cindy Zarnstorff, Anchorage, AK

Prep: 15 min. + chilling
Bake: 25 min. + cooling
Makes: 8 servings

	Dough for single-crust pie
1½	cups sugar
¼	cup plus 1½ tsp. cornstarch
1½	cups water
4	Tbsp. plus 1½ tsp. raspberry gelatin
1	pint fresh or frozen unsweetened blueberries
1	tsp. lemon juice
1	pint fresh or frozen unsweetened raspberries
4	oz. cream cheese, softened
⅓	cup confectioners' sugar
1¾	cups whipped topping

1. On a lightly floured surface, roll dough to a ⅛-in.-thick circle; transfer to a 9-in. pie plate. Trim to ½ in. beyond rim of plate; flute edge. Refrigerate for 30 minutes. Preheat oven to 425°.
2. Line crust with a double thickness of foil. Fill with pie weights, dried beans or uncooked rice. Bake on a lower oven rack until edge is golden brown, 20-25 minutes. Remove foil and weights; bake until bottom is golden brown, 3-6 minutes longer. Cool completely on a wire rack.
3. In a large saucepan, combine sugar, cornstarch and water until smooth. Bring to a boil; cook and stir until thickened, about 2 minutes. Stir in gelatin until dissolved. Divide mixture in half. Stir blueberries and lemon juice into 1 portion; spread over crust. Chill until set. Gently fold raspberries into the remaining gelatin mixture; cool to room temperature and set aside.
4. Meanwhile, in a small bowl, beat cream cheese and confectioners' sugar until smooth. Fold in whipped topping; spread over the blueberry layer. Refrigerate until filling is set, about 2 hours.
5. Carefully spread raspberry mixture over cream cheese layer. Chill at least 4 hours.

Dough for single-crust pie
Combine 1¼ cups all-purpose flour and ¼ tsp. salt; cut in ½ cup cold butter until crumbly. Gradually add 3-5 Tbsp. ice water, tossing with a fork until dough holds together when pressed. Shape into a disk; wrap and refrigerate 1 hour.

1 piece 460 cal., 15g fat (9g sat. fat), 21mg chol., 161mg sod., 79g carb. (56g sugars, 3g fiber), 3g pro.

"Made this for bridge last night and it was not only pretty but also awesomely delicious. Additionally, I now can make a much tastier glaze for summer fruit pies than the usual strawberry."

—Karen Hitchcock, tasteofhome.com

Lemon-Berry Shortcake

Bake a simple cake using fresh strawberries, and enjoy this summertime classic with a generous layer of whipped topping and berries.
—Meryl Herr, Grand Rapids, MI

Prep: 30 min.
Bake: 20 min. + cooling
Makes: 8 servings

1⅓ cups all-purpose flour
½ cup sugar
2 tsp. baking powder
¼ tsp. salt
1 large egg, room temperature
⅔ cup buttermilk
¼ cup butter, melted
1 tsp. grated lemon zest
1 Tbsp. lemon juice
1 tsp. vanilla extract
1 cup sliced fresh strawberries

Topping
1 cup fresh blackberries
1 cup sliced fresh strawberries
1 Tbsp. lemon juice
1 tsp. sugar
2 cups reduced-fat whipped topping

1. Preheat oven to 350°. Grease and flour a 9-in. round baking pan.
2. In a large bowl, whisk flour, sugar, baking powder and salt. In another bowl, whisk egg, buttermilk, melted butter, lemon zest, lemon juice and vanilla. Add to the dry ingredients; stir just until moistened. Fold in 1 cup of strawberries. Transfer to the prepared pan.
3. Bake until a toothpick inserted in center comes out clean, 20-25 minutes. Cool 10 minutes before removing from pan to a wire rack to cool completely.
4. For topping, toss berries with lemon juice and sugar. To serve, spread whipped topping over cake. Top with berries.
1 piece 252 cal., 9g fat (6g sat. fat), 42mg chol., 245mg sod., 40g carb. (19g sugars, 2g fiber), 4g pro.

Red, White & Blue Salad

Our striking salad drew plenty of attention at our Independence Day party. I use gelatin to create the shimmering stripes.
Laurie Neverman, Denmark, WI

Prep: 30 min. + chilling
Makes: 16 servings

1 pkg. (3 oz.) berry blue gelatin
2 cups boiling water, divided
2½ cups cold water, divided
1 cup fresh blueberries
1 envelope unflavored gelatin
1 cup heavy whipping cream
6 Tbsp. sugar
2 cups sour cream
1 tsp. vanilla extract
1 pkg. (3 oz.) raspberry gelatin
1 cup fresh raspberries
Optional: Whipped topping and additional berries

1. Dissolve berry blue gelatin in 1 cup boiling water; stir in 1 cup cold water. Add blueberries. Pour into a 3-qt. serving bowl. Refrigerate until firm, about 1 hour.
2. In a saucepan, sprinkle unflavored gelatin over ½ cup cold water; let stand for 1 minute. Add cream and sugar; cook and stir over low heat until dissolved. Cool to room temperature. Whisk in sour cream and vanilla. Spoon over the blue layer. Refrigerate until firm.
3. Dissolve raspberry gelatin in the remaining 1 cup hot water; stir in the remaining 1 cup cold water. Add raspberries. Spoon over the cream layer. Chill until set. Top with whipped topping and berries if desired.
1 serving 179 cal., 11g fat (7g sat. fat), 40mg chol., 46mg sod., 18g carb. (16g sugars, 1g fiber), 3g pro.

Pumpkin Sloppy Joes

When my granddaughter gave me eight pumpkins from her garden, I thought I'd tire of cooking with them. Thankfully, I recalled this recipe from a friend. (If you don't have fresh pumpkins, canned works too!)
—Eleanor McReynolds, Scott City, KS

Takes: 30 min. • **Makes:** 8 servings

- 1 lb. ground beef
- ½ cup chopped onion
- 1 garlic clove, minced
- 1 cup canned pumpkin
- 1 can (8 oz.) tomato sauce
- 2 Tbsp. brown sugar
- 2 Tbsp. prepared mustard
- 2 tsp. chili powder
- ½ tsp. salt
- American and mozzarella cheese slices, optional
- 8 hamburger buns, split

1. In a large skillet, cook the beef, onion and garlic over medium heat until meat is no longer pink; drain. Stir in the pumpkin, tomato sauce, brown sugar, mustard, chili powder and salt. Bring to a boil. Reduce heat; simmer, uncovered, for 10 minutes.

2. Meanwhile, if desired, cut out pumpkin shapes from American cheese slices with a pumpkin-shaped cookie cutter. Cut mozzarella cheese into shapes (triangles, half-circles, etc.) to make pumpkin faces. Spoon meat mixture onto buns and, if desired, top each with a cheese pumpkin.

1 sandwich 250 cal., 8g fat (3g sat. fat), 28mg chol., 607mg sod., 30g carb. (9g sugars, 3g fiber), 15g pro.

Mummy Poppers

I wrapped these spicy jalapeno poppers in puff pastry like a mummy. You can tame the heat by adjusting the amount of chipotle peppers.
—Nick Iverson, Denver, CO

Prep: 30 min. • **Bake:** 30 min.
Makes: 32 appetizers

- 1 pkg. (8 oz.) cream cheese, softened
- 2 cups shredded cheddar cheese
- 2 green onions, finely chopped
- 1 to 2 chipotle peppers in adobo sauce, finely chopped
- 2 Tbsp. lime juice
- 1 Tbsp. honey
- ½ tsp. salt
- ½ tsp. ground cumin
- ¼ tsp. pepper
- 16 jalapeno peppers, halved lengthwise and seeded
- 1 pkg. (17.3 oz.) frozen puff pastry, thawed and cut lengthwise into 32 strips

1. Preheat oven to 400°. Beat the first 9 ingredients until blended. Spoon or pipe cheese mixture into pepper halves.

2. Wrap puff pastry strips around pepper halves. Transfer wrapped peppers to parchment-lined baking sheets. Bake until the pastry is golden brown and the cheese is melted, 30-40 minutes.

Note Wear disposable gloves when cutting hot peppers; the oils can burn skin. Avoid touching your face.

1 popper 133 cal., 9g fat (4g sat. fat), 14mg chol., 159mg sod., 10g carb. (1g sugars, 1g fiber), 3g pro.

Scoop Out the Seeds
A measuring teaspoon is a great tool for removing the seeds from peppers.

Spiderweb Dip with Bat Tortilla Chips

We host a yearly Halloween bash, and everyone looks forward to the spidery taco dip with bat-shaped dippers.
—Sonia Candler, Edmonton, AB

Takes: 30 min.
Makes: about 1½ cups dip and about 7 dozen chips

- 20 chipotle chili and pepper tortillas or flour tortillas (8 in.) Cooking spray
- ¾ tsp. garlic salt
- ¾ tsp. ground coriander
- ¾ tsp. paprika
- ⅜ tsp. pepper

Dip
- 1 pkg. (8 oz.) cream cheese, softened
- ¾ cup salsa
- ½ cup prepared guacamole
- 1 to 2 Tbsp. sour cream

1. Preheat oven to 350°. Cut tortillas into bat shapes with a 3¾-in. cookie cutter. Place tortillas on baking sheets coated with cooking spray. Spritz tortillas with cooking spray. Combine garlic salt, coriander, paprika and pepper; sprinkle over the tortillas. Bake until edges just begin to brown, 5-8 minutes.
2. For the dip, combine cream cheese and salsa. Spread into a 9-in. pie plate. Carefully spread guacamole to within 1 in. of edges. Pipe sour cream in thin concentric circles 1 in. apart over guacamole. Beginning with the center circle, gently pull a knife through the circles toward the outer edge. Wipe knife clean. Repeat to complete spiderweb pattern. Serve with tortilla bats.
2 Tbsp. dip with 7 chips 338 cal., 14g fat (5g sat. fat), 22mg chol., 704mg sod., 44g carb. (1g sugars, 1g fiber), 9g pro.

Meringue Bones

This unique treatment for meringue travels well too! You will certainly get requests for the recipe, and folks will be surprised at how simple it is!
—*Taste of Home* Test Kitchen

Prep: 30 min.
Bake: 1½ hours + cooling
Makes: 1 dozen

- 2 large egg whites, room temperature
- ⅛ tsp. cream of tartar
- ½ cup sugar

1. In a small bowl, beat egg whites and cream of tartar on medium speed until soft peaks form. Gradually add sugar, 1 Tbsp. at a time, beating on high until stiff peaks form. Transfer mixture to a pastry bag fitted with a small round tip.
2. On parchment-lined baking sheets, pipe meringue into a 3-in. log. Pipe two 1-in. balls on opposite sides of each end of the log. Repeat with the remaining meringue.
3. Bake at 225° for 1½ hours or until firm. Remove to wire racks to cool. Store in an airtight container.
1 serving 35 cal., 0 fat (0 sat. fat), 0 chol., 9mg sod., 8g carb. (8g sugars, 0 fiber), 1g pro.

Prime Rib with Horseradish Sauce

When we want to celebrate with friends, a menu featuring tender prime rib is festive yet simple to prepare. A pepper rub and mild horseradish sauce complement the beef's wonderful flavor.
—Paula Zsiray, Logan, UT

Prep: 5 min. • **Bake:** 3 hours
Makes: 8 servings

- 1   bone-in beef rib roast (4 to 6 lbs.)
- 1   Tbsp. olive oil
- 1   to 2 tsp. coarsely ground pepper

Horseradish Sauce
- 1   cup sour cream
- 3   to 4 Tbsp. prepared horseradish
- 1   tsp. coarsely ground pepper
- ⅛   tsp. Worcestershire sauce

1. Preheat oven to 450°. Brush roast with oil; rub with pepper. Place roast, fat side up, on a rack in a shallow roasting pan. Bake, uncovered, 15 minutes.
2. Reduce heat to 325°. Bake 2¾ hours or until meat reaches desired doneness (for medium-rare, a thermometer should read 135°; medium, 140°; medium-well, 145°), basting with pan drippings every 30 minutes.
3. Let stand 10-15 minutes before slicing. Meanwhile, in a small bowl, combine the sauce ingredients. Serve with beef.
4 oz. cooked beef 325 cal., 21g fat (9g sat. fat), 7mg chol., 115mg sod., 2g carb. (1g sugars, 0 fiber), 31g pro.

Deluxe Cornbread Stuffing

When my husband and I were newlyweds and far from family, we invited friends over for a Thanksgiving feast. I searched for dressing recipes and combined several to create this pleasing one.
—Pamela Rickman, Valdosta, GA

Prep: 20 min. • **Bake:** 55 min.
Makes: 12 servings

- 6   cups crumbled cornbread
- 2   cups white bread cubes, toasted
- 1   cup chopped pecans
- ¼   cup minced fresh parsley
- 1   tsp. dried thyme
- ½   tsp. rubbed sage
- ½   tsp. salt
- ½   tsp. pepper
- 1   lb. bulk pork sausage
- 2   Tbsp. butter
- 2   large tart apples, diced
- 1   cup diced celery
- 1   medium onion, finely chopped
- 1¾ to 2¼ cups chicken broth

1. Preheat oven to 350°. In a large bowl, combine cornbread, bread cubes, pecans and seasonings; set aside. Crumble sausage into a large cast-iron or other ovenproof skillet; cook over medium heat until no longer pink, breaking into crumbles. Remove with slotted spoon; drain on paper towels.
2. Add butter to the drippings; saute apples, celery and onion until tender. Add to the bread mixture; stir in the sausage and enough broth to moisten.
3. Spoon mixture into cast-iron skillet; bake, covered, 45 minutes. Uncover and bake just until set, about 10 minutes longer.
1 cup 326 cal., 18g fat (4g sat. fat), 19mg chol., 780mg sod., 35g carb. (8g sugars, 4g fiber), 8g pro.

Classic Turkey Gravy

Making gravy is simple when you have the right proportions of ingredients. This version tastes delicious and will become your go-to gravy for every holiday dinner.
—Virginia Watson, Kirksville, MO

Takes: 15 min. • **Makes:** 2 cups

Drippings from 1 roasted turkey
1 to 1½ cups turkey or chicken broth
¼ cup all-purpose flour
Salt and white pepper to taste

1. Pour turkey drippings into a 2-cup measuring cup. Skim fat, reserving 2 Tbsp. Add enough broth to the drippings to measure 2 cups.
2. In a small saucepan, combine flour and reserved fat until smooth. Gradually stir in the drippings mixture. Bring to a boil; cook, stirring, until thickened, about 2 minutes. Season with salt and white pepper to taste.
¼ cup 45 cal., 3g fat (1g sat. fat), 4mg chol., 127mg sod., 3g carb. (0 sugars, 0 fiber), 1g pro.

"Great base gravy. Came out very rich and flavorful ... then again, Mom's turkey drippings are fantastic to begin with!"

—lady_g, tasteofhome.com

Apple & Herb Roasted Turkey

My daughter loves to help me make this moist roasted turkey with herbs. Her job is to hand Mommy the ingredients—if she doesn't eat the apples first!
—Kimberly Jackson, Gay, GA

Prep: 20 min.
Bake: 3 hours + standing
Makes: 14 servings

¼ cup minced fresh sage
¼ cup minced fresh rosemary
1 turkey (14 lbs.)
1 medium apple, quartered
1 medium onion, halved
1 celery rib, halved
½ cup butter, melted
½ cup apple jelly, warmed

1. Preheat oven to 325°. Combine sage and rosemary. With fingers, carefully loosen skin from the turkey breast; rub herbs under the skin. Secure skin to underside of breast with toothpicks.
2. Place turkey breast side up on a rack in a roasting pan. Place apple, onion and celery in turkey cavity. Brush turkey with butter.
3. Roast, uncovered, 3-3½ hours or until a thermometer inserted in thickest part of thigh reads 170°-175°. (Cover loosely with foil if turkey browns too quickly.)
4. Remove turkey from oven; brush with apple jelly. Tent with foil and let stand 15 minutes before removing toothpicks and carving.
8 oz. cooked turkey 626 cal., 31g fat (11g sat. fat), 262mg chol., 222mg sod., 10g carb. (9g sugars, 0 fiber), 72g pro.

Quick Cranberry Gelatin Salad

Since this tangy salad keeps well, I make it a day ahead for my holiday menu. It's also a perfect choice to take to a potluck—even people who aren't fond of cranberries think it's yummy. I got the recipe from a friend at church who likes to cook as much as I do.
—Betty Claycomb, Alverton, PA

Prep: 10 min. + chilling
Makes: 10 servings

- 1 pkg. (6 oz.) cherry gelatin
- 1½ cups boiling water
- 1 can (20 oz.) crushed pineapple, undrained
- 1 can (14 oz.) whole-berry cranberry sauce
- 1½ cups seedless red grapes, halved
- ¼ cup chopped pecans

In a large bowl, dissolve gelatin in water. Stir in pineapple and cranberry sauce. Refrigerate for 30 minutes. Stir in grapes and pecans. Pour into a 2-qt. serving bowl. Refrigerate until firm.
½ cup 141 cal., 2g fat (0 sat. fat), 0 chol., 119mg sod., 29g carb. (22g sugars, 1g fiber), 2g pro.

"This has become a Thanksgiving tradition. Everybody loves it! I make this instead of cranberry sauce. I omit the pecans but no one misses them. The best cranberry salad ever!"

—TheDix, tasteofhome.com

Eggnog Pumpkin Pie

This pie of my mom's is the absolute best pumpkin pie I have ever tasted. Eggnog is the special ingredient in the creamy custard filling.
—Terri Gonzalez, Roswell, NM

Prep: 10 min.
Bake: 1 hour + cooling
Makes: 8 servings

  Dough for single-crust pie
1 can (15 oz.) pumpkin
1¼ cups eggnog
⅔ cup sugar
3 large eggs
1½ tsp. pumpkin pie spice
¼ tsp. salt
  Whipped cream, optional

1. Preheat oven to 375°. On a lightly floured surface, roll dough to a ⅛-in.-thick circle; transfer to a 9-in. pie plate. Trim crust to ½ in. beyond rim of plate; flute edge. In a large bowl, combine pumpkin, eggnog, sugar, eggs, pumpkin pie spice and salt. Pour into crust.
2. Bake until a knife inserted in the center comes out clean, 60-65 minutes. Cool on a wire rack. Refrigerate until serving. If desired, top with whipped cream.
Note This recipe was tested with commercially prepared eggnog.
Dough for single-crust pie
Combine 1¼ cups all-purpose flour and ¼ tsp. salt; cut in ½ cup cold butter until crumbly. Gradually add 3-5 Tbsp. ice water, tossing with a fork until dough holds together when pressed. Shape into a disk; wrap and refrigerate 1 hour.
1 piece 317 cal., 15g fat (9g sat. fat), 123mg chol., 280mg sod., 40g carb. (22g sugars, 2g fiber), 7g pro.

Gingerbread Cutout Cookies

The smell of these cookies makes me think of going to Grandma's house. My boys always linger around the kitchen when I make them.
—Christy Thelen, Kellogg, IA

Prep: 30 min. + chilling
Bake: 10 min./batch + cooling
Makes: 5 dozen

- ¾ cup butter, softened
- 1   cup packed brown sugar
- 1   large egg, room temperature
- ¾ cup molasses
- 4   cups all-purpose flour
- 2   tsp. ground ginger
- 1½ tsp. baking soda
- 1½ tsp. ground cinnamon
- ¾ tsp. ground cloves
- ¼ tsp. salt
     Vanilla frosting of your choice
     Red and green paste food coloring

1. In a large bowl, cream butter and brown sugar until light and fluffy, 5-7 minutes. Add egg and molasses. Combine flour, ginger, baking soda, cinnamon, cloves and salt; gradually add to the creamed mixture and mix well. Cover and refrigerate until easy to handle, about 4 hours or overnight.
2. Preheat oven to 350°. On a lightly floured surface, roll dough to ⅛-in. thickness. Cut with floured 2½-in. cookie cutters. Place 1 in. apart on ungreased baking sheets.
3. Bake until edges are firm, 8-10 minutes. Remove to wire racks to cool completely. Tint some of the frosting red and some green; leave remaining frosting plain. Decorate cookies.
1 cookie 77 cal., 2g fat (1g sat. fat), 10mg chol., 69mg sod., 13g carb. (6g sugars, 0 fiber), 1g pro.

Get a Jump on Christmas Baking

- **Freeze gingerbread cookie dough:** Tightly wrapped, cookie dough will keep in the freezer for up to 3 months. To use, thaw the dough in the fridge overnight and roll out the cookies the next day.
- **Freeze baked (undecorated!) gingerbread cookies:** Let the cookies cool completely on the baking sheet, then transfer the sheet to the freezer until the cookies are frozen solid. Transfer the frozen cookies to freezer-safe containers, and store in the freezer for up to 6 months. Thaw at room temperature, then decorate and enjoy!

Holiday Cutout Cookies

Pull out your cookie cutter collection and let your imagination soar with these fun cutouts.

—Anne Grisham, Henderson, NV

Prep: 20 min.
Bake: 5 min./batch + cooling
Makes: about 10 dozen

1   cup butter, softened
1   cup shortening
3   cups sugar
4   large eggs, room temperature
6   Tbsp. evaporated milk
2   tsp. vanilla extract
2   tsp. almond extract
6   cups all-purpose flour
1   tsp. baking soda
½ tsp. salt

Frosting

3   cups confectioners' sugar
1   tsp. vanilla extract
4   to 6 Tbsp. half-and-half cream
    Food coloring of your choice, optional
    Assorted sprinkles

1. In a large bowl, cream butter, shortening and sugar until light and fluffy, 5-7 minutes. Beat in eggs, milk and extracts. In another bowl, whisk flour, baking soda and salt; gradually beat into the creamed mixture. Divide dough into 4 portions. Shape each into a disk; cover and refrigerate overnight or until firm enough to roll.
2. Preheat oven to 400°. On a lightly floured surface, roll out each portion of dough to ⅛-in. thickness. Cut with floured 3-in. holiday cookie cutters. Place cutouts 1 in. apart on ungreased baking sheets.
3. Bake until edges are lightly browned, 5-7 minutes. Remove from pans to wire racks to cool completely.
4. For frosting, in a large bowl, beat confectioners' sugar, vanilla and enough cream to reach a spreading consistency. If desired, beat in food coloring. Frost and decorate cookies as desired.

Freeze option Freeze undecorated cookies in freezer containers for up to 3 months. To use, thaw in covered containers and decorate as desired.
1 cookie 87 cal., 3g fat (2g sat. fat), 11mg chol., 36mg sod., 13g carb. (8g sugars, 0 fiber), 1g pro.

Holiday Cutout Cookies Tips

- Don't overmix the dough! Overmixing or overhandling will result in dense, tough cookies.

- To keep cookies intact before and after baking, lift them with a large spatula that supports the entire shape.

- Let baking sheets cool completely between each batch—residual heat will soften the dough and make it spread.

Red Velvet
Candy Cane Fudge

My favorite kind of cake, red velvet, inspired me to create this fudge. If you like, you can spoon the candy mixture into paper-lined mini muffin cups instead of spreading it in a pan.

—Crystal Schlueter, Northglenn, CO

Prep: 25 min. + chilling
Makes: 3¾ lbs.

- 1 tsp. butter
- 2 pkg. (12 oz. each) white baking chips, divided
- ⅔ cup semisweet chocolate chips
- 3 tsp. shortening, divided
- 1 can (14 oz.) sweetened condensed milk
- 1½ tsp. red paste food coloring
- 4 cups confectioners' sugar, divided
- 6 oz. cream cheese, softened
- 1 tsp. vanilla extract
- ¼ tsp. peppermint extract
- 3 Tbsp. crushed peppermint candies

1. Line a 13x9-in. pan with foil; grease foil with butter. Set aside.
2. In a large microwave-safe bowl, combine 3¼ cups white baking chips, the chocolate chips and 2 tsp. shortening. Microwave, uncovered, on high 1 minute; stir. Microwave at additional 15-second intervals, stirring until smooth. Stir in milk and food coloring; gradually add 1 cup confectioners' sugar. Spread into prepared pan.
3. In another large microwave-safe bowl, melt the remaining white baking chips and shortening; stir until smooth. Beat in cream cheese and extracts. Gradually beat in the remaining confectioners' sugar until smooth. Spread over red layer; sprinkle with crushed candies. Refrigerate 2 hours or until firm.
4. Using foil, lift fudge out of pan. Remove foil; cut fudge into 1-in. squares. Store between layers of waxed paper in an airtight container.
1 piece 70 cal., 3g fat (2g sat. fat), 4mg chol., 15mg sod., 10g carb. (10g sugars, 0 fiber), 1g pro.

White Chocolate
Brandy Alexander

A Brandy Alexander combines brandy and creme de cacao into a delicious, creamy drink that became increasingly popular in the '60s. My husband and I love to entertain, so this recipe is a keeper.

—Sharon Delaney-Chronis,
  South Milwaukee, WI

Takes: 15 min. • **Makes:** 6 servings

- 3½ cups whole milk
- ⅛ tsp. salt
- 6 oz. white baking chocolate, finely chopped
- ⅓ cup brandy
- ¼ cup creme de cacao
- ½ tsp. vanilla extract
  Optional: Whipped topping and white chocolate shavings

1. In a large saucepan, heat milk and salt over medium heat just until the mixture comes to a simmer. Remove from heat. Add chocolate; whisk until mixture is smooth. Stir in brandy, creme de cacao and vanilla.
2. Fill mugs or cups three-fourths full. Top with whipped topping and chocolate shavings if desired.
¾ cup 316 cal., 15g fat (9g sat. fat), 20mg chol., 137mg sod., 27g carb. (27g sugars, 0 fiber), 7g pro.

Recipe Index